The Battle for Childhood

The Battle for Childhood

Creation of a Russian Myth

ᖫᖬ

Andrew Baruch Wachtel

Stanford University Press · *Stanford, California*
1990

Stanford University Press
Stanford, California
© 1990 by the Board of Trustees of the
Leland Stanford Junior University
Printed in the United States of America

CIP data appear at the end of the book

Sources of Illustrations

1, *4*, *5*: *Stolitsa i usad'ba*, no. 19–20 (Oct. 10, 1914), pp. 7, 23, 24. *2*: *Stolitsa i usad'ba*, no. 59 (June 1, 1916), pp. 4–5. *3*: *Stolitsa i usad'ba*, no. 55 (Apr. 1, 1916), p. 8. *6*, *7*, *14*: *Iz istorii realizma v russkoi zhivopisi* (Moscow, 1982), plates 126, 116, 75. *8*: *Stolitsa i usad'ba*, no. 14–15 (Aug. 1, 1914), p. 6. *9*: E. Trubetskoy, *Iz proshlogo* (Vienna, 1920?), p. 65. *10*: D. S. Likhachev, *Poèziia sadov* (Moscow, 1982), p. 329. *11*, *12*: S. A. Tolstaia, *Iz zhizni L. N. Tolstogo* (1913). *13*: *Stolitsa i usad'ba*, no. 33 (May 1, 1915), p. 3.

༺༻

To the memory of my grandmother,
Berta Drapkin Rados,
who first interested me in things Russian

Acknowledgments

I owe a debt of gratitude to many colleagues at universities across the country for their careful readings of my manuscript and their suggestions for improving it. Boris Gasparov, Hugh McLean, and Jurij Striedter were among my earliest and most helpfully critical readers. Each of them, in his own way, left a strong imprint on this book. William Mills Todd, III, read the final book draft with amazing care, and suggested many important additions. I would also like to thank the following friends and colleagues who read drafts of the book and offered valuable advice: Terence Emmons, Lazar Fleishman, Michael Flier, Gregory Freidin, Michael Heim, John Kopper, Gary Saul Morson, Irina Paperno, and Michael Wachtel. The book was written with the financial support of the Harvard University Society of Fellows. I am indebted to both the Junior and Senior Fellows of that organization for moral support, good wine, and rigorous questions. I thank Hilja Kukk and the staff at the Hoover Institution Library for assistance in finding the illustrations. Elizabeth Calihan helped to edit the final manuscript and forced me to rethink and improve old material even when I pretended it was unnecessary. Finally, I wish to thank Helen Tartar, Julia Johnson Zafferano, and the rest of the Stanford University Press staff for turning a manuscript into a book.

I have done all translations except where otherwise indicated. Russian words are transliterated using the Library of Congress system, except for "sky" and "skoy" at the ends of personal names.

A.W.

Contents

Ten pages of photographs follow p. 110

The Battle for Childhood

Happy, happy, irretrievable time of childhood. How can one not love, not cherish memories of it. Those memories freshen and exalt my soul. They are a source of great pleasure.

—Lev Tolstoy, Childhood

Childhood is looked upon as the happiest time of life. Is that always true? No, only a few have a happy childhood. The idealization of childhood originated in the old literature of the privileged. A secure, affluent, and unclouded childhood, spent in a home of inherited wealth and culture, a childhood of affection and play, brings back to one memories of a sunny meadow at the beginning of the road of life. The grandees of literature, or the plebeians who glorify the grandees, have canonized this purely aristocratic view of childhood.

—Lev Trotsky, My Life

Introduction

The books from which I have drawn my epigraphs should have
next to nothing in common. Lev Tolstoy's *Childhood*, a work of
prose fiction, marked its 23-year-old aristocratic author's literary
debut. It was published in the leading Russian literary journal in
1852, a time of political stability and great national self-confidence,
just before the debacle of the Crimean War and the subsequent reforms of Alexander II. Lev Trotsky's *My Life,* which has yet to be
published in the Soviet Union, is nonfictional—the autobiography of an embittered and aging Russian-Jewish exile. It was written in a period of intense national dislocation, after World War I,
the Russian Revolution, and the first years of Stalinism. And yet,
as soon as Trotsky discusses childhood, he feels constrained to attack Tolstoy's literary conception, a conception that by the 1930's
should have been as irrelevant as the ancien régime that Trotsky
and his revolutionary comrades had swept away. How is it that
a view of childhood proposed in a work of fiction in the 1850's
was the relevant point of departure for a nonliterary autobiography written almost a century later? What can explain the long-
term hold of Tolstoy's interpretation of childhood on the Russian
imagination?

Trotsky's dialogue with Tolstoy points to a common pattern in
Russian cultural history: in the course of time, a theme or idea first
expressed in a work of literature ceases to be a mere literary problem and becomes a sociocultural myth. In this case, the process of
transformation was extremely complex: for almost 100 years,
echoes and reworkings of Tolstoy's *Childhood* can be found migrat-

ing back and forth, from genre to genre, from ideological camp to ideological camp, acquiring more significance with each succeeding generation. The interpretation of childhood proposed in fiction influenced writers of autobiographies, and, in its turn, the autobiographical tradition enriched subsequent works of fiction.

Tolstoy claimed universal validity for his picture of the happy childhood, and many members of the gentry class agreed. In the period 1860–1905, however, competing interpretations of the meaning and purpose of childhood began to appear. Eventually, childhood (which could be defined in various ways, although Tolstoy's version was almost always used as a point of reference) became a kind of membership badge, confirming its holder's right to belong to a specific social class or literary faction.

The purpose of this book is to trace the literary, social, and cultural mechanisms by which the theme of childhood developed in Russia from the 1850's to the 1930's. Since works of imaginative literature played a leading role in this process, I will concentrate on the purely literary problems of genre formation and generic evolution. At the same time, however, I will pose questions about the relationship between literature and the broader social system in order to explain the increasingly strong ideological and cultural importance of conceptions of childhood in this period.

The advent of a specifically Russian conception of childhood can be dated to September 1852, when Tolstoy's *Childhood* appeared anonymously in the journal, *The Contemporary*. Although there are signs that a peculiarly Russian attitude toward childhood was forming slowly before 1852, the publication of Tolstoy's work marks a watershed.[1] Of course, Russians may well have experienced childhood as a differentiated period of life before 1852. Nevertheless, until this time Russian culture lacked a coherent integral model for the expression and interpretation of this stage of life,[2] a recognition and means of expressing the child's point of view—and, as Philippe Ariès has suggested, there is an important sense in which, in the absence of a generally accepted cultural model, members of a society are not conscious of having had a childhood.[3] In short, for the Russian imagination, childhood was a gigantic *terra incognita*, waiting to be discovered. Until Tolstoy created Nikolai Irten'ev, the Russian child lacked a voice of his own; he was a literary mute, sometimes seen but never heard.

The Russian awakening to childhood was fairly late, considering that childhood and children had been an almost constant presence on the West European sociocultural scene at least since the appearance of Jean-Jacques Rousseau's *Emile* (1762) and the first part of his *Confessions* (1782).[4] Once it appeared, however, the theme of childhood spread quickly into a number of genres, both fictional and nonfictional. Before 1852 there were practically no first-person accounts of childhood in Russia. The next 70 years saw scores of writings devoted to the subject. These include a number of seminal literary works as well as a host of now-forgotten autobiographies by members of Russia's gentry class.

Childhood, like its sequels *Boyhood* (1854) and *Youth* (1857), belongs to an exceptionally flexible type of fictional narrative that was unknown in Russian literature before 1852. I call narratives of this type *pseudo-autobiographies*. Speaking generally, a pseudo-autobiography is a first-person retrospective narrative based on autobiographical material in which the author and the protagonist are not the same person.[5] The author of *Childhood* is Tolstoy, but the narrator calls himself Nikolai Irten'ev. Yet, in many respects, Irten'ev is Tolstoy's autobiographical double; much of the fictional character's life was drawn from Tolstoy's experience. At the same time, Irten'ev is his own double; throughout the narrative the older and more mature Irten'ev examines and comments on the actions of his past self. While there is a sense in which the two Irten'evs are the same person, they are separated and differentiated by an abyss of time and space that can be bridged only by imperfect memory. As a result of this double doubling, the pseudo-autobiography is an inherently ambiguous genre. The author, narrator, and protagonist (the narrator's past incarnation) each have their own voice in the pseudo-autobiographical text, but the relationship between the voices is fluid and purposely ill-defined.

Childhood proved to be an unavoidable point of departure for future generations of Russian writers. Most of the great Russian literary discussions of childhood were written as pseudo-autobiographies. These include S. T. Aksakov's *The Childhood Years of Bagrov's Grandson* (1859), M. E. Saltykov-Shchedrin's *Old Times in Poshekhonie* (1881), M. Gorky's trilogy *Childhood, Among the People,* and *My Universities* (1913–20), A. Belyi's *Kotik Letaev* (1922), and I. A. Bunin's *The Life of Arsen'ev* (1927–30). Each of these works represents a dialogue both with Tolstoy/Irten'ev and, more broadly, with the pseudo-autobiographical genre that *Childhood* initiated.

It would be a mistake, however, to examine the pseudo-autobiography solely in a high-cultural context. The great debate as to the meaning and purpose of childhood that marks the three twentieth-century pseudo-autobiographies mentioned above would never have occurred had Tolstoy's interpretation of childhood (and, to a lesser extent, Aksakov's) not inspired generations of Russian autobiographers. Members of the Russian gentry class perceived Tolstoy's idyllic picture of life on a country estate, of the child's family and surroundings, and of the child himself not as the description of an individual life but as the paradigmatic Russian childhood.[6] As a result, when they sat down to write autobiographies they recalled childhood, consciously or unconsciously, through the filter of Tolstoy's work. Words, phrases, and even entire scenes from *Childhood* were superimposed onto supposedly nonfictional texts.

In effect, then, Tolstoy created what could be called the myths of Russian childhood, myths that were developed and canonized not in fiction but in autobiography. The Tolstoyan myths of childhood became so strongly embedded in the Russian cultural mind that they could not be ignored, even by those members of the gentry class who had had unhappy childhoods and by writers from other classes. In their autobiographies the Tolstoyan myths took on a negative connotation; these autobiographers constantly contrasted their own experiences to those of Irten'ev/Tolstoy in a generally unsuccessful attempt to create an alternative model for childhood.

Thus, the interpretation of childhood that Tolstoy proposed in *Childhood* became both a literary and a sociocultural theme in Russia. By analyzing the manifestations of that theme between the 1850's and the 1930's, I hope to define the battle for childhood, a late echo of which can be heard in Trotsky's plaint, "only a few have a happy childhood."

L. N. Tolstoy and His *Childhood*

In the summer of 1851, when Tolstoy began writing the work that was to become *Childhood*, he was not quite 23 years old. Although he had harbored vague literary plans for years, there was as yet no sign that he would become a professional writer.[1] Since turning eighteen, he had tried his hand at a number of occupations and had, in his own estimation and in that of his family, failed miserably at all of them. He had not gotten a university degree, his efforts to reorganize the family estate had produced no results, he had accumulated gambling debts, and, finally, he had gone off to join his brother as an officer in the Russian Army of the Caucasus. Throughout this period he recorded his thoughts and activities in a remarkably precocious journal. As soon as this journal became available to scholars, it was apparent that it constituted a kind of experimental laboratory, a testing ground on which the young Tolstoy could try out some of the narrative strategies that he used so effectively in his later work.[2] Nevertheless, although Tolstoy the journal writer had already mastered a number of crucial techniques, the transition from diary writer to published author was an arduous one. This transition occurred during the year in which he wrote *Childhood*.

In the final version of *Childhood*, two conflicting impulses are held in delicate equipoise; very generally, they might be called the autobiographical and the novelistic. Throughout his life, Tolstoy was troubled by the tension caused by his desire to speak generally as the teacher of mankind and his talent as an observer of the particular details of the individual life (his own and others). It was this tension, resolved for a time in favor of the general, that after 1877 led to his rejection of almost his entire literary oeuvre. In the 1850's, however, Tolstoy saw the matter somewhat differently. At this stage, he evidently identified autobiography with the specific, while fiction was equated with the general. *Childhood* was something of a synthesis of these two impulses. On the one hand, the narrative is particular and individualized; the autobiographer Irten'ev recounts experiences that relate to him and to him alone. On the other hand, the lyrical tone that pervades the whole, coupled with the fact that Irten'ev is a fictional creation, lend it a feeling of generality; it seems as if Irten'ev's childhood could have belonged to anyone. This balance seems entirely effortless in the published version, but Tolstoy's comments on his work as it was developing indicate that finding a middle ground between the particular and the general, between the autobiographical and the novelistic, was both his most important concern and a source of much difficulty.

It took Tolstoy some time and a number of false starts before he arrived at his ultimate formal conception of *Childhood* in particular and the trilogy in general.[3] Originally, he thought the work would be in four parts and intended to call it *The Four Epochs of Development*. Although the plot of the initial version of the section on childhood is similar to that of the final one, there are significant differences as well. For one thing, the original version is less autobiographical.[4] For another, the first version covers a much larger span of time; some of the scenes included would later be incorporated into *Boyhood* and even into *Youth*. Far more important, the complicated relationship between author, narrator, and protagonist still remained to be clarified. The story is told in the first person by an anonymous narrator. However, at the beginning of the first surviving draft there is a small section signed "G.L.N." (that is, Count [in Russian, "Graf"] Lev Nikolaevich). It is in the form of a letter addressed to an unnamed (and quite possibly nonexistent) correspondent and, despite containing a number of conventional formulas, it provides clues to the evolution of Tolstoy's thoughts on the relationship of author to text:

> I wrote them [the "notes," as he calls them, A.W.] for myself, never thinking that there would be a time when I would wish to let anyone read them—Why did I write them? I cannot give you any definite account. I found it pleasant to jot down scenes that illustrate childhood memories so poetically. I found it interesting to examine my development and, most important, I wanted to find some kind of single source in the outline of my life—an aspiration that could guide me.[5]

Since, presumably, this paragraph was destined for publication, the first sentence should be seen as a bow to literary convention. By pretending to have written the "notes" only for himself (even as he is publishing them), Tolstoy attempts to remove the stamp of literariness from them. This device makes them seem more personal, more spontaneous. After the opening disclaimer, however, the introduction becomes more suggestive. It was "pleasant" to "illustrate childhood memories so poetically." The absence of a possessive pronoun attached to childhood (the possessive is, of course, emphatically present in the two sentences that follow) hints at a certain generalizing tendency in the proposed work; a suggestion to take what follows as a depiction not merely of the childhood of G.L.N., but of childhood as such.

The next two sentences, on the other hand, link the work and G.L.N. very closely. He claims that it was interesting "to examine *my development*" and "to find a single source in the outline of *my life*" (italics mine). Despite the fact that the life described in *The Four Epochs of Development* was not Tolstoy's own, he felt (or, at least, pretended to feel) that the patterns of thought and development in it belonged to him. One hesitates, however, to draw sweeping conclusions from this introduction, because it is difficult to see exactly how it was to have been connected to the text that follows. The narrator of the first redaction is never named, so it is possible that Tolstoy originally intended to present the work as an autobiography. It is also conceivable that the introduction was never intended for publication. Either way, the introduction marks a false start; Tolstoy would never identify himself so closely with his text again. Nevertheless, this aborted beginning is important because it suggests that from the very outset, in June or July of 1851, Tolstoy saw his work both as an outlet for the expression of autobiographical material and as a description of childhood in general. A tension between autobiography and fiction, between Tolstoy's presence as an author and as a narrator, was part of the trilogy from its inception.[6]

In January 1852 Tolstoy finished a second draft of *Childhood*. By this time, the work had taken on a fairly coherent shape. The story was told by a narrator who was differentiated from the author by name, and a system of chapters (absent in the first draft) had been introduced. Many of the scenes that would appear in the fourth and final version were already included, as was the idea of presenting a few crucial days in the life of the young boy (instead of attempting a full chronology of the child's life, as had been envisioned in the first version). At the end of the new manuscript, Tolstoy appended two short chapters entitled "To the Readers" and "To Those Esteemed Critics Who Wish to Take This Personally." In the former, Tolstoy made the following programmatic statement: "In my opinion the persona of the author, the writer (creator) is an antipoetical persona. Since I wrote in the form of an autobiography and wanted to interest you in my hero as much as possible, I wished him to have no imprint of authorship and, therefore, I avoided all authorial devices—learned expressions and constructions" (1: 208–9).

In the first version of the introduction, Tolstoy had emphasized the connection between himself and the narrator. Now, however, he underscores the nonautobiographical nature of his work. He disassociates himself from his main character and reminds the reader that this is a work of fiction. The phrase "I wrote in the form of an autobiography" (as opposed to having written a true autobiography) and the words "my hero" are crucial for defining Tolstoy's attitude toward the text here. Yet at the same time, a direct address to the reader is nothing if not the kind of "authorial device" that

Tolstoy claims to have avoided. It is not clear what he means by "scholarly expressions and constructions." Perhaps he has in mind didactic generalizations à la Rousseau. Whatever the case, this entire afterword is a clear example of the author's voice intruding on his text to make didactic comments (the following chapter addressed to the critics does the same thing to an even greater extent). As such it flatly contradicts the avowed purpose of the book. It would seem that Tolstoy came to understand the problem himself, for this type of heavy-handed authorial intrusion was eliminated in the third and fourth redactions.[7]

Tolstoy's discomfort with the mix of autobiography and fiction in *Childhood* did not disappear even when he had finished the story. After the final version of *Childhood* had been accepted for publication by *The Contemporary* in the September 1852 issue, Tolstoy wrote a letter to N. A. Nekrasov in response to the latter's request for a sequel: "The autobiographical form that I chose and the obligatory link between the following parts and the preceding one so constrain me that I often feel the desire to abandon them and leave the 1st part without a continuation" (1: 330). This was, in effect, the first "public" statement that Tolstoy made about his work. He continued to emphasize the fictive element ("autobiographical form") just as he had in the abandoned afterword to the second redaction. It is worth noting, however, that Tolstoy might well have felt constrained to play up the fictive here because, as a beginning author, he wanted to emphasize the literariness of his work. In this period prose fiction was the most prestigious type of writing, and Tolstoy naturally wanted to make a career as a writer of belles lettres, not as a memoirist. Like most journals, *The Contemporary* did not tend to publish autobiographies by beginning authors, so the unknown writer might have simply been trying to make an impression on the editor-in-chief. Even so, his complaint that the form of the work was "constraining" bears investigation.

All of Tolstoy's early published works employ first-person narrators; as a beginning writer he clearly found it easier to speak in the first person. This preference is probably a legacy from his early literary laboratory: the diary. However, while a first-person narrator can both analyze himself and pronounce general judgments, those judgments are fated to seem subjective. They obviously emanate from a single viewpoint and express the opinions of an individual. Although Tolstoy's favorite eighteenth-century writers, Rousseau and Laurence Sterne, reveled in subjectivity, by the mid-nineteenth century the expectations of writers and readers had changed radically. In England, France, and Russia novelists were attempting to erase their overt presence from the text insofar as possible. As it turned out, this kind of realism never suited Tolstoy; he needed and wanted direct authorial presence. Later in his career, particularly in *War and Peace* and *Anna Karenina*, he succeeded in creating forms that combined seemingly objective narration with a strong authorial presence. In 1852, however, Tolstoy evidently found it expedient to compromise with the expectations of the public and the critics. Nevertheless, despite severely limiting his direct presence in *Childhood*, he never entirely excised the authorial voice. After the success of *Childhood*, Tolstoy could worry less about pleasing his readers. In *Boyhood* and *Youth* he made increasing use of generalizing statements, and the first-person narrator became more and more constraining.

The tension between the autobiographical and the fictional boiled over in comically naive fashion when Tolstoy saw *Childhood* in print for the first time. It turned out that Nekrasov had, for some unknown reason, published it under the title *The Story of My Childhood*. Tolstoy was furious and dashed off a letter to Nekrasov (although he never mailed it) in which he said, "The very title *The Story of My Childhood* contradicts the sense of the work. Who cares about *my* childhood" (1: 332). Of course, the complaint is illogical, since a reader who believed that the narrator wrote the whole work could just as easily be expected to think that the narrator had written the title as well. Nevertheless, Tolstoy's complaint is telling; immediately, and rather childishly, he connected the word "my" in the title to the author and not to the narrator, thus indicating that he himself did not believe in the illusion he had created. Although this incident might appear simply as an example of bruised authorial self-esteem, it also illustrates the extent to which fiction and autobiography were intertwined for Tolstoy when he was writing *Childhood*.

Perhaps the best formulation of the dual nature of the project can be seen in a diary entry for November 30, 1852: "The 4 Epochs of Life constitutes *my* novel before Tiflis. I can write about him because he is so distant from me" (46: 150–51). Since many of the facts of Irten'ev's life do not coincide with those of Tolstoy's, in what sense could Tolstoy call the work "*my* novel"? It is significant, of course, that he did not say "my life." The italicized "my" indicates that Tolstoy closely identified himself with his work and its hero. At the same time, the words "novel" and "him" indicate that Tolstoy was able to distance himself from his story, to accept it as a fictional construct. The obvious internal contradiction here is one that Tolstoy was evidently never able to solve.

The second sentence deserves special consideration, especially in connection with a diary entry from a slightly earlier period:

Everyone describes human weaknesses and the humorous side of people by transferring them to invented personages, sometimes successfully, if the author is talented, but more often unnaturally. Why? Because we know mankind's weaknesses in ourselves and in order to show them faithfully we must show them in ourselves, because a particular weakness is appropriate only for a particular person. Very few people have the strength to do this. We try to distort the personage on whom we project our weaknesses as much as possible in order not to recognize ourselves. (46: 76)

Tolstoy berates others for cowardice and insincerity, yet at this time he himself was not able to write without the help of a mediating character. After all, who was Irten'ev if not an "invented personage" who could stand for his creator? At this point in his career, Tolstoy could only write about someone who "was distant." In fact, his greatest challenge as a beginning writer lay in creating a literary form that would have the effect of an autobiography, the ring of truth that only unmediated authorial presence can produce, while allowing him to retain a certain narrative distance. Later in life, when Tolstoy talked about the trilogy, it was precisely the presence of a fictitious narrator and the mix of *Dichtung* and *Wahrheit* that he felt called upon to criticize:

In order not to repeat myself in the depiction of childhood I reread what I had written under that title and regretted that I had written it: it is so bad, so literary, so insincerely written. It could not have been otherwise, first of all because my idea was to write the story not of my childhood but of that of my friends and so the result was a clumsy mix of their childhood and mine, and, second, because at the time of writing I was not at all independent in terms of expression and was under the influence of two writers who strongly affected me then: Sterne (his *Sentimental Journey*) and Töpffer (*Bibliothèque de mon oncle*).
   I particularly don't like the last two parts—Boyhood and Youth—
. . . I hope that what I write now will be better and, more important, more useful for other people. (34: 348–49)

This passage comes from the "Memoirs" (1903) that P. I. Biriukov requested in order to fill out the writer's childhood biography. By then Tolstoy had either forgotten or chosen to ignore the literary and personal reasons that had caused him to write his trilogy in its original form. Why is it that *Childhood* still does not utterly displease its author, as do the two later parts? Probably because even in 1903 Tolstoy retained nostalgic feelings for early childhood. If anything those feelings deepened as he compared them with the following periods of his life.[8] Later in "Memoirs," when describing the basic chronology of his life, he calls the early years "the joyful, poetic period of childhood until the age of 14." The events described in *Boyhood* and *Youth*, on the other hand, are part of "a horrible 20-year period of coarse dissipation" (34: 347). It was, in part, Irten'ev's relatively unjudgmental stance toward the events of his boyhood and youth that bothered the older Tolstoy.

Of course, the very fact that Tolstoy was outraged by Irten'ev's comparatively lenient attitude suggests the degree to which he felt a personal connection to the actions described in the trilogy. Had Irten'ev been a wholly fictional creation, Tolstoy could not have feared that he might "repeat himself" when describing his own childhood. Although he correctly remembers that his "idea" had been to write a work of fiction, the older Tolstoy now judges his work as an autobiography (albeit an untrue and poorly written one). It is bad because it fails to tell the truth about Tolstoy (an intent that did not exist in 1852). The presence of *Dichtung* and *Wahrheit* is still recognized in the trilogy, but these categories are interpreted in a new context, as falsehood and truth, respectively. It is not the extent to which a section is factual that counts, however (for the second two parts of the trilogy are factually closer to Tolstoy's life than is the first); what is crucial is the interpretation of those facts. *Childhood* depicts a period of innocence in a way that the older Tolstoy sees as ideologically proper; it is therefore not all bad. Although *Boyhood* and *Youth* are more autobiographical, they do not emphasize the horrors of these periods sufficiently; consequently they are insincere and bad.

To sum up Tolstoy's attitude toward the trilogy, I would say that he always regarded it as a group of texts through which he could express extremely personal material in a mediated literary form. Neither purely factual nor purely fictional, the trilogy was a kind of compromise. Sometimes, while writing the work and especially in later life, Tolstoy found such compromises distasteful, but it is clear that for the young writer they were necessary if he was to turn his already well developed self-analytic ability into a literary work.

The Genre of *Childhood*

After long and sometimes painful experimentation, Tolstoy created the Russian version of a narrative form that combined the immediacy of autobiography with the creative freedom of the novel; I call this form the pseudo-autobiography. For the next 70–80 years, most Russian literary descriptions of childhood would be pseudo-autobiographies. This section is primarily devoted to an analysis of the innovative narrative techniques that Tolstoy used in his trilogy. However, I will also quote passages from later Russian pseudo-autobiographies in order to show the ways in which Tolstoy's work inspired the creation of a new literary genre in Russia.

The pseudo-autobiography is an autobiographically based work that imitates the autobiography in all respects but one: its author and narrator are not the same person. Although the formal distinction might seem trivial (after all, lacking the title page, it can be impossible to tell a "real" autobiography from a pseudo-autobiography), it is not. For both author and reader the lack of identity between author and narrator means that the work is to be treated as fiction, read and judged by a set of criteria different from those applied to nonfiction. Although the pseudo-autobiography often sticks quite close to the facts of the author's life (and must include substantial amounts of autobiographical material), it cannot simply be considered a subset of the autobiography proper. In an influential book on autobiography published in 1975, Philippe Lejeune defines the genre as follows: "A retrospective narrative in prose by a real person about his or her own life. It emphasizes the individual life and, in particular, the development of one's own personality."[9] According to Lejeune, if the author hides behind the mask of an independent narrator, he breaks the unspoken "autobiographical pact" that exists between himself and his reader. Once this pact is broken, the reader perceives the work as fiction, no matter how much autobiographical material it contains.

I believe that Lejeune is only partially correct here. It is true that the author loses some of the immediacy of autobiography when he chooses a fictional narrator. On the other hand, if the fiction produced is in the form of an autobiography, and if it contains autobiographical material, certain narrative advantages that would be lost in a third-person text are retained. Thus, the pseudo-autobiography frees the novelist from a too-close association with his text while partially retaining the special bond that links the reader of an autobiographical text and its narrator.[10] In effect, the pseudo-autobiography denies the identity of author and narrator while enticing the reader into believing in its existence.

The interpretive uncertainty that inevitably results when a work straddles generic boundaries in this way has been vividly characterized by Gary Saul Morson. In what he calls "boundary works,"

Morson claims, "it is uncertain which of two mutually exclusive sets of conventions governs a work. When this kind of ambivalence obtains, it is possible to read the work according to different hermeneutic procedures and hence, all other things being equal, to derive contradictory interpretations. Doubly decodable, the same text becomes, in effect, two different works." [11] Morson believes that there are two types of boundary works: those whose ambiguities were basically unintentional, and those that were designed specially to be ambiguous. He calls the latter "threshold works." [12] When other Russian writers began to take advantage of the generic ambiguities that Tolstoy had exploited in *Childhood*, his "threshold work" became the source of what I would call a "threshold genre."

Since the pseudo-autobiography depends for its peculiar effect on its ability to seem to be both fiction and autobiography simultaneously, it should be clear that the genre cannot be defined only in terms of form; not every first-person narrative is a pseudo-autobiography. If, for example, the competent reader cannot imagine that an identity exists between author and narrator, the pseudo-autobiographical ambiguity is lost. Thus, the narrator of *Notes from the Underground* cannot be confused with Dostoevsky, and, consequently, the work cannot be considered a pseudo-autobiography even though it is narrated in the first person. On the other hand, Dostoevsky's *Notes from the House of the Dead* should be seen as a pseudo-autobiography because its narrator, Gorianchikov, shares a good portion of Dostoevsky's experience. Indeed, from the very beginning, part of the interest readers have taken in this work can be traced precisely to their attempts to see Dostoevsky hiding behind his fictional narrator.

Since the pseudo-autobiography cannot be defined by purely formal considerations, it is tempting to understand the genre entirely in terms of its content. Such an approach would claim that a work in this genre is characterized by a partial identification of the life of its author with that of one or more fictional characters. It seems to me, however, that there are compelling reasons not to ignore formal characteristics when defining this genre. Both *Childhood, Boyhood, Youth* and *Anna Karenina* are highly autobiographical. Nevertheless, from the point of view of response, the first-person work engenders certain expectations in the reader that the third-person novel does not (whether such expectations are justified is, of course, an entirely different matter). In addition, from the writer's point of view, the degree of identification with the autobiographical character is stronger if that character is the narrator of his own story rather than the object of a narrator's account. An examination of Tolstoy's diaries and letters indicates that there was a stronger and qualitatively different bond between Tolstoy and Irten'ev than between Tolstoy and Levin.

From what has been said above, it should be obvious that the pseudo-autobiography is not the same as what other scholars have called the "autobiographical novel," the "poetic autobiography," the "memoir novel," or the "roman autobiographique." [13] Most of these terms were invented by scholars whose primary interest was autobiography. For them autobiography is a genre, a specific literary mode that has its own norms and that creates certain expectations in writers and readers. They were understandably not interested in formulating a strict and positive definition of works that they did not consider autobiographies. Instead, their definitions tend to be negative: everything that is not an autobiography is an "autobiographical novel" or a "roman autobiographique." [14] The result is a catch-all category containing a large number of heterogeneous works. In fact, the pseudo-autobiography can be considered a subset of any of the aforementioned categories, but it is a subset that is defined positively.

The pseudo-autobiography affords the novelist an unusual opportunity. He can use material from his own life in a form that has traditionally engendered an illusion of truth in readers, yet he is not bound by truth and is able to create the kind of fictional world characteristic for the novel. He can describe "something general, representative, within his own experiences, the deeper logic within his character, which life itself may in certain respects distort, or within some dominant aspect of his character." [15] Simultaneously, however, he need never lose the protection of a fictional mask.[16]

The Russian literary scene of the second half of the nineteenth century was particularly conducive to the production of pseudo-autobiographies. As B.M.Eikhenbaum and L.Ia.Ginzburg have pointed out, the period just before the publication of *Childhood* was marked by a flowering of previously marginal literary genres, such as autobiography, the journal, and letters. The demand on the part of literary critics (the all-important tastemakers of this period) for autobiographies was particularly strong.[17] Paradoxically, throughout this period the most prestigious literary form remained prose fiction, particularly the novel. The novel, however, could not be about just anything; it was expected to be a vehicle for telling the truth about society. In these circumstances the appearance of the pseudo-autobiography was completely logical. It was written in the style of an autobiography and on the basis of autobiographical material. In these respects it met the public's demand for works in marginal genres. On the other hand, such works contained fictional narrators. This allowed pseudo-autobiographies to be included in the prestigious category of prose fiction. As novels they could make more general statements on the human condition than would be appropriate for the more subjective autobiography.

In the original draft of his *Old Times in Poshekhonie*, Saltykov-Shchedrin eloquently summarized the advantages of the pseudo-autobiographical form: "I considered it unsuitable to write a so-called autobiography: first, because autobiographical details are too frequently of no general interest, second, because it is not always comfortable to touch on those details with complete frankness."[18]

The author of the pseudo-autobiography consciously mixes material taken from his own life with material taken from the lives of others, from the literary tradition, and from his imagination. To succeed he must create a convincing central figure who sets down his life retrospectively in the form of an autobiography. The reader perceives the autobiographical form of the work immediately and, at some point, must also have the possibility of confirming the factual authenticity of some of its portions. The contemporary reader often cannot do this (especially if the pseudo-autobiography is a first book by an unknown author), but later readers almost always have access to such information.[19] From my point of view, then, the reception of a work on its first appearance is not always a good indication of whether it is or is not a pseudo-autobiography. Only with the passage of time is the curious reader allowed the opportunity to discover more about the author in question and to perceive the genre in which the work was written. Of course, the author himself is conscious of what he is doing from the very beginning.

The Narrative Possibilities of the Pseudo-Autobiography

From the point of view of narrative, the most interesting possibility opened by the pseudo-autobiography is for a polyphonic interplay of voices in the text. An autobiography is always dialogic; it must be written in the present by a person describing his past incarnation. As one scholar has stated: "The events recorded in an autobiography have a double relevance, a relevance both to the author's historical life, and a relevance to his present self; they are symbolic of both."[20] The autobiography is based on a continual dialogue between the past and present selves of its author. Often those two selves are quite dissimilar. The pseudo-autobiography opens the potential for a complex relationship involving the author, the narrator, and the protagonist. The protagonist is supposed to be the narrator's past incarnation, but, because the pseudo-autobiography is always based on autobiographical material, he is also a partial incarnation of the author's own past self. In the text of a typical pseudo-autobiography, all three voices have the opportunity to interact.

One way to imagine the positions of the three voices in a pseudo-autobiography is by using a theoretical concept proposed by M. Bakhtin: the chronotope. Put as simply as possible, a chronotope is the space/time orientation typical for a text or genre.[21] I take the liberty of extending Bakhtin's basic definition to include the space/time orientation of the individual voices within a single text. Each of the three voices in the pseudo-autobiography can be said to have its own characteristic chronotope. The narrator's time is the present reviewing the past; it is a time of recollection and can potentially include any and all moments from the time of writing the text back to the narrator's first conscious memory. Sometimes, through the use of written documents, family legends, and other material, the narrator's time can stretch even farther back into the past. His space can be the entire real world; in practice, however, at the time of writing he is usually physically separated from the part of the world in which the narrated events took place.

The protagonist's time is exactly the reverse of the narrator's; it is the past recreated as the present. The protagonist relives past events, making them present again. The narrator's present time does not exist for the protagonist; his time extends only until the moment being treated in the narrative. The protagonist's space is also limited in comparison to the narrator's; he can know only the space in which the narrated events took place. In pseudo-autobiographies of childhood, this space is generally the closed world of the Russian estate.

The author exists in a space/time continuum that has nothing to do with that of the world depicted in the text. His voice speaks in the present tense, but it is a generic present tense with no defined "now"—the author's statements are meant to be universal, and essentially they exist outside of time. His space is equally undefined, for he occupies no clear position in the world of the narrator or in that of the child. He is merely present, a disembodied voice hovering somewhere above the surface of the real world.[22] The overall unity of the pseudo-autobiography is not created by a single narrative point of view, but, rather, by the constant interplay and alternation of the three chronotopes in the text.[23]

Although Tolstoy was a literary novice in 1852, the three-voiced system he developed in *Childhood* remained the typical narrative mode of the Russian pseudo-autobiography. The first voice is that of the child Irten'ev, expressing the impressions of his life as they seemed to him at the time of their occurrence. Of course, the reader knows consciously that the text was written by an adult writer (whoever it may have been) and that it is impossible for the narrator to remember the exact wording of conversations, or even to recall precisely events that occurred years before. Despite these caveats, however, the text is often narrated by the supposedly unmediated voice of the child, boy, or youth. The second voice is that of Irten'ev, the narrator and putative writer of the text. The older Irten'ev explains the actions of his protagonist (his younger self) and comments on them. Finally, there is the authorial voice; this is usually extremely close to the voice of Tolstoy himself as we know it from the diaries and his later work. The author's voice makes generalizing comments that go far beyond the commentary provided by Irten'ev.[24]

The Narrator's Voice

In *Childhood* (and throughout the trilogy), Nikolai Irten'ev is the narrator. Although he never states it directly, his purpose in writing seems to be to recapture his past self and, through an analysis of his life, to understand his present position. To achieve this, he looks back on his actions and attempts to relive them through conscious memory. Because Irten'ev duplicates the function of the narrator of almost any autobiography, his voice is, from the point of view of narrative technique, the most common presence in *Childhood* and the least interesting. Irten'ev has two primary modes of narration. One is a first-person, past-tense account recalling events in the past while expressing some ex post facto knowledge: "On the day after the events which I have described, after eleven o'clock in the morning, a barouche and a light carriage stood at the porch" (Tolstoy, 1: 39). The narrator recalls a past action through the prism of his present consciousness. Irten'ev not only describes the scene of his departure for Moscow, but he also reveals an awareness of his activity as a writer ("the day after the events which *I have described*"). In terms of both space and time, he is clearly outside the world being described.

Not surprisingly, sentences of this type are common in both autobiographies and pseudo-autobiographies. The following examples are taken from S. T. Aksakov's *The Childhood Years of Bagrov's Grandson* and O. E. Mandel'shtam's *The Noise of Time*, respectively:

> Beneficent fate soon sent me a new and unexpected enjoyment which made the strongest impression on me and greatly broadened the circle of my contemporary ideas.[25]

> The whole orderly mirage of Petersburg was only a dream, a shining shroud thrown over the abyss, while all around stretched the chaos of Judaism; neither fatherland, nor home, nor hearth but precisely chaos, an unknown fetal world from which I emerged, which I feared, about which I surmised inchoately and avoided, I always avoided.[26]

In both cases the narrator emphasizes the dichotomy between his past and present selves. Bagrov, in preparing to describe his new source of enjoyment, speaks of the future effect that it would have (information to which the child could not have been privy). Mandel'shtam interprets his inchoate childhood feelings in terms of categories that he developed as an adult.

The second mode of narration is a present-tense narrative voice that comments on, analyzes, or otherwise characterizes past actions. In *Childhood*, it too belongs to the older Irten'ev: "When I try to remember mama the way she was at that time only her brown eyes come to me" (1: 39). The "now" of this present-tense, first-person voice is the moment of writing. Such a voice helps set the "epic situation"[27] in which the story is narrated and separates the description of the events being narrated from the time of their occurrence. This sentence type is also common in both pseudo-autobiographies and autobiographies:

> I don't exactly know what the "activity" of my brother consisted of and how precisely he spent his university years.[28]

> Here, on the sheer-cutting brink—I hurl long, mute glances into the past...
> I am thirty-five years old.[29]

The latter quote, from Belyi's *Kotik Letaev*, is particularly evocative. It comes from the very beginning of the work and emphasizes both the physical and temporal abysses that separate the narrator from his past incarnation. Whether speaking in the present or the past tense, the narrator's purpose is to recount what happened in the past. The narrator's past and present selves are, of course, connected by a bridge of conscious memory, but that bridge is a flimsy one. In fact, the event itself and the recollection of it belong to qualitatively different worlds, and, try as it might, the narrator's voice can impart only a pale reflection of original experience. On the other hand, the loss of immediacy is partially recouped by a gain in self-understanding. The narrator's present self sees the broader implications of past events in ways the experiencing self never could have.

The Child's Voice

It would seem, then, that the ideal situation would be one in which the narrator's perspective could be enlivened by the excitement of actual experience. To bring the past alive is the function of the narrator's past incarnation: the protagonist. In *Childhood* this role belongs to the young Irten'ev. Although the narrator often speaks for extended sections without interference from other voices, passages presented from the child's point of view are usually framed by narrative commentary and are comparatively brief. This is unavoidable, because, at least in Tolstoy's conception, the narrator must prepare the reader for the scenes that the child will relive.[30]

Here, for example, is a relatively extended section reproducing the child's consciousness from chapter 24 of *Childhood*. Having first met the pretty Sonechka at his grandmother's birthday party, Irten'ev goes to bed, filled with memories of the evening. He cannot understand how he had been able to love his childhood idol Serezha and thinks only of Sonechka:

How could I have loved Serezha so passionately and for so long?—I thought while lying in bed—No! He never understood, couldn't appreciate and wasn't worthy of my love... But Sonechka? How wonderful she is! "Do you want to?" "You begin."

I jumped up on all fours and vividly imagined her little face, covered my head with the blanket, tucked it under myself on all sides and, when there were no openings left, lay down and, feeling a pleasant warmth, plunged into sweet dreams and memories. (Tolstoy, 1: 75)

The first section is presented as a quoted reminiscence. Although it is clear that Irten'ev could not have remembered the exact words he used as an eleven-year-old, his recreation of past events is unmediated by any commentary on the part of the narrator. The narrator is present in order to note time (past-tense "I thought") and space ("lying in bed"); his function is to frame the child's vision, not to qualify it or to analyze the child's thoughts. The second section, although narrated as a past event, follows the child's train of thought and action quite convincingly. The very undefinedness of the child's feelings, "sweet dreams and memories," represents an attempt to recapture a time when feelings were not analyzable because there was nothing to compare them to. The image of the excited child wrapping himself in his blanket and feeling the warmth of his own body is convincingly child-like as well. It is important that the child defines himself as a "reminiscing" being from an early age, for this capacity to reminisce motivates the narrator's ability to recall detailed pictures of his childhood after the passage of a number of years. It seems that Irten'ev internalizes experience and creates "memories" of it almost immediately.

Scenes presented as if through the child's consciousness have a freshness and immediacy that sets them apart from the narrator's more measured presentation. Instead of being simply recalled, the moment is reexperienced. In the following passage from *Childhood Years*, for example, the reader can feel the young Bagrov's excitement when he saw the nomadic tribes of the steppes for the first time: "It was with curiosity that I looked over the summer living quarters of the Bashkirs, which could be seen in the distance, and at their grazing herds and flocks. I had heard about all of this from my father, but I was seeing it with my own eyes for the first time. There the river appeared and a multitude of lakes" (Aksakov, 1: 284).

In some pseudo-autobiographies the child's voice can speak in the present tense. This is Belyi's favorite technique in *Kotik Letaev*.

However, he mixes present knowledge with past reality in such a way as to form a sort of past/present continuum:

It seemed to me—
    —the passages of the apartment lead to an abyss of darkness; and everything breaks off there. (*Kotik Letaev*, p. 40)

Here past tense ("it seemed to me") indicates the fact of the narrator's present knowledge, while present tense recreates the inchoate feelings of the child in the child's here and now.

Whether the narrator's past incarnation speaks in the present or past tense, the reader interprets the scene as recreating the "now" of the past incarnation. That what is narrated in the past tense can be perceived as present-tense action has been recognized to be a characteristic feature of third-person narration since the appearance of Käte Hamburger's study, *The Logic of Literature*. Hamburger argues that this feature (which she calls "the epic preterite") occurs only in third-person texts because they are the sole texts of narration.[31] First-person texts are excluded, because they are seen as part of the system of discourse in which tenses imply pastness or nonpastness as in speech. However, as Ann Banfield argues in *Unspeakable Sentences*, the assimilation of all first-person texts to the category of "discourse," as opposed to "narration," is a mistake. The assumption that the past tense implies past time is created, not by the mere presence of an "I," but by a relation between narrator and interlocutor/reader, an "I" and a "you."[32] In true discourse, as in speech, tenses situate the action described with respect to the present, the reference point in common between narrator and reader/interlocutor. In cases like the pseudo-autobiography, the assumption that the narrator's present tense is the same as the reader's breaks down. The voice of the narrator's past incarnation, even when expressed in the past tense, is understood as expressing the present—just as in a novel, "the preterite is no longer perceived as stating the past.[33]

This self in the past is, in pseudo-autobiographies dealing with childhood, the child. In works that do not deal with childhood, the self in the past is the narrator before he had the experiences from which he is separated by time and space and about which he is writing.[34] In either case the self in the past is and must be felt to be distinct from the narrator. This separation between the voices of narrator and past self is sustained in a variety of ways. First and most obviously, there must be between them an epistemic gap: sentences in the child's present must contain nothing that is incongruous with what the child could have *known* at the time. If they do, they become sentences that are attributed to the adult narrator.

Second, the child's consciousness can be recreated through a number of techniques. Recreations of past consciousness can contain fragments of conversations, bits of poetry, and stories. All of these are embedded in the child's mind and help create the illusion that the actions being recreated by the past self's consciousness are happening here and now. In order to convey a child's thoughts, authors occasionally try to use the exact words he might have uttered. However, this is not necessary—it is the child's consciousness that must be reproduced, not his exact mode of expression. For example, Tolstoy achieves an evocation of the child's world without directly "quoting" the child's thoughts or speech in a number of "stop action" descriptions. In these descriptions the adult narrator is present only through iterative verb markers like *byvalo* or *sluchalos'* (which can both be translated as "it would often happen"). Iterative markers indicate that the remembered scene is a composite, one that happened so many times as to have been indelibly impressed on the memory. Here the sequence of perfective past-tense verbal structures that the narrator generally uses to move the text forward is replaced by imperfectives in past or even present tense. These verbs give the effect of stopped time or of the simultaneity of action and its expression; they are the ultimate expression of the protagonist's chronotope. At such points the narrative often switches from first- to second-person singular verb forms:

It often happened that, after having had your fill of running around the big room downstairs, you would sneak upstairs to the classroom on tiptoes and you'd look—Karl Ivanych is just sitting alone in his armchair and, with a peacefully majestic expression, he is reading one of his favorite books. Sometimes I'd catch him in moments when he wasn't reading: his glasses would have slid down his big aquiline nose. . . . It would happen that he didn't notice me and I would stand in the doorway and think: the poor, poor old man! There are lots of us, we are playing, enjoying ourselves, but he is all by his lonesome and there's no one to comfort him.[35] (Tolstoy, 1: 6)

Only the last section of the quote, after the colon, could really be considered the actual thoughts of a child. Even so, the whole passage is imbued with a spirit of past time that has been successfully recaptured in the present. It is as if Irten'ev has access to a video tape of his childhood and is able, upon viewing it, to relive his memories. The reader watches the child watching; he sees Karl Ivanych just as the child used to.

In later pseudo-autobiographies, such passages have a definite purpose; they are used to express nostalgia for lost time and space. In fact, the iterative construction could be called the grammatical expression of nostalgia.[36] The iterative allows the narrator to go into a kind of trance; while in that trance he can bring his past incarnation back to life and reexperience long-past events.[37] In one sense, the creative power of memory to conflate a group of related scenes into a single narrative unit makes the reliving of experience more intense than the original impression could have ever been. At the same time, the iterative past-tense markers emphasize the pastness of the scene. They remind the reader that the past can never be really made present again, no matter how convincingly it can be recreated through narrative. The iterative, used as a vehicle for the recreation of time past, can therefore be considered a central grammatical construction of the pseudo-autobiography.[38]

Thus far I have considered passages in which there is little or no interaction between the voices of the narrator and the child. The narrator's voice frames that of the protagonist, but their respective chronotopes remain essentially separate. However, there are also sections in which there is a dialogue between the child's recreation of past actions and the narrator's recollection of them. The following passage from *Childhood*, illustrating the child's feeling for music and his way of perceiving it, provides a good example. Irten'ev recalls his mother playing the piano: "Maman was playing the second concerto of Field, her teacher. I was dozing and some sort of light, bright, and transparent memories appeared in my imagination. . . . Maman often played those pieces; therefore I remember the feeling that they awakened in me very well. That feeling resembled memories; but memories of what? It seemed you were recalling things that never happened" (Tolstoy, 1: 31).

Initially the child's response is portrayed without commentary. The feelings evoked are purposely indeterminate, fluid. The description of memories as "light," "bright," and "transparent" mimics the lack of definition of the child's pre-analytic experience. Then the scene receives a kind of commentary from the narrator Irten'ev, who feels that unmediated memory is, for some reason, not entirely satisfactory. To mark such passages he often inserts himself directly into the text (here when he says, "therefore I remember the feeling they awakened in me very well"). Such insertions serve as a kind of "guarantee" of the genuineness of the memory, and they allow for a smooth transition from childhood memories to adult analysis. Having reentered the text, the narrator can now question his reminiscences: he can provide a more concrete account of them. In this case he comes to a dead end. There were definitely memories evoked, but they are memories that (despite their having existed in the child's consciousness) do not have any concrete referent ("memories of things that never happened").

The Author's Voice

The pseudo-autobiography, as I have defined it, requires the possibility of yet another voice in the text: the voice of the author. The author is the person who actually writes the text as a whole, and ultimately, of course, the reader knows that all the voices in the text are written by him. However, as producer of the entire text, the author remains outside it. What I call the authorial voice within the text, on the other hand, appears at those moments when neither the narrator nor the child is speaking, characteristically in order to make general statements that go well beyond what the narrator or child (whose conclusions, to be convincing, must be based on personal observation and motivated by the material used in the work) can say. Indeed, the author's statements, while linked to the actions described by the narrator or the child, are not fully motivated by them and, to some extent, emanate from a point of view beyond or outside the text.

The non-Russian reader might be excused for concluding that the author's voice is simply the incarnation of the Russian author's inevitable desire to preach, to draw cosmic conclusions from individual experience. However, certainty of an exact equivalence between the views of the actual author and those expressed by the authorial voice should not be expected at the level of individual remarks or passages. First, because such equivalence is, of course, inherently difficult to prove. But more important, because it is unnecessary. Although too large or decisive a gap between the point of view of the real author and that of the authorial voice would tend to break down the identification needed in a pseudo-autobiography, one can imagine individual cases in which an identity does not obtain. In such cases one would want to speak of author and "author." Thus, the identity or nonidentity of the two is not really important. What is crucial is that a separate voice position which fulfills what can be called the "authorial function" can be shown to exist in the pseudo-autobiography.

Because *Childhood* was signed simply L.N. when it was first published, it should have been clear to the first readers (and is certainly clear to any present-day reader) that both of the Irten'evs were fictional constructs. That is to say, neither the child's reminiscences nor the adult's commentary are necessarily linked to any unmediated reality. It is the author's voice that organizes the text as a whole, that links external elements from the real world with the internal logic of the fictional *fabula*, and that makes generalizing comments beyond those of which Irten'ev is capable. Its purpose is not to ask questions and seek temporary or provisional answers, but to make statements, to teach others, and to point out the extent to which the life described here is typical for all mankind. It is often difficult to separate the author's voice from that of Irten'ev, because both speak in the first person and both survey the same events. Despite this inherent difficulty, it is important to note the existence of the two and to try to define what separates them.

The clearest distinction between the two voices is hierarchical. Irten'ev's statements grow out of the child's experience. As such they pertain to the specific facts of Irten'ev's life. The author's statements, on the other hand, are concerned with Truth. They are authoritative in tone and fundamentally monologic. The reader has the choice only of agreeing or disagreeing: modification is impossible.

In addition, there are stylistic devices that serve to separate the author's voice from that of Irten'ev. In order to recognize them, it is helpful to return for a moment to the first redaction of the work. Under the clear influence of Sterne, it is filled with digressions. For example, we find descriptions of the physiological signs of good breeding (1: 105), of different types of smiles (1: 106), of what the arrangement of rooms in a house says about the owner's character (1: 114–15), and of the usefulness of hunting (1: 125). These digressions clash quite obviously with the reminiscing voice of the narrator. One example is sufficient to illustrate the general style: "It is impossible to request of God from the soul in any other way than we request of man: in language most simple, accessible and understandable for that man from whom we are requesting something. To seek for prayers and expressions of thought that would be worthy of God is the highest task for the human mind" (Tolstoy, 1: 132).

With each successive redaction, the number and length of these digressions decreases. More and more attention is concentrated on the remembering and analyzing voice of Irten'ev. The authorial voice, with its tendency to make general statements not exactly related to or motivated by the reminiscences, is muted. In fact, at one point Tolstoy seems to have intended to do away with the author's voice altogether. This can be inferred from a diary entry in which he writes that the novel will be "instructive but not dogmatic," as opposed to his proposed novel about a Russian landowner that will be "dogmatic." [39]

The break between Irten'ev's voice and that of Tolstoy is often quite abrupt, as in this section where Irten'ev remembers his attempts to recite the verses he had written for his grandmother's birthday:

> Then my turn came. Grandmother turned to me with an approving smile. Those who have experienced shyness know that the feeling increases in direct proportion to time and that resolution decreases in inverse proportion: that is, the longer the state continues, the more it becomes unconquerable and the less resolution remains. The final bit of courage and resolution left me at that time. (1: 49)

Here the description of how shyness works is motivated to some extent by the narrator's description of his feelings before reading his poem. Still, the author's style is at odds with that of the narration as a whole. The strict parallel constructions, the almost mathematical arrangement of the text, betray an attempt to explain the world differently than Irten'ev would. In fact, anyone who has read Tolstoy's diary can recognize how close this explanatory attempt is to the voice used there. Irten'ev is concerned with his own actions. His examination of childhood is motivated by a desire to understand how he came to be what he is at the time of writing. The authorial voice looks at Irten'ev's childhood (and the autobiographical details of Tolstoy's childhood when they are present) as specific incarnations of the general state of childhood that have universal validity. Such generalizing passages are comparatively rare in *Childhood*, which makes them all the more obvious when they do occur.

Most remarkable of all in *Childhood* are those sections in which all three voices coexist. For example, in the following scene in which the narrator recalls the behavior of Natal'ia Savishna after his mother's death:

> At the time I was amazed at the change from touching emotion, with which she spoke to me, to grumbling and trivial calculation. [*The first voice has been speaking here: it does not analyze or seek to explain, but merely to present what happened. Of course the words "at the time" show that there is a sense of lost time.*] Thinking about it later, I understood that despite what was happening in her soul she still had enough spirit left to take

care of her work. . . . Grief had affected her so strongly that she did not find it necessary to hide the fact that she could take care of other things: she wouldn't have even understood how such a thought could arise. [*Here we are in the presence of the second voice, which looks back on the raw material of the child's perception, interprets it, and sometimes even tries to "correct" the child's impression.*]

Vanity is the feeling most incompatible with true grief but, at the same time, the feeling is so deeply imbedded in human nature that it is very rare that even the strongest grief can drive it out. Vanity in grief is manifested in the desire to seem either afflicted or unhappy or firm. [*This is the third voice, the author's, which extrapolates from the story of Natal'ia Savishna and the child's reaction to it in order to show a general truth about mankind.*] (1: 91)[40]

Of course, Tolstoy realized that the form he had chosen was not perfectly suited to express such general truths; that is why he spoke of the form as "constraining" and threatened not to write the sequels to *Childhood*.[41] On the other hand, *Childhood* had been a major success, and Nekrasov kept badgering Tolstoy for the promised continuation. For a beginning writer with literary ambitions, such requests were too flattering to ignore, so Tolstoy continued to write. After the first part, however, he did not feel it quite as necessary to hide the authorial voice; in *Boyhood* and *Youth* its presence becomes increasingly obvious.

At times the reader is addressed directly (a device that Tolstoy strictly avoided in *Childhood*): "Did it ever happen, oh reader, that at a certain time of life you suddenly noticed that your view of things was changing completely?" (2: 15). Or later, "Who has not noticed those secret nonverbal relations that appear between people who always live together?" (2: 17). Or, "Do not disdain, oh reader, the society into which I lead you. For if the strings of love and sympathy in your soul have not weakened, then even in the maids' room you will discover sounds to make them resonate" (2: 52). Whereas movement from the voice of the child to that of the narrator and back again was typical for the organization of *Childhood*, in *Boyhood* the interaction of the narrator's and the author's voices becomes more common. The voice of Tolstoy the teacher of mankind, so typical of his later works, begins to assert itself.

The relationship of child's voice, narrator's voice, and author's voice characteristic for the trilogy as a whole is projected onto a different plane in *Boyhood*, when Irten'ev writes down Karl Ivanych's autobiography. For a few chapters Irten'ev takes the position of the author and Karl Ivanych takes that of Irten'ev. When writing his own autobiography, Irten'ev never seems aware of the problems of form and distance that Tolstoy agonized over in his diaries and letters. However, as soon as he begins to record Karl Ivanych's life, Irten'ev recognizes their existence. Because Karl Ivanych had told him the story many times, he says, "I hope to relate it word for word." Then he goes on to say, "To this day I have not decided if this was actually his life story or a work of fantasy, born during his lonely life in our home, in which he himself started to believe from repeating it so often, or if he merely touched up the real events of his life with unbelievable facts" (2: 25). As Irten'ev notes, there can be no definite answer to the problem of truth in autobiography; any of his proposed schemata could be valid. Of course, this problem was of constant concern to Tolstoy while he was working on the trilogy. It is one that should interest the reader as well, and its formulation by Irten'ev seems designed to attract the reader's attention specifically (and subtly) to the question of autobiographical truth.

As the age of Irten'ev the child approaches that of Irten'ev the narrator, the distinction between their voice positions becomes blurred. More and more frequently reminiscence and analysis become one and the same, and material and judgment are fused. So, for example, Irten'ev the youth describes how he watches a servant removing the storm windows in early spring. "Allow me to help you, Nikolai—I said, trying to give my voice a most humble expression, and the thought that I was doing a good deed . . . strengthened the humble mood of my spirit even more" (2: 81). The young child had not been capable of analyzing his own actions. Only in hindsight could the older Irten'ev discern their meaning. By the time of his youth, however, Irten'ev portrays himself as being capable of acting and reflecting simultaneously. The narrator's job becomes more one of selection than analysis, and the constructive principle that had held *Childhood* together becomes more difficult to adhere to. Eventually, in fact, it becomes impossible, which is probably why the fourth volume of *The Four Epochs of Development*, the one that was supposed to bring events in the narrator's life up to the time of writing, was never written. Having lost the fictional distance that separated him from Irten'ev (surviving plans indicate that the final volume was to have been more autobiographical than the preceding ones), Tolstoy was unable to continue writing.

There is one other possible way to introduce authorial presence in a pseudo-autobiography. It can be done through the use of some kind of framing device that allows the author (identified either by name or masquerading as the editor of a "found" manuscript) to incorporate his voice directly into the text. Tolstoy did not employ this technique, but it was used by Aksakov in *The Childhood Years of Bagrov's Grandson*, by Dostoevsky in *Notes from the House of the Dead*, and by Leont'ev in *The Egyptian Dove*. In these works, the author reminds the reader of his controlling presence through an introduction, footnotes, or addenda. Leont'ev takes the process even farther, occasionally commenting on the narrator's tale in the course of the narrative: "I was completely unable to find the conclusion of this excerpt: but on the very same page, written in pencil, was: *Is this necessary?* And that is all. It is obvious from everything that the author of these memoirs began, more and more, to be burdened by his labor and, for a long time, did not know how to free himself from it."[42] Although this sort of authorial masking was common in both the European and Russian literary traditions, it takes on a special poignancy in the pseudo-autobiography. Because the events described are, in fact, autobiographical to some extent, such an authorial insertion can be a confession. In the passage above, for example, it is difficult not to read the author's commentary on the narrator's text back onto Leont'ev himself.

In the twentieth century, as pseudo-autobiography became a recognized genre among Russian writers and readers, the presence of an external authorial voice became less intrusive. This pattern fits well with what we know from the behavior of other genres.

Talking specifically about autobiography, for example, Elizabeth Bruss says: "As a genre becomes more familiar to the reading public, there is less need for the author to provide internal signals to ensure that his text will be read with the proper force."[43] Thus, although Belyi provides no authorial voice within his text, the situation of the child described in *Kotik Letaev* is similar enough to that of the young Belyi (Bugaev) in other, directly autobiographical works as to hint at the presence of an extra-textual voice. Vladimir Nabokov, in *Look at the Harlequins!* (which can be considered a parody of the entire pseudo-autobiographical genre), keys the authorial presence by, among other things, providing a list of "other books by the narrator" at the beginning of the novel. The titles are parodic puns on the names of Nabokov's own books.

Thus, in all pseudo-autobiographical novels there is some stylistic factor which reminds the reader that there is an authorial presence controlling the "memories" of both narrator and child. This is, of course, in addition to the inescapable fact that the author's real name or his accepted pseudonym always differs from that of the narrator.

The European Sources of *Childhood*

There is one other question that should be addressed before beginning an analysis of *Childhood*: it concerns the degree to which Tolstoy's first published work was dependent on foreign models. Despite 125 years of discussion, the question of how and to what extent Tolstoy was influenced by other literary works when writing *Childhood* is a controversial one. Although everyone is aware of Tolstoy's statements, critical opinion has run the gamut from opinions that descry very strong influence to those that practically deny it altogether.[44] Many attempts have been made to prove that Tolstoy did or did not borrow specific elements from specific works. Because my primary concern is with Tolstoy's importance for the Russian tradition that grew up after the publication of *Childhood*, I do not propose a full-scale investigation of its potential sources. Nevertheless, there is a compelling reason for examining the narrative forms and accounts of childhood that Tolstoy might have had at his disposal when he began writing his first published work. By doing so it may be possible to understand why, despite a number of obvious influences, *Childhood* seemed so fresh and original to Tolstoy's contemporaries.

As I have already mentioned, in both form and content *Childhood* was unlike anything that had appeared previously in Russian literature. It was, however, similar to a number of European works of the previous 70 years. Suspicions that *Childhood* was not "original" have been voiced in connection both with Tolstoy's age and inexperience in 1851–52 and with several statements he made in later years. One of those statements has been quoted previously: "at the time of writing I was not at all independent in terms of expression and was under the influence of two writers who strongly affected me then: Sterne (his *Sentimental Journey*) and Töpffer (*Bibliothèque de mon oncle*)." The other is a list that Tolstoy provided in response to the question, "What books most influenced you at different periods in your life?" There are a number of works that have clear parallels with *Childhood* in the list of books that Tolstoy said exerted the greatest influence on him from the ages of fourteen to twenty. These included Sterne's *Sentimental Journey*, Rousseau's *Confessions*, Pushkin's *Evgenii Onegin*, and Dickens's *David Copperfield*.[45] Also present are such didactic novels as Rousseau's *Emile* and *La Nouvelle Héloïse*.

It is impossible to overestimate the influence of Rousseau's thought in general and his *Confessions* in particular on French first-person narratives in the first third of the nineteenth century. There is a consensus among scholars of autobiography that *Confessions* marked a new era in literary self-portraiture. Rousseau's concern with self-analysis instead of mere self-description, his realization of the conflicting impulses that can exist simultaneously within an individual mind, and his continual attempts to probe beyond the surface in an attempt to understand the real motivations for his actions set *Confessions* apart from its predecessors. In addition, his concern with "romantic" love and his preference for "unspoiled" nature as opposed to "corrupt" civilization (or, on the level of human beings, his preference for the "innocent" state of childhood) became articles of faith for many Romantics. Tolstoy acknowledged his debt to Rousseau on many occasions, perhaps nowhere more forcefully than in his 1905 letter accepting membership in the newly founded Rousseau Society: "Since I was fifteen, Rousseau has been my teacher. Rousseau and the Gospels have been the two great and benevolent influences on my life" (75: 234). As important a literary model as *Confessions* was, however, Rousseau's work was not fiction. It was meant to be read (and was in fact read) within the conventions of autobiography.[46] It was not until the following generation that French writers transformed many of Rousseau's themes and literary techniques from the world of autobiography into that of fiction.

Vicomte de Chateaubriand's *René* (published 1802) is an early example of this trend. A number of Rousseau-influenced themes are treated in this first-person narrative, including the escape from civilization and the noble savage. In addition, the overall form of the work is that of a confession; a tendency to confession is typical for many of the French works I will discuss. Although *René* does rely to some extent on observations that Chateaubriand made in America, it is not autobiographical. Therefore, from the point of view of the history of the pseudo-autobiography, it is not nearly as important as two novels that appeared somewhat later: Benjamin Constant's *Adolphe* (published in 1816) and Alfred de Musset's *La confession d'un enfant du siècle* (published in 1836). Both of these novels can be called pseudo-autobiographies.

Adolphe is a first-person account of the love of a young man for a woman ten years his senior. The novel is framed by an introduction signed by Constant. There he claims merely to be the editor and publisher of Adolphe's manuscript, which was found among papers left after the young man's untimely death. The work's subtitle, "A Story Found Among the Papers of an Unidentified Man," reinforces the illusion of separation between Constant and his narrator. The "found manuscript" device did not, of course, originate with *Adolphe*, but it proved particularly useful for writers of pseudo-autobiography: it motivated their presence in the text as an autonomous editorial voice while reinforcing the illusion that the work had actually been written by someone else. Constant's novel is remarkable chiefly for the subtlety of Adolphe's self-analysis. He possesses an uncanny ability to depict his contradictory emotions toward his mistress Ellénore. A typical passage occurs early in the novel when he tries to convince himself to make his love known:

In the end, I searched for a justification that would allow me to get out of the battle honorably, at least in my own eyes. I told myself that one should never rush anything, that Ellénore was too little prepared for the step I was contemplating, that it would be better to wait some more. Almost always, in order to live at peace with ourselves we disguise our impotence and weaknesses by means of calculations and systems. This satisfies that part of us which is, as it were, spectator to the rest.[47]

The disjunction seen here between the reminiscing voice and the explaining or analyzing voice (marked in this case by a shift from first-person singular to first-person plural) is a trope typical for the pseudo-autobiography and one that Tolstoy in particular was to use with telling effect.

That *Adolphe* was strongly autobiographical was obvious to many contemporary readers. One acquaintance of Constant's expressed the general sentiment when he wrote: "I recognized the author on every page. . . . No confession has ever placed a truer likeness before my eyes."[48] On the other hand, *Adolphe* is far from being completely autobiographical. For example, Constant exploited the freedom offered by the fictional form to construct a composite portrait of Ellénore: in personality she is Madame de Staël, but in appearance she is another of Constant's mistresses.

Musset's *Confession* tells a very similar story. Here the young hero, Octave, has been corrupted intellectually by the malaise that he attributes to the epoch in which he was born (the Empire), and physically by his debauched life in Paris. After his father's death, he moves to the countryside where, a short time later, he falls in love with Brigitte, a widow almost ten years his senior. The bulk of the novel chronicles their affair. Their love is problematic from the beginning, since Octave cannot bring himself to trust his mistress; true to the Romantic dualism so fashionable at the time, he alternately loves and hates her. The influence of Rousseau is apparent throughout the work, especially in the condemnation of the corrupting power of society and the frequent panegyrics to nature. In the end, having tortured himself and Brigitte for more than six months, the hero decides to separate from her. He leaves France, a melancholy and broken man who realizes that he is incapable of love. As was the case with *Adolphe*, the narrator's self-analysis, here overlaid with a bit of Romantic demonology, provides the central narrative interest. In addition, as with *Adolphe*, contemporary readers were quick to note autobiographical parallels, here between Octave and de Musset and between Brigitte and George Sand.

Thus, both Constant and Musset provided potential models for Tolstoy. However, although the form of the French novels was similar to the one he eventually used, the content was completely different. First of all, the central theme of both novels is love, and the central character is a young man in his twenties. This theme, so dear to the hearts of the Romantics, found almost no echo in Tolstoy's work or in the subsequent Russian pseudo-autobiographical tradition. The somewhat bitter, confessional tone of the French examples is in strong contrast to the nostalgic and elegiac mood of the Russian tradition. Finally, the French novels are far more self-absorbed than their Russian counterparts. In Russian pseudo-autobiographies, elements of the surrounding world (what Russians call *byt*) always play a significant role, whereas the French are far more concerned with the narrator's ratiocinations. Thus, French pseudo-autobiographies provided examples of how first-person, semi-autobiographical prose could be handled, but they did not have much of an influence in Russia. Indeed, I mention them here primarily to show how important the influence of national tradition can be in the development of a genre. The French tradition continued to evolve in the direction of greater contemplativeness in the nineteenth century, and it culminated in Marcel Proust's *Remembrance of Things Past*. The Russian tradition, on the other hand, which began later, evolved in very different ways, despite having some common early models (particularly Rousseau).

If the most famous French pseudo-autobiographies of the early nineteenth century had little influence in Russia, another first-person narrative, now practically unknown, was far more important. That work, *La bibliothèque de mon oncle*, by Rodolphe Töpffer, had a great effect on the young Tolstoy. *La bibliothèque de mon oncle* is in three parts, and it describes the childhood and adolescent years of a contemplative young man. It is not clear how autobiographical the work actually is, but it is narrated in the style of a pseudo-autobiography: the writer is identified as Rodolphe Töpffer and the narrator calls himself Jules.

Although *La bibliothèque de mon oncle* is concerned with the narrator's young years, the urban childhood described is very different from Irten'ev's. The majority of the scenes describe Jules's unrequited love for a succession of young women. Töpffer follows the French tradition of contemplative first-person narration. His world is focused inward; Jules participates only minimally in the world around him, observing it, for the most part, from a window in his uncle's apartment. The only real exception is the group of scenes in part 1, in which Jules sneaks into a neighboring apartment. He lies about having been there and that lie leads to others, eventually causing a chain reaction of catastrophes. The episode ends with Jules being punished by his tutor. It seems probable that Tolstoy modeled chapters 11–14 of *Boyhood* on these scenes from Töpffer.

For the genesis of Tolstoy's trilogy, *David Copperfield* (published in Russian translation in the 1851 edition of *The Contemporary*) is also important.[49] Like *La bibliothèque de mon oncle*, it is cast in the same pseudo-autobiographical form as Tolstoy's work. In *David Copperfield* the implied division between narrator and author is apparent on the title page, which reads (in an English translation of the Russian version that Tolstoy apparently read):

The Adventures, Experiences, and Observations
of David Copperfield
The Younger
(Autobiography)
A Work
of Charles Dickens

There are, however, crucial differences between *David Copper-field* and *Childhood*. First of all, *David Copperfield* lacks the nostalgic tone that is characteristic of Tolstoy's *Childhood* and that became typical of the whole pseudo-autobiographical genre in Russia.[50] Although Tolstoy experienced more than his share of tragedy in his own early years, he chose to remember only the lyrical sides of childhood. Certainly, there was no room for the Murdstones or the blacking factory in Tolstoy's work. In addition, as Eikhenbaum pointed out, Tolstoy's *Childhood* is practically plotless: it consists of a series of loosely connected sketches. In this it differs strongly from the complicated novelistic structure of *David Copperfield*.[51] Although the honesty of Dickens's portrayal must have impressed Tolstoy, he had other goals in mind for his autobiographically oriented first work. *David Copperfield* reads like an autobiography, whereas *Childhood*, at least in part, was meant to be a much more general statement on human development.

In addition, Tolstoy's use of the authorial voice distinguishes his work from that of Dickens or Töpffer. Of course, both in eighteenth-century literature and in the Romantic period, an overt authorial voice was commonly employed. Sterne and Rousseau used it frequently, and it was also a favorite trick of Pushkin's. The Realists, however, tended to deemphasize the overt role of the author in the text. *David Copperfield* and *La bibliothèque de mon oncle* are consistently narrated from the point of view of David and Jules, respectively. As mentioned earlier, however, in *Childhood* Irten'ev's point of view is often overruled by an authorial voice. Thus, Tolstoy's narrative was unusual insofar as he chose, in an otherwise realistic narrative, to incorporate an authorial voice typical of the late-eighteenth-century authors he so loved.

In his discussion of the genesis of *Childhood*, Eikhenbaum claims that it was merely one of a series of similar works that had appeared in the Russian journals in the late 1840's and early 1850's. He cites such examples as A. de Lamartine's *Confession*, A. T. Bolotov's *Notes*, P. A. Kulish's "The Story of Iul'iana Terent'evna," I. A. Goncharov's "Oblomov's Dream," and Aksakov's *Family Chronicle* and *The Childhood Years of Bagrov's Grandson*.[52] Since then, many critics have repeated this assertion, apparently without bothering to verify it. However, an examination of the works in question shows that they could not have had much influence on Tolstoy.[53] The works of Lamartine and Bolotov are straightforward auto-biographies with minimal descriptions of childhood.[54] "Iul'iana Terent'evna" was published almost simultaneously with *Childhood*.[55] *Family Chronicle* is in the third person and has no description of childhood. *The Childhood Years of Bagrov's Grandson* is certainly a pseudo-autobiography, but it was published six years after *Childhood*; in fact, there is some evidence that Aksakov may have borrowed a few things from Tolstoy. The only work in the entire series that has anything to do with Tolstoy's is "Oblomov's Dream"; it will be discussed in Chapter 3. It is true, then, that autobiography and childhood were "in the air" at the time, but contemporary Russian works seem to have had little influence on the young Tolstoy.[56]

The question of the originality of *Childhood* can now be answered in two ways. There is no doubt that Tolstoy borrowed from a large number of sources when writing *Childhood*. Some might claim that this fact alone proves that he was merely a "timid follower" (to quote Eikhenbaum again). In this view, all Tolstoy did was to recombine a number of preexisting motifs. Although this interpretation has been espoused by many competent scholars, I cannot agree with it. The mere existence of a large number of sources cannot be taken as proof of a work's lack of originality. The important question is how the sources are used. In *Childhood*, Tolstoy managed to synthesize a number of genres that had previously been thought to belong to separate spheres. He melded Rousseau's idyllic conception of childhood and the ferocious analytic insight of *Confessions* with the more lyrical strains of the French pseudo-autobiography, and he used this synthesis to describe a purely Russian situation. In this sense *Childhood* is a deeply original work. To some extent, Tolstoy's originality can also be seen in the further development of Russian views of childhood. Before 1852 there were scores of European works that could have influenced the form and content of Russian works on the subject. Yet

Tolstoy's work became the sole model; almost every account of childhood published in Russia after 1852 turned to Tolstoy (and not to Rousseau, Dickens, Töpffer, or others) for inspiration.

Childhood in *Childhood*

If there is a single overarching message in *Childhood*, it is that childhood is an essentially happy period. This does not exclude unhappy moments, of course, but the overall impression is and—Tolstoy implies—should be one of joyous innocence. While it is perhaps unnecessary to point out that Tolstoy borrowed his theoretical conception of childhood from Rousseau, it is noteworthy that Tolstoy applied this concept more extensively than did its inventor. Although Rousseau may well have had a happy childhood, he devoted less than twenty pages of *Confessions* (a work of approximately 600 pages) to a description of it. When Tolstoy provided Irten'ev with a happy childhood, he clearly was making a conscious choice. The author's own childhood could not have been a happy one, at least in any conventional sense. His mother died before he was two, and, in his own words: "I don't remember my mother at all" (34: 349). His father died when Tolstoy was eight, and thereafter he was shuttled between the homes of grandmothers and aunts. Nevertheless, despite personal experience (or, perhaps, because of it), Tolstoy both considered childhood the happiest time of life in theory and provided Irten'ev with a lyrically joyful version. Through Irten'ev he was finally able to have the childhood he had probably always wanted. Incidentally, Tolstoy's selective use of autobiographical material in *Childhood* illustrates one of the advantages of the pseudo-autobiography. Had he claimed to be writing an autobiography, he might have found it difficult to rewrite his childhood memories so radically.

The perception of childhood as time in paradise is expressed at various points in the work. It is in chapter 15, however, that this theme receives its most elaborate treatment. It is not difficult to discern that this chapter is the key one for the entire story. For one thing, it bears the same name as the title of the book; for another, it is placed between the descriptions of the two days in Irten'ev's life around which the entire narrative is structured. Finally, it lies at the physical midpoint of the work: preceded by fourteen chapters and followed by thirteen.

The chapter begins with two sentences in the author's voice: "Happy, happy irretrievable time of childhood! How can one not love, not cherish its memories?" (1: 43). For the Russian cultural mind, these may have been the most unforgettable sentences Tolstoy ever wrote. For the next 80 years, practically every first-person description of childhood in Russia, whether in fictional or in nonfictional form, was oriented to them. As is typical of authorial statements throughout *Childhood*, these lines are unmotivated by anything preceding them. They are not modified by a personal pronoun or a time marker. Instead, they are simply meant to express the abstract, universal truth about childhood.

The author's statement is followed by one sentence in the voice of the narrator: "Those memories freshen, exalt my soul, and are a source of great enjoyment for me." This sentence defines Irten'ev's personal reasons for writing about childhood. Through recollections of childhood happiness, he hopes to recapture a part of himself that has, evidently, been lost in the process of growing up. His soul in the present needs to be "freshened" through reminiscence. He perceives the world of childhood as an idyllic one, fundamentally different from the world in which he now lives. It is not the case that things simply got steadily worse in the course of Irten'ev's life. He experiences moments of happiness in *Youth* and even in *Boyhood*, but childhood is the only period that he sees as happy in and of itself, regardless of what he may have experienced at a given instant. Of course, it would be a mistake to assert that every moment of Irten'ev's childhood is happy. Tolstoy did not provide Irten'ev with a saccharine childhood. Nevertheless, moments of unhappiness, or even of personal tragedy, do not prevent Irten'ev from recalling his childhood as a golden age, just as moments of happiness in later life do not modify the essentially unfortunate character of boyhood or youth.[57] Tolstoy's model, in which childhood is perceived as a golden age, the highpoint of a person's life, dominated Russian autobiographical conceptions of childhood until well into the twentieth century.

Having characterized childhood from the point of view of author and narrator, Tolstoy proceeds to an extended recreation of a childhood scene from the perspective of Irten'ev the child. The scene described (the child falling asleep at evening tea) seems unremarkable in terms of content. Nothing dramatic happens here, and there is no obvious reason why this particular scene should have impressed itself indelibly on the child's mind. However, the choice of a scene of uneventful domestic bliss is quite logical. It emphasizes Tolstoy's eschewal of traditional plotting techniques and forces the reader to concentrate solely on the mood induced by the recollection:

Having had your fill of running around, it would happen that you would be sitting at the tea table on your high chair; it's already late and sleep weighs down your eyes, but you don't move from your place, you sit and listen. And how could you not listen? Maman is talking to someone and the sounds of her voice are so sweet, so welcoming. How much those sounds say to my heart! I look at her face with eyes clouded over by sleepiness and suddenly she has become all itsy-bitsy—her face is no bigger than a button. (1: 43)

The iterative "it would happen" indicates that the scene is a composite, but, with this exception, the rest of the paragraph (indeed, practically the rest of the chapter) stays entirely in the voice of the child.[58] This is by far the most extended section narrated from the child's point of view in *Childhood*. In fact, the successful narrative recreation of such a large chunk of childhood material would almost seem to belie the author's characterization of childhood as an "irretrievable time."

The recreated state of childhood happiness cannot last, however. It is destroyed by the same mind that resurrected it, as soon as that mind begins to question and analyze its own recollections. As the second and third parts of the trilogy will show, childhood innocence was lost under the twin onslaught of civilization and sexuality; the adult narrator's hope that he can recreate it disappears as soon as time and space intrude on the narrative. For the child, only the here and now exist. The narrator, on the other hand, is conscious of the spatial and temporal abyss separating him from his past self. As soon as the consciousness of the reminiscing narrator enters the text, the illusion that the past can be permanently recaptured is destroyed. Thus, at the end of chapter 15, the narrator asks himself: "Will the freshness, the insouciance, the need for love and the strength of belief that one possesses in childhood ever return?" (1: 45). The answer, of course, is that those things cannot return. The chapter, which began on such an ecstatic note, ends in a minor key with the narrator's realization that the "irretrievable time of childhood" is just that: "Is it possible that life has really left such deep scars in my heart that those tears and joys have gone forever? Do only memories remain?" (1: 45). The desire and ability to summon up a past, happy world, coupled with the realization that the world thus recreated is only an illusion, lies at the very core of *Childhood*.

As a number of critics have noticed, *Childhood* has no plot in the normal sense of the word.[59] In fact, for all intents and purposes, nothing really happens in the course of the narrative.[60] The structure of a typical nineteenth-century novel can be likened to that of a motion picture: individual sections are linked in a continuous flow of narrative. The structure of *Childhood*, in contrast, is that of an album of still photographs. Each page contains a certain number of moments captured in time, but, between these moments, there are unavoidable gaps. Each chapter presents a new set of images, but there is no reason to expect that these images should be connected to the ones in the previous chapter in anything but the most general way.[61] The success of *Childhood* was due, most of all, to Tolstoy's ability to use these loosely connected scenes in order to open up the minds of his protagonist and his narrator. The technique he employed—what N. G. Chernyshevsky, in his famous 1856 essay on *Childhood*, called the "dialectic of the soul"—was effective precisely because the absence of a conventional plot ensured that the reader's attention would be focused almost entirely on the younger Irten'ev's perceptions of the world and on the older Irten'ev's analysis of his past self. In order to strengthen the motivation for this powerful psychological presentation of the world, Tolstoy endowed Irten'ev with a prodigious capacity for reminiscence.

In a previous section I quoted the child's description of his feelings when he heard his mother play the piano. "That feeling resembled memories; but memories of what? It seemed you were recalling things that never happened" (1: 31). The image of a young child desperately searching for memories of an even earlier time would play an important role in subsequent Russian accounts of childhood. Most Russian gentry autobiographers recall having been sensitive, precocious children, a perception that this image of the preternaturally responsive Irten'ev certainly helped to form. Nor is this the only instance in which the child evinces a precocious tendency to reminiscence. For example, having just left home for the first time, Irten'ev sits in the carriage and thinks about his mother: "Every reminiscence led me to think about her. I remembered the mushroom that I found the day before in the birch walk, I remembered how Liubochka and Katen'ka argued over who should pick it, and I remembered how they cried saying goodbye to us." He does not remember his mother directly. Instead, he brings her to mind through a string of associative memories.[62] Indeed, it would seem that even as a child Irten'ev had a tendency to convert every experience into a "memory."

Earlier, I characterized the structure of *Childhood* in terms of a photo album. In view of the interlocking memories that hold the narrative together, a different and perhaps more appropriate metaphor suggests itself: one could say that *Childhood* is structured like the wooden "matreshka" dolls with which all Russian children play. The younger Irten'ev remembers something that happened to him; the adult narrator remembers the child remembering; finally, if the scene is autobiographical, one can imagine Tolstoy himself remembering it before placing it in the narrative.

Excluding Irten'ev himself, the central figure in *Childhood* is that of the mother. She is present on the very first page (in the form of a picture that Karl Ivanych hits with a fly swatter), and it is her death that marks the end of Irten'ev's childhood. It is not surprising, therefore, that she should be the only person, other than the child himself, to appear in the chapter called "Childhood." Her character is fully developed in chapter 2, which is entitled "Maman." As with the work as a whole, what is striking about this chapter is its total lack of conventional narrative interest. Instead of being organized around a specific event or events, material is presented in a series of static portraits: mother pouring tea, mother giving a piano lesson to Nikolai's sister, mother smiling, mother asking Nikolai how he slept. The series of portraits is, of course, a particularly effective way to evoke the child's perception of the world. For the child, scenes like this are repeated every day; there is no expectation that they will cease some time in the future, nor any remembrance of a time before they began. In this sense the child's perception of time is cyclical; there are but a limited number of possible events, and these are constantly repeated. The child's apprehension of the world is implicitly opposed by the narrator's. The older Irten'ev is always aware of just how fragile the child's world really is.

The attributes with which Tolstoy endows Irten'ev's mother were destined to be repeated in scores of Russian autobiographies and pseudo-autobiographies. Some of these attributes were part and parcel of a gentry upbringing. These include the ability to play the piano, to embroider, and to speak fluent French and German. Other qualities could not have been inculcated solely through education, but they too became de rigueur for the Russian autobiographical mother. Her eyes express "kindness and love" (1: 8). Her smile makes everyone who sees it happier. She is deeply religious but not fanatically so. She pities and helps the poor and religious pilgrims. She is scrupulously fair and is always good to her serfs. Indeed, in chapter 13, the narrator flashes back to the time before he was born and describes how his mother tried to free her nanny, Natal'ia Savishna. When Natal'ia Savishna refused to accept and expressed a desire to remain with the family, she became the unofficial nanny of all her mistress's children and the majordomo of the household.

Most important of all for the subsequent development of Russian accounts of childhood, Tolstoy emphasizes the close bond connecting mother and son—clearly the closest bond that ever existed for Irten'ev. The narrator describes the scene of parting from her as follows: "It is strange that, while I vividly remember all the faces of the servants . . . I am completely unable to recall Maman's face or her position: maybe this is because for all of that time I couldn't work up the courage to look at her. It seemed to me that had I done so, my and her grief would have certainly reached impossible proportions" (1: 41). In these few pages of description and commentary, Tolstoy was able to create the pattern for almost all the mothers of Russian autobiography. This is all the more remarkable if we recall that, unlike much else in *Childhood*, the relationship of mother and child was entirely fictional.

While Irten'ev's mother is portrayed quite simply as "an angel," his father is a more complicated figure. In large measure this is due to the fact that the narrator knows his father better. His mother died before he was old enough to judge her or even to remember her very well. The father, on the other hand, is present from time to time throughout the trilogy, and the narrator has evidently had the chance to recognize his father's faults and his virtues. There are two separate chapters in *Childhood* devoted to a description of Irten'ev's father (chapter 3, "Papa," and chapter 10, "What Kind of Man Was My Father?"). The latter begins with a straightforward characterization that captures most of the father's important traits: "He was a man of the previous century and had the elusive combination of character traits typical of the youth of that century: chivalry, resourcefulness, self-confidence, amiability, and love of debauch [*razgul*]. . . . His two great passions were cards and women (1: 28–29).

The most important trait that Tolstoy gives Irten'ev's father is *razgul*, a kind of devil-may-care insouciance coupled with the ability to do nothing at all. In the course of the entire trilogy we never see the father do anything. He does not work and he never did (he was formerly an army officer). He manages his estates but, as we see in chapter 3, he has little control over what is actually done; all his arrangements are altered by his estate manager. Although it seems that Irten'ev feels close to his father, he does allow himself to judge him. Thus, he finishes his characterization as follows: "God only knows, whether he had any moral convictions. His life was so full of various enthusiasms that he never had the time to form any for himself. What is more, his life was so happy that he did not see any need for them" (1: 30). As was the case with the traits that Tolstoy gave Irten'ev's mother, his description of the father was destined to be repeated in many Russian autobiographies and pseudo-autobiographies.

The fact that the portraits of Irten'ev's mother and father are not based primarily on Tolstoy's own memories inevitably leads to the question: In what sense is *Childhood* autobiographical? To some extent, this question can be answered by examining the development of the work in the course of four drafts. Overall, the first draft of *The Four Epochs of Development* is less autobiographical than the trilogy as we know it. It is in two parts: the first describes childhood, and the second deals with the periods of boyhood and youth, although there are no divisions into defined periods as such. The description of childhood contains, in a rather condensed form, much of the material that would later go into *Childhood*. There are, however, some crucial differences. Irten'ev was to be an illegitimate child (his mother had left her husband to live with her lover, Irten'ev's father), and much of the work's plot as well as the child's reactions to it hinged upon the difficulties inherent in the position of an illegitimate child in Russia. This situation clearly draws on the story of the Islenev family, neighbors of the Tolstoys and relations of his wife-to-be. Even more important, the second part of this first version has almost nothing to do with the remaining parts of the trilogy as it eventually came to be written. In the first draft, the children were brought to Moscow to be educated at a "commercial school." After the death of the mother, the father changes his plans and enrolls them in a "gymnasium." They live in the house of a professor of physiology who is an old acquaintance of the father's. Their life at his house and the problems of being poor and illegitimate form the central thread of the second part of the proposed text. Of the secondary characters present in the trilogy, we see only Karl Ivanych and Grisha. The French tutor is absent, as is the grandmother. Natal'ia Savishna is mentioned, but her character is not developed at all. In short, the life of the narrator of the proposed novel *The Four Epochs of Development* had little in common with Tolstoy's own. As Tolstoy revised the novel, he began to eliminate some scenes that had nothing to do with his life and to add new scenes (or develop previously existing ones) with an autobiographical resonance. The description of life with Karl Ivanych is lengthened, and, in *Boyhood*, three entire chapters are devoted to his biography. In his *Memoirs*, Tolstoy was later to write: "In *Childhood* I described the German, our teacher Fed. Iv. Rössel, in as much detail as I could under the name of Karl Ivanych" (34: 370). The French *gouverneur* St. Jerome (St. Thomas in real life) appears. So does the grandmother, and, although she is made the mother's mother and not the father's, many of her characteristics are those which Tolstoy describes in his *Memoirs* more than 50 years later. I mention these examples merely to show that, in the course of writing, the trilogy became increasingly autobiographical.[63]

Nevertheless, even in the final version of *Childhood*, it would seem that there are not enough points of contact between the lives of Irten'ev and Tolstoy to justify calling the work a fictionalized autobiography. Rather, it is a hybrid work, a true pseudo-autobiography, which liberally mixes facts from Tolstoy's life with invented situations. This free mixture has prompted Ginzburg to say that the trilogy is composed of "works that are more auto-psychological than autobiographical."[64] Nevertheless, there is evidence showing that the final version of *Childhood* contained enough autobiographical material for Tolstoy's immediate family to recognize themselves. A. V. Goldenveizer describes the moment of recognition quite dramatically. It seems that I. S. Turgenev read *Childhood* aloud to Tolstoy's sister and brother before the identity of the author had been revealed: "From the very first lines Mariia Nikolaevna and Sergei Nikolaevich were stunned: 'But that's us he described! Who is this?' 'At first we just couldn't think about Levochka,' continued Mariia Nikolaevna. 'He had gotten into debt and been taken off to the Caucasus. In all probability we thought about brother Nikolai.'" [65]

There was only one other feature of the content of *Childhood* that was as important for the future development of Russian autobiography and pseudo-autobiography as Irten'ev's portrait gallery. This was the child's attitude toward the physical world around him. The estate on which Irten'ev is depicted as growing up was, in many respects, typical for the estates of the middle rank of Russian gentry. Its most important single trait is self-sufficiency. For the child Irten'ev, the world of the estate is the entire world. It is a telling fact that, on the way to Moscow at the beginning of *Boyhood*, the young Irten'ev finds it hard to believe that there are people who do not know who he and his family are. On the estate, as the child of the master, Irten'ev is the center of the universe. He lives in the midst of the natural world, and the landscapes of rural central Russia have a special meaning for him. Much of the action of *Childhood* (and of the trilogy as a whole) takes place in the city, but the cityscape never makes a positive mark on the boy's consciousness. It is the countryside that resonates within the boy's soul, and Irten'ev's special relationship to nature plays an important role in determining the "plot" of the trilogy.

The natural world is perceived as a sphere of goodness standing against both social evils and personal problems. It is here that the influence of Rousseau on the young Tolstoy is felt most strongly. The idea that childhood innocence is a paradise lost that can best be recaptured through reminiscences of the natural world is repeated from time to time throughout the trilogy. [66] It is not only that nature opposes the baneful influence of civilization. For Tolstoy, nature defies time and space; its beauty, which changes at every season but always returns, recalls a time before the child understood the meaning of death and decay. Of course, since for both Tolstoy and Irten'ev this natural world was connected to a context of a Russian gentry estate, the experience of the golden age is expressed by reference to the specifics of what a Soviet critic might call the "feudal-patriarchal order." The intense nostalgia evoked by memories of nature on the estate is not merely personal. By the early 1850's it was already clear that an era was drawing to an end; thus, not only would Tolstoy not experience his childhood again, but no one would ever grow up as he had. The system that had been operative at least since the days of Catherine the Great was passing. It is the combination of personal and collective loss that lends the nature scenes such a powerful resonance in the trilogy.

Irten'ev describes himself in the natural world for the first time when he recalls the hunt on the day before his departure for Moscow. If Irten'ev's ability to recall the tiniest details of long-past events seemed amazing when he described people, then his photographic recall of the scene before the hunt is completely beyond the realm of the possible. The description is meant to be in the voice of the child, but it is so hyperrealistic that it cannot possibly be read as a remembered moment. At moments like these, Tolstoy's realism of description ends up contradicting his psychological realism: "There were swarms of ants swarming over the uncovered roots of the oak tree under which I was sitting. They went over the dry gray earth, through the dried oak leaves and the acorns, the desiccated, moss-covered twigs, the yellow-green moss, and the rare thin blades of green grass" (1: 25).

It is not merely the detail with which Irten'ev is able to recall the scene that is unusual. Even more surprising is his conviction that he can commune with nature in a personal way. He looks at a butterfly and notes: "I don't know whether the sun had warmed her up, or whether she had taken the juice from that little grass, but it was clear that she was feeling fine" (1: 25). Nor is Irten'ev's ability confined merely to understanding the moods of lower animals. Nature speaks directly to him. For example, at the beginning of *Boyhood*, when the grieving family is returning to Moscow after Irten'ev's mother's funeral, they are overtaken by a thunderstorm. Naturally, the thunder and lightning scare the boy, but what he feels is not merely a child's normal fear of thunder. He interprets the storm as an apocalyptic moment: "Troubling feelings of anguish and fear grew in me as the storm strengthened, but when the grandiose moment of silence arrived—the moment which usually precedes the outbreak of a thunderstorm—those feelings increased so much that if this state had lasted another quarter of an hour I am sure I would have died of agitation" (2: 10). But nature, which has the power to bring the boy to the point of death, also has the power to change his mood almost immediately. The thunderstorm passes and, with it, so does the boy's anxiety. Indeed, the state of his soul is directly connected to that of the external world: "I experience that inexpressibly joyful feeling of hope in life, which quickly replaces the heavy feeling of fear. My soul is smiling, just like refreshed and newly merry nature" (2: 11–12).

In addition to being powerfully affected by the actual experience of the natural world, Irten'ev (both the child and the adult) can be moved by the mere recollection of the scenery of his childhood paradise. In *Childhood*, after Irten'ev has embarrassed himself by dancing incorrectly at his grandmother's, he consoles himself with intertwined memories of his mother and of the estate's natural surroundings. The whole passage is in the voice of the child:

For if Maman had been here, she would not have blushed for her Nikolen'ka ... and my imagination floated far beyond that dear image. I recalled the meadow in front of the house, the tall lindens in the garden, the clean pond which the swallows soar over, the blue sky in which white transparent clouds stand still, the aromatic stacks of fresh hay, and many other peaceful and joyful memories floated through my roiled imagination. (1: 72)

The link between memories of the mother and those of the unspoiled land is a symbolically logical one. In later Russian autobiography the mother figure (who can also be a grandmother or a nanny) frequently takes on the overt characteristics of a pagan mother-earth goddess combined with those of an angel in human form.[67] The perfection of the mother and the healing power of nature will become two of the central myths of gentry childhood.

Nor is it only the child who is capable of feeling the refreshing power of nature. In the chapter entitled "Youth," the older Irten'ev senses it as well. He says, "That summer I was young, innocent, free and, therefore, almost happy" (2: 175). Then he begins to reminisce. He looks at the birches, which "hiding behind one another retreated from me into the distance of the pure forest," and he enjoys "exactly the same fresh young strength of life which nature breathed all around me." The chapter ends with the statement: "At that time it seemed as if nature and the moon and I, that we were all one and the same thing" (2: 180).

In a number of important respects, the relationship between Irten'ev and nature corresponds to that which is characteristic for what Bakhtin calls the idyll: "Finally the third characteristic of an idyll . . . is the combination of human life with the life of nature, the unity of their rhythm, a common language for natural phenomena and events of human life."[68] If the trilogy is to be considered an idyll, however, it is an idyll of a specific type: the paradise lost. The narrator has grown up and has left the estate. He can recapture its charm only through memory. In this sense, the estate and childhood are analogous. Memories of one are inextricably linked to memories of the other, and both types of memories "freshen and exalt the soul."

In *Childhood*, Tolstoy presented Russian literature with a model for writing about childhood and proposed an interpretation of the meaning and purpose of this stage of life. From the first, he had hoped that his work would be read as a general statement, not simply as a fictionalized version of his own early years. He must have been gratified when most early reviewers singled out the universality of his portrayal for praise. He would probably have been even more gratified had he known the extent to which his literary method and his myths of childhood permeated Russian autobiographies and pseudo-autobiographies for the next 70 years.[69]

As I noted earlier, in a discussion of *Childhood* in *Diary of a Writer*, Dostoevsky called Tolstoy the poet and historian of the upper-middle gentry class.[70] We are now in a better position to see just how perceptive this statement was. It is true that the kinds of experiences Irten'ev describes were typical of a gentry childhood. In this sense Tolstoy was a kind of historian. But these kinds of experiences had not been expressed in Russia previously, nor (and this is even more important) had they been given a general interpretation. In his overall conception, in his descriptions and interpretation of Irten'ev's surroundings, of his parents, and of Irten'ev himself, Tolstoy invented a Russian gentry attitude toward childhood. In time, his personal myths of childhood became the foundation on which practically all future Russian works on the subject were constructed. In this sense he was not the historian of gentry childhood, but rather its creator, a poet first and foremost.

Chapter Two

S. T. Aksakov: A Broader Vision

Tolstoy provided Russia with a powerful interpretive model of childhood. Yet, despite favorable reviews and instant popularity, certain characteristics of *Childhood* ensured that future writers would not use the Tolstoyan model in an unmediated form. First of all, there was Tolstoy's decision to organize all the action of his novella around two days in Irten'ev's life. From a literary point of view, this innovative structure was one of Tolstoy's triumphs; it allowed him to deemphasize plot intrigue and to concentrate primarily on Irten'ev's psychology and view of the world around him. As a model for the presentation of childhood memories, however, this approach was evidently too risky for less talented writers to adopt. The development of Russian childhood accounts (both autobiographical and pseudo-autobiographical) shows that writers, however much they borrowed from Tolstoy in other areas, preferred to conceive their lives as more conventionally plotted. Rather than describe a crucial group of days, they tend to begin with birth or earliest memories and continue chronologically through selected events of early life.

The second deficiency in *Childhood* (from the point of view of later Russian writers) was Tolstoy's almost complete lack of concern with the history of the Irten'ev family. Once again, this "deficiency" was a source of strength in *Childhood*, because it allowed Tolstoy not to waste precious space describing things that the young Irten'ev did not experience. On the other hand, especially for autobiographers, the ahistoricism of *Childhood* made it an unsuitable model. As a rule, autobiographers did not wish merely to create subtle psychological self-portraits (even if they had the ability to do so). Rather, they saw themselves as one link in a long chain of family history, a history in which their own childhood years played only one part. Taken by themselves, Tolstoy's myths of childhood were too personal and specific for general consumption. To become generally accepted, they needed to be placed in a wider context.

As it happened, Russia did not have long to wait for a work that echoed many of the themes of *Childhood* while being imbued with a strong sense of familial and personal chronology. Just six years after Tolstoy's literary debut, the reading public welcomed the final work of the aging Aksakov: *The Childhood Years of Bagrov's Grandson*. It is difficult to determine whether Tolstoy's work or Tolstoy himself had anything to do with the way Aksakov portrayed childhood. Most probably, Aksakov had read *Childhood* when it first appeared, although there is no record of his reaction.[1] The two writers first met in January 1856 and became friendly almost immediately.[2] Aksakov read excerpts from *A Family Chronicle* to the younger writer, and he evidently took Tolstoy's criticism seriously.[3] It is quite conceivable that the two talked about *Childhood Years* before it was completed. One thing we know for certain, however, is that Tolstoy was impressed with *Childhood Years* even before its publication: in a diary entry for January 1857, he wrote: "A reading at S. T. Aksakov's. Childhood, wonderful!"[4]

As soon as *Childhood Years* appeared in print, Russian readers and critics echoed Tolstoy's sentiments. Almost immediately, they noticed the links connecting the new work with Aksakov's previously published *A Family Chronicle* and *Memoirs*. Indeed, for the most part they saw the works as a trilogy that one critic dubbed *The Bagrov Family*.[5] This reading was given "official" approval by Aksakov's son Ivan, who, in the preface to the posthumous edition of his father's works, informed the reading public that "the exact same personages appear in *Excerpts from the Bagrov Family Chronicle . . .* and in *Childhood Years . . .* and, finally, in the *Memoirs* that were appended to the *Chronicle* and published simultaneously with it."[6] The three works are to be considered together as a grand family autobiography. In some sense such a reading is correct: it is true that all three works are based on the biography of Aksakov and his family. Yet, while this approach brings out many common thematic points, a "holistic" reading has drawbacks as well. It is, first of all, entirely in keeping with the unfortunate Russian and Soviet tendency to read only for content, ignoring the formal and stylistic devices that make a work of art. In addition, such a reading ignores the intent of the author himself, who went to great pains *not* to write a standard autobiography. In fact, no two of the works that make up the "trilogy" belong to the same genre: despite obvious similarities and points of connection, each work calls for a different type of reading. Since what differentiates these works has been largely ignored, this will be the primary subject of my analysis. Only *The Childhood Years of Bagrov's Grandson* is a pseudo-autobiography, and, because of its influence on the Russian literary and autobiographical traditions, it will be the primary text discussed. However, both *A Family Chronicle* and *Memoirs* will be treated as well, in order that the particularities of *Childhood Years* may be seen more clearly.

It should be mentioned that, although all Soviet editions of Aksakov publish the works in autobiographical chronological order (that is, *Family Chronicle, Childhood Years, Memoirs*), such an arrangement does not reflect the order in which the works were written, published, and read by Aksakov's contemporaries. *A Family Chronicle* was begun as early as 1840. It did not appear as a whole, however, until 1856, by which time *Memoirs* had also been completed. The two were published together in a single volume in 1856. *Childhood Years*, the so-called middle volume of the "trilogy," was not completed until 1858. Of course, the fact that the works were written over a long period and out of order does not necessarily disqualify them as an autobiographical trilogy; after all, Tolstoy published his trilogy over five years and Gorky's stretched over ten. Nevertheless, despite the extent to which Tolstoy's or Gorky's trilogies evolved in the course of writing, in each case the three volumes share a narrator and a broadly similar point of view and structure. This is not the case with Aksakov. *A Family Chron-*

icle is a biography. It describes the actions of two generations of the Bagrov family and is narrated, mostly in the third person, by a member of the third generation, Sergei Bagrov. *Childhood Years* is a classic pseudo-autobiography: it is narrated, this time in the first person, by the same Sergei Bagrov, who tells the story of his early childhood. Finally, *Memoirs* is typical autobiography: it is narrated in the first person by Sergei Aksakov and describes his life from ages eight to sixteen.

A Family Chronicle has often been called an epic, and its central character, Stepan Mikhailovich Bagrov, has been likened to an Old Testament patriarch. While the novel does contain both Biblical and epic elements, neither of these characterizations captures the structure on which the work is based: the Russian fairy tale or folk tale. The fairy tale is a particularly appropriate model for a biographical novel based on old family stories from a semi-legendary past. One can imagine the young Bagrov hearing about the old days and transforming these stories in his mind to fit the patterns of the fairy tales he knew. Later, perhaps, he would have been unable to separate family legends from his reinterpretations.[7] In any case, *A Family Chronicle* is filled with folk- and fairy-tale structures.[8]

The first two sections of *A Family Chronicle* are modeled on Russian folk tales of the warrior hero, or *bogatyr'*. The central character is Stepan Mikhailovich Bagrov: short, squat, broad-shouldered, and strong as a rock, he reminds one of Il'ia Muromets.[9] His qualifications for the hero's role become clear in his struggle with Kurolesov. Kurolesov is the evil sorcerer: specifically, he is a vampire (at one point his actions are described as "bloodsucking" [1: 106]). He wins his wife by charming Stepan Mikhailovich's family (in the latter's absence) and manages to keep his wife and all her family under his evil spell. When his power finally wanes and his wife unmasks his way of life (the scene of discovery is described as a sort of satanic ball, complete with drunkenness, half-naked women, singing, and wild dancing), he throws her into a dark dungeon. She is rescued by the *bogatyr'*, who, appropriately, breaks down the door of her prison and carries her away to safety.

The story of Sof'ia Nikolaevna's early life belongs not to the

Russian folk epic, but to a well-known fairy tale: "Cinderella." The lovely young girl is good, virtuous, beautiful, and the favorite of her father. However, after her mother dies, she is persecuted by the inevitable evil stepmother. The situation is changed by the death of the stepmother and Sof'ia's return to her father's favor. Immediately after her fairy tale concludes, we learn how Aleksei Stepanovich fell in love with and eventually married her. Aleksei Stepanovich is a latter-day version of the simple son of Russian folklore: *Ivan durachok*. Everyone considers him dull, uneducated, and intellectually inferior (except, of course, the magical Cinderella, who is capable, it turns out, of turning this frog into a prince). In the end, his virtues become clear to all and he marries Cinderella. The "Fourth Excerpt" of the novel describes how the virtuous heroine charms the crusty old *bogatyr'* despite the evil machinations of her sisters-in-law (troublemaking sisters or sisters-in-law are also stock fairy-tale characters). Finally, as all fairy tales must, *A Family Chronicle* ends happily with the birth of a son to the married couple.

By emphasizing folk elements in *A Family Chronicle*, I do not mean to imply that the work is not biographically accurate. However, the way in which Aksakov organizes the text shows that he has chosen to relate his family history to fairy- and folk-tale structures. Real-life stories are projected onto these structures and derive additional meaning from them. As I mentioned before, this form is appropriate, considering that the work's narrator supposedly heard these family stories as a child, a time when fairy-tale structures are strongly embedded in the mind.

Although it would seem difficult not to notice the folk- and fairy-tale elements in *A Family Chronicle*, they were unimportant for Aksakov's contemporaries. Instead, early readers saw the work as an autobiography, and they felt that Aksakov's talent lay in his ability to use his family story to illustrate general truths about Russian life. One contemporary reviewer praised Aksakov's ability to find the general in the specific as follows: "This is all raised by him to a level of typical expression. The internal and the general shine through in everything, whether in the character of a single person, or even in the character of an entire way of life." [10] It was precisely this peculiarly Russian tendency to see literary characters as models for or models of human behavior that allowed Aksakov's family fairy tale to influence the development of Russian gentry autobiography. [11]

Rather than beginning their autobiographies with their own memories, as they might have had they followed the Tolstoyan model of childhood, Russian autobiographers usually started with a discussion of their entire family history. In the course of the nineteenth century, there were at least five autobiographies that bore the subtitle "A Family Chronicle" and many more in which this phrase was used in the text. Of course, the reading of Aksakov whereby *Childhood Years* was seen as nothing more than a continuation of *A Family Chronicle* sanctioned this type of approach. The opening lines of T. Tolycheva's memoirs indicate the importance of Aksakov's influence: "The interest and importance of notes and family reminiscences of all types has long been appreciated. As long as they are compiled sincerely. . . . You don't even need talent. S. T. Aksakov is an exception; but everyone has a family chronicle." [12]

For the original readers of *A Family Chronicle*, *Memoirs* that followed it must have seemed surprising. Suddenly, instead of the voice of Bagrov setting down his family history, the narrator becomes Aksakov himself. He reviews his life, in the first person, from the beginning of his formal education at the Kazan' gymnasium to his early university days. As an autobiographer, Aksakov is prepared to vouch for the accuracy of his statements (this, of course, does not exclude the possibility of accidental errors), something he was clearly not prepared to do in his novels. In *Memoirs* he is already a "historical" person who interacts with real people in a verifiable world. Gone are the Gogolian flights of lyricism, gone the epic/heroic/fairy-tale elements so characteristic of *A Family Chronicle*. [13]

In place of the divisions into "excerpts" (which gave *A Family Chronicle* the illusion of being fragmentary, the incomplete retelling of dimly remembered family stories), *Memoirs* is in four chapters, three of which are set in the city and one in the country. The narrator describes his earlier self, sometimes carefully analyzing his actions from his present perspective, sometimes presenting large chunks of material almost without analysis. The first two chapters concentrate closely on the boy and his small world, whereas the latter two look more to the outside world.

This work has generally been considered the weakest link of the "trilogy," and I am inclined to agree. It sometimes seems that Aksakov did not quite know what he wanted to do here. Were these reminiscences to be a description of his life and times (that is, an outward facing set of memoirs, a sort of prehistory for his *Literary and Theatrical Memoirs*)? Or, were they to be the latter part of *Childhood Years*, a novel he had not yet written but about which he was already thinking? In the end, *Memoirs* contains elements of both, but in a not completely felicitous combination.

There is, however, one moment at the beginning of *Memoirs* that, because it echoes the central Tolstoyan myth of childhood so strongly, deserves to be mentioned. Before describing his departure from the country estate for school in the city, Aksakov interrupts his narrative and inserts an apostrophe to childhood:

O, where are you, magical world, the Scheherazade of human life. . . . You, golden time of childhood happiness, the memory of which stirs an old man's soul so sweetly and sadly! Happy is he who had one, who has something to remember! For many it passes unnoticed or joylessly and in their mature years all that remains in the memory is the coldness or even the cruelty of people. (2: 10)

Clearly, just as did Tolstoy, Aksakov recalled childhood as the happiest time of his life (and, ideally, as the time that should be the happiest of any life). Of course, this is not to say that childhood is without problems, fears, and unhappy moments. There would be plenty of those described in Aksakov's pseudo-autobiography. Still, this panegyric to childhood in *Memoirs* could have hinted to readers that, at least in general outline, Aksakov's eventual work on childhood would not differ too greatly from Tolstoy's.

When, two years after the publication of *A Family Chronicle* and *Memoirs*, readers opened Aksakov's newest work, *The Childhood*

*Years of Bagrov's Grandson: Serving as a Continuation of 'A Family
Chronicle,'* they could have reasonably expected to see a third-
person narrative. One imagines that they might have been per-
plexed at Aksakov's choice of still another narrative form for his
latest effort. Of course, for those readers who had been following
recent developments in Russian literature, the basic formal conceit
of *Childhood Years* should have recalled Tolstoy's trilogy. Just as
Nikolai Irten'ev had recounted the story of his early years, Stepan
Mikhailovich's grandson (the third-person narrator of *A Family
Chronicle*), Sergei Bagrov, narrates the story of his childhood in the
first person. Aksakov, in a preface to the work, takes credit merely
as Bagrov's amanuensis: "Stepan Mikhailovich Bagrov's grandson
told me the story of his childhood years in great detail; I took down
his stories as accurately as possible" (1: 63).

Since, as we now know, the work is autobiographical, why did
Aksakov choose to use the pseudo-autobiographical form? The
standard explanation, and the one put forth by Ivan Aksakov in his
posthumous edition of his father's works, is that the form was
chosen to protect relatives who were still alive. This seems unlikely. While it is true that some of Aksakov's relatives were unhappy about the family's literary appearance, it should not be forgotten that the family had already appeared, with names named,
in *Memoirs*. That is, when Aksakov wanted to write a real autobiography, he did so without worrying about family propriety. In
fact, there were a number of purely literary reasons for Aksakov's
choice of genre.

The first, and perhaps the most important, was his conviction
that fictional form would give his work a more general character.
Instead of being the story of the writer Sergei Aksakov, a real man
with a past, present, and future, the novel becomes the description
of a fictional world, a world that any reader can enter at will in
order to empathize with the fictional characters. From Aksakov's
letters during this period of his work on *Childhood Years*, it seems
clear that, no matter how much autobiographical material the
novel contains, he did not think of it as an autobiography. Thus, in
a letter to Turgenev, he wrote: "I am writing a book for children. . . . I could think of nothing better than to write the history

of a child's life, beginning from legendary, prehistorical times and following it through all the impressions of life and nature." [14] One obvious advantage of the fictional form was the possibility of beginning the work at a "prehistorically early age": were it a "real" autobiography, readers might not accept such a beginning. In another letter, Aksakov calls the work "the life of a person in babyhood." [15] Aksakov repeats his plea for a generalized reading in the preface to the novel: "These stories present a rather complete history of a babe, the life of a person in childhood, and a childhood world that is created gradually under the influence of daily new impressions" (1: 263). Clearly, Aksakov felt more at ease writing about the child's world when he did not have to worry about whether all the details were exactly the same as those of his own childhood. As we will see later, the fictional form also allowed him to provide his work with a definite structure, one that might have seemed too contrived in a "real" autobiography. Finally, Aksakov felt that the reader would find it more interesting to read a book about childhood itself, rather than about the author's childhood in particular.

Therefore, despite the opinion of Ivan Aksakov, there are compelling reasons to consider *Childhood Years* not as an autobiography but as a pseudo-autobiographical novel in the tradition of Tolstoy's trilogy. In addition to the fact that in so doing we respect the wishes of the work's author, reading *Childhood Years* as a work of fiction ensures that we will pay more attention to its literary qualities. Instead of wondering about who is who, or trying to decipher Aksakov's attitude toward such issues as serfdom and education, we can appreciate other qualities in the work.

First of all, let us examine Aksakov's attempt to disassociate his voice from that of Bagrov. I have already mentioned the preface in which the author claims merely to have transcribed the oral accounts of Bagrov. In addition, the novel concludes with the following sentences: "Here ends Bagrov's grandson's narrative of his childhood. He insists that further stories relate not to his childhood, but to his boyhood. S.A." (1: 554). Together with the preface, these lines serve to frame the entire narrative, emphasizing the separation of text from author. The last sentence may well be a sort of polemical riposte to Tolstoy. Bagrov dates the end of childhood before his ninth birthday; Irten'ev's begins three days after his tenth birthday. This chronological discrepancy brings out an important difference between the works of Tolstoy and Aksakov. It has often been noted that Irten'ev is a more introspective, self-analytic narrator than Bagrov; I do not think, however, that anyone has noticed that this is simply a function of age. Bagrov tells us how he came to know the world around him. Irten'ev, by the time he begins his story, is almost fully self-conscious. He has already discovered the world and is trying to come to terms with it. As far as Aksakov was concerned, the Irten'ev of *Childhood* was not a child at all.

For Aksakov the frame is a necessary but not sufficient device for separating himself from his narrator. To further emphasize their separation, he sprinkles a series of authorial footnotes throughout the text. These serve both to clear up potential sources of misunderstanding and to remind the reader of the author's existence. Their content is quite varied. Sometimes they merely indicate where a certain story spoken of by Bagrov can be located.[16] At other times they are longer and speak of Bagrov in the third person, qualifying his observations. For example, after Bagrov speaks of crossing the ice-covered Volga, we read the following footnote: "It is rare for a big river to freeze over without snow. I saw the Volga as young Bagrov describes it only one time" (1: 550). Still other footnotes serve to define technical terms or dialect words.[17]

The most complicated series of footnotes is connected to the fairy tale "The Scarlet Flower." First, the story is mentioned in the text. Then there is a footnote, supposedly belonging to Bagrov (although how Bagrov could have provided a footnote in the course of his oral narration is not made clear). This is followed by another note, signed S.A.: "So as not to interrupt the story of childhood this fairy tale has been placed in an appendix" (1: 468). Finally, the fairy tale itself appears at the end of the novel as promised. This kind of give and take between author/editor and narrator is an important formal device used periodically to remind the reader that he is reading a novel and not the autobiography of Aksakov. A separation of the voices of author, narrator, and protagonist is, of course, one of the hallmarks of the pseudo-autobiography.

Although Aksakov used the same literary form as Tolstoy, he treated essentially different literary and personal problems. In *Childhood*, the young Tolstoy was attempting (among other things) to find his personal voice and to "Russianize" some of his favorite European literary works. As Tolstoy grew into his task, the story became more autobiographical—always remaining, formally, a pseudo-autobiography. *Childhood* is constructed around single days in the child's life that, like narrative snowballs, incorporate information and observations as they roll. The child's voice is augmented both by the adult narrator's comments and by the general statements of an authorial voice that was to become Tolstoy's trademark. Aksakov also makes use of a triple division into author/editor, narrator, and child, but he structures the narrative quite differently. While he claims simply to have recorded the tales of Bagrov, the novel is built on a number of devices that reveal the care with which Aksakov arranged his material.

Just as did Tolstoy, Aksakov exploits the possibility of shifting back and forth from the child's point of view to that of the adult. In *Childhood Years* the narrator's function is to punctuate the narrative from time to time, pointing out the novelty of what is being described from the point of view of the child. The sense of discovery that permeates the novel is achieved, not only through the freshness of the child's observations, but also through the narrator's interjections that emphasize the child's point of view. For example, beginning his description of the scene in Ufa when news of Catherine the Great's death was received, the narrator says: "And that day brought me new, hitherto unknown concepts, and forced me to feel feelings that I had never experienced" (1: 378). This introduction, as it were, reminds the reader to imagine what all of the rumors surrounding the accession of Paul and all the attendant ceremonies must have meant to the young child.

Often such interjections introduce new experiences in the sensory world: "We galloped quickly along the smooth road and I experienced the previously unknown pleasure of fast driving" (1 : 381). The mere fact that winter sleigh-riding is pleasant would not have been surprising to Aksakov's reader. However, the narrator's comment invites the reader to experience the scene from the child's point of view, to relive his or her first sleigh ride. This ability to make the reader reexperience familiar scenes through the eyes of the child lends Aksakov's prose its freshness and vitality. Most important, narrative interjections mark new stages in the child's development. Whereas Irten'ev is old enough to make big discoveries (pertaining to important philosophical and moral issues), Bagrov is still young enough to make little discoveries in the natural world. Each new encounter (and there are hundreds of them in the novel) broadens the child's horizons. It is the narrator's function to point out these little epiphanies. Thus, Bagrov had always disliked winter because it prevented him from running around outside. But, in his first winter at Bagrovo, he comes to appreciate the winter scenes. The narrator adds: "For the first time I sensed that winter scenes could have a specific beauty too" (1 : 393). This observation is part of a larger pattern of discoveries about nature that the child makes in the course of his first eight years. In fact, his development is marked by a broadening appreciation of the natural world.[18] Aksakov carefully alternates scenes of the natural world with domestic scenes in order to create the illusion of a widening spiral of time and perception.[19]

The narrator's function is hardly limited to preparing the reader for the child's descriptions. He also takes an active role in commenting on and explaining the child's impressions. Often the commentary and the description are so intertwined that it is difficult to define where one leaves off and the other begins. This, for example, is how the narrator describes his feelings in connection with his first spring in the country: "At that time, understanding nothing, not discriminating or appreciating, not even using any names, I felt new life within me and became a part of nature. It was only at the mature age of conscious memories of that time that I consciously appreciated all of its charming wonder, all of its poetic beauty" (1 : 475). This passage has important implications for the work as a whole. First of all, there is the child's ability to become a "part of nature." This was a quality that Irten'ev remembered, and it became a typical component of the gentry childhood myth. The loss of this quality was always lamented, and one of the functions of autobiographical memory was to revive it. On the other hand, although the child is a part of nature (perhaps because of it), he does not realize or fully appreciate his position. Only the adult narrator, thinking back on childhood, can appreciate what the child had. Although he cannot become a child again, he can, through memory and the written word, recreate that feeling for himself and the reader. The adult narrator is vital for the expression of loss, of nostalgia for time past that is always present in the Russian gentry autobiographical tradition. Unlike Irten'ev, however, the adult narrator in *Childhood Years* notes his childhood feelings and his nostalgia for them without trying to analyze one or the other. Where Irten'ev must consciously express *why* he feels something, Bagrov is content merely to express *what* he feels.

The irretrievability of past time and space is sometimes felt quite openly. Thus, for example, after a description of the arrival of migratory birds at Bagrovo in the spring, the narrator interjects: "In fact, it is impossible to imagine what was happening in the air, on land, and on water without having seen it, *and it is no longer possible to see it in the places I am speaking about*" (1: 466; italics mine). It is not only perception that is changed by time; the actual physical circumstances are different. One cannot see such flocks of birds both because first impressions can never be repeated and because there simply are not the same quantities of birds anymore. Of course, the narrator in *Childhood Years* is the secondary voice. He is a long way, for example, from the Gogolian flights of the narrator of *A Family Chronicle* (although he is, in fact, supposed to be the same Bagrov), who, in a similar passage, cries: "My God, how wonderful, I imagine, was that wild, virgin, luxuriant nature then!... No, you are no longer the same now, you are not even as you were when I came to know you" (1: 67). Such lyrical apostrophes are out of character with the Bagrov who narrates *Childhood Years*. Even so, the narrator's presence is a constant reminder of time past, the reminiscing and controlling force in the novel.

The narrator plays one other important role. From time to time he is allowed to make the kind of cosmic generalizations that, in *Childhood*, are made by the author's voice. In Aksakov's work these general truths are closely connected to matters being discussed and are motivated quite clearly. Still, given Aksakov's statement that he wanted to avoid any semblance of preaching,[20] their presence is somewhat surprising. It is also notable that such statements are basically absent in *A Family Chronicle* and *Memoirs*. Perhaps they are used here to enhance the feeling of generality that Aksakov wished to create: *A Family Chronicle* described a fairy-tale never-never land that had little connection to the real world; *Memoirs* was the record of an individual from whose life it would have been inappropriate to draw general inferences; *Childhood Years*, however, was the story of "a child," a representative life. It is also possible that there is a certain influence of Tolstoy here, although there is no proof. In addition, general statements by the narrator are another device used to show the difference between the child's perception and the adult's; once again, they serve to underscore the freshness of the child's vision.

An interesting example occurs when the child expresses his indignation that his father did not discipline a certain Mironych (the overseer of an estate owned by Aleksei Stepanovich's aunt); this person seemed both cruel and venal to the child, but all the adults felt that, since he did his job well and since anyone else in the same position would probably be worse, he should remain in his post. Later the narrator comments: "The wisdom of experience cannot be comprehensible to a child; voluntary concessions are incompatible with the chastity of his soul, and I was utterly incapable of accepting the thought that Mironych could beat people without ceasing to be a good man" (1: 303). The idea that the child's soul is purer than the adult's is a standard component of the "happy childhood" myth. Tolstoy clearly borrowed the concept from Rousseau. Aksakov might have gotten it from Rousseau as well, although, once again, the mediation of Tolstoy is possible.

Such narrative intrusions are quite frequent in the novel. Sometimes they even sound like avuncular advice to those parents who might be reading. This is the case, for example, when the child (who had always been truthful) remembers how he once failed to tell the whole truth to his mother. At the time he rationalized his omission by citing an incident when his mother had specifically requested him to withhold the whole truth. The narrator then adds: "Children are unusually retentive and, often, a word spoken carelessly in their presence can serve as encouragement for the kind of action they would never have committed had they not heard the approving word" (1: 515).

Sometimes, the adult narrator provides a psychological analysis of the actions of his former self. This is, of course, one of Tolstoy's most common narrative techniques. Irten'ev's self-analysis can often completely engulf the child's memories; in fact, one frequently suspects that the memory is recalled merely to provide food for analysis. In *Childhood Years* the technique is used with reserve; analysis flows logically from memory and serves as an effective reminder of the time and space separating the adult narrator from the child. The following passage describes the child's actions while his grandfather lies dying: "After dinner my cousins came into the living room and I began, quite animatedly, to chatter and to tell them all manner of things. Unconsciously, I wished to suppress the constant presence of the thought of my grandfather's death with empty conversation" (1: 387). The function of Bagrov's self-analysis is to explain his former actions, not to judge them. He notes the psychological cause and goes on with the narration. It is not an exercise in self-flagellation à la Irten'ev. This difference is undoubtedly a function of the relative personalities of Tolstoy and Aksakov. Irten'ev, like Tolstoy, is a young man not completely at peace with himself. Psychological analysis reveals the darker sides of his personality and destroys illusions. Through this destruction he hopes to slough off the accumulated dross of civilization and to find his true self. The reminiscing Bagrov, like his creator, is an older man who is basically at peace with himself. He uses psychological analysis not to tear up his soul, but rather to explain feelings and emotions that the child did not fully understand.

Thus, the narrator's voice (the voice of the older Bagrov) plays a varied and active role throughout the novel: he corrects the child's

misperceptions, analyzes his actions, and makes general statements motivated by the child's memories. Given the narrator's
constant presence, it is a bit difficult to imagine how readers and
critics have been able to say things like: "This is not a memoir
about the past, but a story about events that unfold before our very
eyes. In other words, Aksakov does not reminisce—he makes the
reader a sort of contemporary and eyewitness of the episodes." [21]
Such naive misreadings, which simply ignore the presence of
the narrator (let alone the voice of the author) do a disservice to
Childhood Years and to Aksakov. They help perpetuate the myth
that, while Aksakov may describe landscapes wonderfully, there is
nothing literary about him. Certainly, part of the novel's charm lies
in the freshness of the scenes presented by the child's unmediated
voice; nevertheless, those scenes are shaped and made much more
effective by the constant interplay between the voices of child, narrator, and author.

Having established the presence of a complex pattern of voices
in the novel, I can turn to the dominant one, that of the child, and
examine the linguistic and structural devices that make his part of
the narrative so fresh and memorable. Perhaps the best characterization of the child's voice is provided by the adult narrator. He describes why, as a child, he was able to impress his family with imi-
tations of a certain insane young man whom he had seen. He
desired "to pass on my impressions to others with the exactitude
and clarity of real life, so that the hearers would come to understand the described things just as I myself did" (1: 432). How,
then, does the child's voice succeed in creating the feeling of reality,
a feeling that all readers of the novel have remarked, but few have
attempted to explain?

First and foremost, the secret is in the quantity of detail. Where
Tolstoy, for example, will focus on a few images and bring them
out with the force almost of caricature, Aksakov includes practically everything in his descriptions, without emphasizing specific elements, thereby imitating the child's sponge-like ability to
absorb new scenes. The novel becomes a record not of what happened to the child or of what he did (because nothing particularly

dramatic happens here, in opposition to the event-filled plot of *A Family Chronicle*) but of what the child saw and remembered. The unusually tactile quality of young Bagrov's descriptions gives them the illusion of photographic reality. Here, for example, is his depiction of a river-bank landscape:

The bird-cherries, thick as logs, were covered with already darkening fruit; the bushes of ripe black currants diffused their aromatic smell through the air; the flexible, sticky stems of blackberries, covered with big, still-green berries, wrapped themselves around everything that they touched; there were even lots of raspberries. (1: 286)

Every tree and bush is given a name. The reader is so immersed in the wood that he can practically taste the berries.

Another example of the child's narrative ability can be seen in the following description of falconing. Once again, the effect of photographic accuracy is achieved by piling up detail. The present tense is used here, creating the illusion of a moving picture. This is appropriate for the action of the hunt, as opposed to the still life of the berry patch:

I loved everything about the hunt: the way the dog, having scented the trail of the quail, begins to get excited, wags his tail, snorts and presses her nose right to the ground; the way she gets ever more excited as she approaches the bird; the way the hunter, himself excited, holding his hawk on his raised right hand and holding back his dog on the leash with his left hand, whistling, almost runs after her. (1: 422)

It is in passages like these that the influence of Aksakov's earlier works on hunting and fishing can be felt. In his nonfictional work he had honed a style of writing that was perfect for such set pieces. However, in the earlier works, such scenes sometimes had a slightly pedantic natural-historical tone. Here, in the mouth of the child, they seem fresher because the autobiographical form encourages the reader to experience the scene not as the description of a well-known sight, but as a newly discovered world viewed for the first time.

Nor is the child's keen glance focused exclusively on nature. His curiosity is piqued by everything around him, by books, for example, and by the peasants in the field. When young Bagrov is taken to see the peasants threshing buckwheat, he describes the scene with his usual concern for detail:

A threshing-floor, swept smooth, had been cleared on one of the plots; more than thirty flails went back and forth across a tall pile of buck-wheat stalks. In amazement, I watched this work, which I had never seen, for a long while. I was enraptured by the harmony and dexterity of the quick, measured blows. The flails shimmered, rising and falling one beside another, never becoming entangled; meanwhile, the peasant women did not stand in one place—first they moved forward, then stepped back. (1: 426–27)

It is interesting that the picture as seen by the child is interrupted by the narrator, who mentions the fact that the child was seeing the work for the first time. As I mentioned earlier, this is one of the narrator's most common tropes; here it focuses the reader's attention on the child viewing the threshing, not simply on the process itself.[22]

Thus, behind the seemingly smooth and effortless narration of Aksakov's novel, there turns out to be a complicated interplay of voices. Taken together, these voices simultaneously create the illusion of a world seen through a child's eyes and call our attention to the distance between the child's world and that of the adult narrator. The novel's structure also seems simple at first glance. It appears that the narrator sticks to chronological order, speaking about those people and events that interested him or shaped his life. Behind the chronological façade, however, is a carefully modulated and structured text based on spatial and personal contrast (primarily on binary oppositions like city/country, mother/father) and temporal continuity (the rhythmic flow of the seasons, the cycles of life from birth to death). These spatial and temporal worlds are bound together by the image of the road.

Of course, the comparison of life with a road is one of literature's oldest and most hackneyed metaphors; Aksakov, however, revitalizes the image by using it both literally and metaphorically. The road is important in and of itself. This is apparent from the very beginning of the novel when Bagrov recalls his earliest childhood memories. He was a weak and sickly child but, for some reason, felt better in a moving carriage. He says: "Having noticed that the road seemed to do me good, my mother constantly went out driving with me" (1: 269). It was during one of these drives that he began to feel stronger, and Bagrov credits the road for saving his life. As is often the case in *Childhood Years*, personal experience motivates a general statement of Truth: "The miraculous healing power of the road cannot be doubted. I have known many people, for whom doctors had given up hope, who are indebted to it for their recovery" (1: 271).

Although the influence of the road on Bagrov's life is apparent from the start of the novel, its importance is emphasized at the beginning of the fifth chapter, entitled "The Road from Parashino to Bagrovo." The chapter begins with a hymn in praise of the road, whose elevated style and syntax is unusual for this work. Both in theme and style one can discern the shadow of N. V. Gogol, Aksakov's friend and literary idol: [23]

The road is an amazing thing! Its power is irresistible, calming and healing. It tears a person away from his surroundings (be they nice or even be they unpleasant), away from the many things that constantly distract him, away from the constantly varied flow of life. It concentrates his thoughts and feelings within the small world of his equipage, at first directing his attention to himself, then to memories of the past and, finally, to his dreams and hopes for the future. (1: 302)

The road serves not only as a symbolic path connecting one time and place to another, but as the source of inspiration for self-contemplation and memories: it is at the root of the autobiographical process itself. The road both circumscribes the boundaries of the young Bagrov's little world and allows him to retrieve his memories. Although the physical distance is the same each time that the road is traveled (i.e., it forms a straight line through space), in terms of time it describes a spiral, moving through the years of his life and connecting the adult narrator to the child.

Even without the panegyric to the road, the importance of the travel motif in *Childhood Years* would be obvious from a reading of the table of contents. Of the novel's twenty chapters, seven are concerned specifically with journeys. They have names like "The Winter Road to Bagrovo," "A Summer Trip to Churasovo," and "The Autumn Road to Bagrovo." From the titles it is also clear that the time of year when the trips take place is crucial. These differences ensure variety in the landscapes described and allow the child to observe, and the reader to appreciate, the natural flow of the seasons. In addition, journeys undertaken at the same season a number of years apart allow the child to measure his slow but steady development. Thus, for example, describing his second mid-summer trip from Ufa to Bagrovo, the narrator says: "We left Ufa at about the same date as two years before. . . . For a second time my soul drank in the same pleasant impressions; while they weren't so new and fresh and didn't amaze me as much as the first time, now I understood them more clearly and felt them more deeply" (1: 414). The repetition of the journey allows the narrator to notice changes, both internal and external, and to express them in a completely natural and seemingly artless way.

Nor are the child's renewed perceptions connected only to the natural world. Upon arriving back in the city, he rereads his old books: "I understood much that was in them more clearly than before. I even saw things that I had completely missed earlier and, therefore, in part, the books seemed new to me" (1: 401). The impression of novelty evoked by the child's ability to see different things each time he passes a certain landmark or milestone is the foundation for the characteristic and unusual structure of the novel. Instead of presenting one completely new scene after another (as Tolstoy does in the trilogy and as is traditional for autobiography), Aksakov presents a few simple scenes time and again (city occupations, field work, fishing, etc.) and makes them seem fresh each time by allowing the child narrator to discover more and more in them. The child uncovers the world as he journeys through it, and the reader can follow his progress and compare it to his or her own childhood experience.

Physically, the road is the connecting link between the provincial city of Ufa and various country estates. The contrast between rural and urban, between the patriarchal Russian estate and the more Westernized city, is quite significant for nineteenth-century Russian literature in general. For gentry pseudo-autobiography and autobiography, it is perhaps the central theme. Tolstoy's Irten'ev, for example, spends his earliest years on the estate. He does not begin to notice the painful conflicts within himself and society until he is uprooted from the quiet country way of life. His tortured self-analysis is connected mostly to city life; conversely, in the country he generally finds peace and solace. In *Childhood Years* the contrast between city and country is externalized and is observed by the child as a conflict between the personalities and preferences of his parents.

Contemporary readers already "knew" Bagrov's parents from the descriptions in *A Family Chronicle*. There the reader was introduced to Sof'ia Nikolaevna, the well-educated daughter of a provincial judge and the jewel of Ufa society, and her husband, the country born and bred, unpolished son of Stepan Mikhailovich. In *A Family Chronicle*, however, Aksakov's choice of a third-person narrator forced him to illuminate their misunderstandings from the outside, concentrating on illustrating their mutual incomprehension through their reactions to various events and situations. Thus, we observe Sof'ia Nikolaevna's despair at her fiancé's inability to conform to the laws of "good" behavior. On the other hand, we see Aleksei Stepanovich annoyed when his wife stirs up trouble in the family. However, the real extent of the gulf separating them is not clear in *A Family Chronicle*. Both Sof'ia Nikolaevna and Aleksei Stepanovich are firmly in the camp of the good fairy-tale characters and, although they can have misunderstandings, nothing can stand in the way of their happiness. In *Childhood Years* things are quite different. The first-person narration filters their conflict through the consciousness of the naive child. As he begins to understand himself, he gradually comes to understand his parents as well.

As a young boy, Bagrov felt more at home in the city; arriving back in Ufa after his first, unpleasant stay in the country, he sensed, "an indescribable joy and then a calm assurance when I felt myself transported to completely different people, when I saw different faces and heard different accents and voices" (1: 332). In Ufa all of Bagrov's attention is turned to his mother. He watches eagerly as she bakes her famous almond torte. As in his descriptions of nature, every detail is lovingly described; the reader can almost figure out the recipe. He waits eagerly to hear the guests praise the torte: "I was exultant and couldn't sit quietly in my highchair. I would always whisper in the ear of the guest sitting next to me that mama had done it all herself" (1: 334). For as long as the family stays in Ufa, Aleksei Stepanovich is a shadowy figure, hardly penetrating Sergei's consciousness. Indeed, the father's only appearance in the first chapter describing city life occurs when he describes some new land he has acquired in the country. His descriptions, according to Sergei, "carried me away and so fired my imagination that I even raved about the sublime new land in the night!" (1: 340).

As soon as the family leaves the city, the mother retreats into the background. Through their common love for nature, Sergei and his father forge new ties. The bond with his mother weakens. For example, the boy becomes passionately involved with fishing and, naturally, wants to tell his mother about his exploits. To his disappointment she appreciates neither his stories nor the pail of fresh fish. He adds with a sigh, "Alas, our fish did not make the slightest impression on my mother" (1: 359). As he appreciates and understands the world around him better, he begins, as it were, to outgrow his mother. It is not that he loves her less; he simply realizes that whole areas of experience are closed to her. Despite his father's assurances that everything will be quite innocent, his mother will not let him see the reopening of the mill, claiming that he will be exposed to the peasants' unseemly behavior there. Sergei says, "I couldn't help believing my mother, but I wanted to believe my father more" (1: 483).

Eventually he comes to judge his mother, at least her attitude toward nature and the world of the estate. A particularly telling scene takes place when the mother comes to visit the little island where Sergei often goes to fish:

> At first she liked it and she had them bring the big leather blanket so that she could sit on it on the riverbank. She never sat right in the high grass, saying that it was damp and there were millions of bugs that would crawl right up on you. . . . We all sat down on it, but, I don't know why, such a cautious and artificial approach to nature dampened my ardor and I didn't have nearly as much fun as I usually did alone with my sister or my aunt. (1: 489–90)

The way these judgments are expressed illustrates the advantages of the pseudo-autobiography. The real autobiographer, looking back from his present vantage point, must judge openly. He cannot pretend not to understand something that is now obvious. When he wants to express his past view he must make it clear that he is speaking from his past self. In the novel, by exploiting the child's incomprehension, the judgment can be made more subtly. Aksakov makes us feel the boy's bewilderment. The effect of the mother's presence on the boy's perception of the world shows us that she is wrong, but it is up to the reader to make the judgment. The narrator does not judge her and the boy simply doesn't understand why he feels the way he does. [24]

In addition to themes connected with the road, another structurally important constellation of motifs surrounds the actions of reading and storytelling. Since the pseudo-autobiography is always, at least implicitly, the autobiography of a writer, it is not surprising that themes like creativity, imagination, and the literary tradition appear frequently. This is the case even when the narrator does not say that he is himself a writer (as is the case in both Aksakov's novel and in Tolstoy's trilogy). In the twentieth century, the narrator's vocation as a writer will often play a crucial role; here, however, literary themes are present and important, but not central.

I have already mentioned the child's retelling of the stories from *Arabian Nights* and his attempts to portray realistically the speech and gestures of an insane man. These are not isolated incidents; the child's propensity for imaginative story-telling is a constantly recurring theme. When he and his sister are left alone at their grandparents' house, he amuses her by relating "various adventures that I had never had. Events that I had heard about or read in books served as some kind of basis or model for them" (1: 321). As he grows older, Bagrov's creative approach to the literary tradition remains unchanged; he simply begins to transform serious literature. Most amusing is his reworking of M. M. Kheraskov's poem "Rossiiada": "I usually read with such burning sympathy, my imagination reproduced my favorite characters—Mstislavsky, Kurbsky, and Paletsky—with such vividness that I seemed to have seen them and to have known them for a long time; in great detail I explained what they did before and after battle, how the tsar asked their advice, how he thanked them for their brave deeds, etc., etc." (1: 375).

Bagrov's parents' reaction to his literary achievements is one more illustration of the differences that separate them. The naive Aleksei Stepanovich, unable to distinguish between creativity in the world of literature and in real life, fears that his son is becoming a liar. Sof'ia Nikolaevna assures him that there is nothing wrong with Sergei's imaginative flights, but, ever mindful of social propriety, she forbids the child "to tell guests about the domestic life of Paletsky, Kurbsky, and Mstislavsky" (1: 375). Books and literature provide one more level on which the conflict between the mother and father is worked out. Whenever Bagrov is in the city or is forced inside, he reads greedily and with pleasure. As soon as he can go out fishing or wandering in the country, however, his books are forgotten completely. Still, literature is clearly in his blood, and the reader is not surprised that Bagrov could grow up to be an autobiographer.

While *Childhood Years* does indeed form the middle link of Aksakov's biographical/autobiographical trilogy, there are good reasons why he chose to write it as a work of fiction. Most important, the pseudo-autobiographical form allowed him to distance himself from his own life. Like Tolstoy, Aksakov found it difficult to write about himself directly.[25] This is attested to in a letter written while he was beginning work on *Childhood Years*: "I'm giving in to the general desire to learn how the young Bagrovs will begin their own life, although this is very difficult and ticklish for me." [26] He never hid from his friends the fact that *Childhood Years* was autobiographically based. [27] He did, however, insist that it was "an artistic reworking" of his childhood and wanted it to be read as such. He realized full well that readers would never notice anything except facts in an autobiography and hoped that they would not neglect the literary qualities of *Childhood Years*.

Aksakov went to great lengths to make his novel not merely the story of his own life, but that of a Russian gentry child. Quite consciously he structured the novel differently from his previous work. The pseudo-autobiographical form was used because it retained the immediacy of autobiography while allowing the writer the freedom to construct a well-balanced and generalized picture from the raw autobiographical material. In fact, however, Russian readers never really did perceive *Childhood Years* as a novel. Although it was recognized as having artistic merit, Aksakov's final work was simply considered an autobiography. Thus, for the Russian literary tradition, Tolstoy's trilogy became the model pseudo-autobiography (the work that had to be taken into account by others who wished to write in the genre) while Aksakov's was underrated.

By a strange paradox, however, the Russian misreading of Aksakov led to his great popularity among gentry autobiographers. Autobiographers evidently found Tolstoy's exclusive concern with Irten'ev too restrictive. Although they borrowed Tolstoy's childhood myths (myths that, for the most part, Aksakov believed in as well), they turned to Aksakov when they wrote their own life histories. Because they ignored the generic differences separating the three volumes of Aksakov's "trilogy," they were able to see it as an organically connected family and personal saga. In the end it was Aksakov, not Tolstoy, who provided the basic model for the gentry autobiographies that were written in Russia up until the Revolution.

Chapter Three

၄၄

Canonizing the Myths of Russian Gentry Childhood

With the appearance of *Childhood* and *The Childhood Years of Bagrov's Grandson*, would-be Russian autobiographers had, for the first time, well-known native literary models on which to base accounts of childhood. There is plenty of evidence, both direct and indirect, to indicate that the pseudo-autobiographies of Tolstoy and Aksakov did in fact provide inspiration for future Russian autobiographers.[1] Indeed, my analysis of Russian gentry accounts of childhood indicates that practically all of them are indebted to *Childhood* and *Childhood Years*.[2] To get some idea of the extent of the influence of Tolstoy and Aksakov, one can start by looking at the number of first-person accounts by gentry writers either wholly or partially devoted to childhood: before 1860 practically none were published; between 1860 and 1916 there were more than thirty.[3] Numbers alone, however, do not tell the whole story. It is far more significant to note the frequency with which gentry autobiographers incorporated material borrowed from literary sources into the framework of their autobiographies.

Evidently, when members of the gentry class recalled their childhood, they projected their own memories onto patterns proposed by Tolstoy and Aksakov. Indeed, it would be fair to say that the pseudo-autobiographies of Tolstoy and Aksakov became the source of a certain number of myths of Russian childhood. These myths range in scope from those governing the interpretation of childhood as a whole (what I call the myth of the happy childhood) to those concerning selected aspects of the child's life (myths relating to mothers, fathers, servants, nature, etc.).

It could be argued that the similarities I have noted between gentry autobiographies and the literary works of Tolstoy and Aksakov are accidental, the result of the fact that writers of both fiction and nonfiction were describing the realities of Russian estate life. There is undoubtedly some truth to this assertion. The Russian landed gentry were, in general, conservative, and there was a certain unanimity in their child-rearing practices and their attitudes toward their children. Gentry children did share many experiences with their peers, and, in the course of this chapter, I will discuss some of the most important ones. However, my claim that there is a literary/mythological basis for Russian autobiographical childhoods does not rest on the fact that many of them depict similar incidents. Instead, I am concerned with the way these incidents are interpreted and the language with which they are described. Thus, while it is true that every gentry child grew up surrounded by an army of serfs (or servants after emancipation), this does not explain why every autobiographer asserts that relations between his or her parents and their serfs were ideal. The estates where gentry children grew up were in fact in the countryside, but this fact fails to explain why almost all autobiographers describe the natural surroundings of their childhood in arcadian terms. Finally, the common-circumstances argument fails to explain the existence of a central myth linking all of these autobiographies: the myth of the happy childhood. The existence of shared childhood experience can neither explain why practically all Russians felt that their childhoods were (or, at least, should have been) happy, nor the fact that they expressed this feeling in remarkably similar language.

What happened in the course of the second half of the nineteenth century was that the stories of childhood proposed by Tolstoy and Aksakov became canonized in the Russian cultural mind. Naturally, as the theme of childhood moved from works of fiction (pseudo-autobiographies) to works of nonfiction (autobiographies), certain aspects of it were transformed. In general terms, one could say that gentry autobiographies used the myths of childhood that Tolstoy and Aksakov had proposed while ignoring the formal ambiguity inherent in the pseudo-autobiography.[4]

The canonization of myths of childhood derived from literary texts was undoubtedly an ideological process. The Russian gentry class was subject to constant pressure from below from the 1860's through the Revolution. Members of other social classes (particularly educated non-nobles, the so-called *raznochintsy*) assertively demanded a share of social and political power. From the point of view purely of intellectual and administrative ability, it was, of course, difficult to deny that the "new men and women" were the equals of the gentry. If the gentry were to defend their position in Russian society, it became extremely important for them to discover virtues that non-nobles did not possess. A gentry childhood, which, according to the myths of Tolstoy and Aksakov, endowed a person with certain positive principles that were retained for a lifetime, became just such a possession. Although ambitious "upstarts" from among the *raznochintsy* could, and did, make up for the deficiencies in their early education, they could never close the childhood gap. In a sense, then, for many gentry autobiographers a "proper" childhood became a substitute for the "blue blood" in which the positivist nineteenth century no longer believed. Childhood eventually became a mark of class solidarity, a rallying point, and a way to differentiate the gentry class from other classes.

The extent to which gentry autobiographers were consciously aware of the ideology that underlies their autobiographies (not to mention the literary origins of that ideology) is difficult to determine.[5] Sometimes acknowledged citations appear and the use of literary myths is clearly intentional. This was a particularly common tactic after the Revolution: émigré writers tried to prove that theirs had been the only true Russian childhood and that, therefore, they were the legitimate heirs to the Russian cultural and social traditions. Their autobiographical reminiscences of childhood paradise are conscious reworkings of earlier literary models, and they stand in opposition to a group of Soviet autobiographies in which childhood is interpreted by means of a new set of myths based, for the most part, on the work of Gorky. In at least some works written before the Revolution, however, one suspects that gentry writers projected their lives onto those of Irten'ev and Bagrov unconsciously. Most autobiographies were produced by nonprofessional writers; their structure and style indicate that they were not extensively reworked. It is likely that the autobiographers in question had neither the literary sophistication nor the ideological interest to use Tolstoy and Aksakov consciously. Instead, they merely wrote what they thought they remembered, and their memories turned out to be colored both by real-life events and by the books they knew and loved.

I am not suggesting that people necessarily had to modify large portions of their childhood memories in order to conform to the gentry myths. Nevertheless, it is clear that they selected, organized, interpreted, and even verbalized their memories of childhood experience in accordance with patterns drawn from works of literature.[6] Because there were practically no gentry autobiographical accounts of childhood published before the 1860's, it is hard to determine whether the patterns of childhood proposed by Tolstoy and Aksakov reflected preexisting cultural myths or whether they created them. Most probably, both processes were at work. At the very least, however, the pseudo-autobiographies of Tolstoy and Aksakov crystallized the myths relating to happy childhood in literary form. The task of the Russian gentry autobiography was to canonize these myths.

The Middle Rank of the Russian Gentry

The vast majority of autobiographical descriptions of childhood were produced by persons whose families belonged to the middle rank of the Russian gentry: this is true for writers of fictional accounts (Tolstoy, Aksakov, and Bunin) and for most of the writers of nonfictional autobiography whose work I have examined.[7] In the period before emancipation, a gentry family of the middle rank owned between 100 and 500 male serfs.[8] In effect, their holdings allowed them to live comfortably without working, but did not provide enough income to live full-time in Petersburg or Moscow. For the most part, they lived on their country estates, overseeing the agricultural production of their serfs and living off a percentage of that production; the serfs fulfilled their obligations either directly, by working corvée (called *barshchina* in Russian), or indirectly, through the payment of quitrent (called *obrok*). After emancipation the rural gentry continued to live in basically the same manner. This was possible because, although the peasants had been freed, the landowners retained a good portion of their pre-emancipation holdings. These remaining lands were cultivated by former serfs, who now worked as sharecroppers or, less frequently, as paid laborers.[9] In addition, the landowners were compensated by the government for the land that was "given" to their former serfs. This compensation was in the form of bonds, which they generally sold at a discount in order to raise hard cash.[10]

For all practical purposes the estates were entirely self-sufficient, as A. A. Fet's *Memoirs* attest: "With the exception of candles and beef, and a small quantity of dry goods, everything, beginning with woolens, shirt-cloth, and table linen and ending with every conceivable comestible, was either made in our home or collected from the peasants."[11] In the winter months, when there was less work to be done on the estates, the wealthier of these families could afford to go to one of the "capitals" for a month or two, usually staying with bachelor male relatives or widowed or spinster female relatives. Even in the city they tried to save money by supplying their own provisions: "During the winters in Petersburg we were brought caravans of provisions from the country: entire frozen steers, whole pigs, hams, masses of chickens, geese, and game-birds and, what we liked best, jugs of foamy iced cream."[12]

For most of the year, however, the middle-rank gentry family lived an isolated life. Roads were legendarily atrocious (during spring flood and fall rains they often did not exist at all), and, except during holiday periods (Christmas and Easter), contacts with neighboring gentry families were few and far between. F. F. Vigel' likens the estate to an enclave separated from the rest of the world by an ocean and impassable mountains.[13] He was, of course, describing the early 1800's, but things changed little in the course of a century. This, for example, is how an anonymous autobiographer described her mother's estate where she grew up in mid-century: "Her estate lay far from the centers of the educated world. Communications were so bad that years passed without anyone dropping in to see us."[14] Even the coming of the railroad, which greatly improved communications between urban centers, did not drastically decrease the isolation of the outlying estates until the end of the century. This, then, was the general socioeconomic situation of the middle rank of the Russian gentry class. Between the 1780's and the 1880's this group developed a way of life and, more important, an attitude toward it that was extremely conservative and resistant to change. One of the pillars of their lifestyle was the belief that childhood was a privileged state. The English maxim that a child should be "seen but not heard" (not to mention French and German practice, where the child was often neither seen nor heard) never reached the Russian countryside. Of course, this is not to say that there were no unhappy gentry childhoods or that the gentry child was happy all of the time; however, the happy childhood became a definite part of gentry "folklore" (the same role filled by the unhappy childhood in the English tradition).[15]

The Myth of the Happy Childhood

The driving force for most Russian gentry autobiographies is nostalgia; practically every writer seems determined to return, at least in thought, to a past that is perceived as having been happier than the present. Although it might seem natural for autobiographers to have a rosy view of the past in general and of childhood in particular, an examination of autobiographical accounts of childhood from other countries fails to reveal such a pattern. For example, M. J. Chombart de Lauwe's study indicates that there was no such myth in France. R. N. Coe's analysis of almost 500 literary childhoods worldwide also fails to uncover a pattern of happiness in childhood memoirs.

Of course, the Russian gentry had some specific historical reasons for idealizing the recent past. In fact, each generation of autobiographers was able to point to a historical break that had occurred at some point in their youth, a break that made the world of the present fundamentally different from the one in which they grew up. Those who wrote in the 1860's, 1870's, and 1880's still remembered the days before the emancipation of the serfs. They believed that a major structural change had taken place in Russian village life after 1861 and that, consequently, no one would ever experience a childhood like theirs again. Unexpectedly, it turned out that, despite the reforms, change came far more slowly than had been anticipated. In fact, the generation born in the 1860's and 1870's grew up in conditions that were remarkably similar to those their parents had known (even if their parents failed to see this). By the time this second generation began to write autobiographies, it was commonly believed that the gentry class was all but defunct. As adults, the members of this generation often found themselves in the position of A. P. Chekhov's Madame Ranevskaia, forced to sell the "cherry orchard" in which they had spent their childhoods. Naturally, the loss of the family property marked the end of an era as far as they were concerned. Nevertheless, the dispossession of the gentry class was far from complete even at the time of the Revolution. The last group of gentry autobiographers (those born between the 1890's and the 1910's) wrote their autobiographies in Paris, London, Belgrade, Berlin, and Constantinople. Their nostalgia was far more motivated than that of their parents and grandparents: for them, the image of childhood inevitably became intertwined with images of Russia itself. In fact, for émigrés like Nabokov who left Russia as youths, memories of childhood eventually became the only connection to a lost homeland.

That Russians perceived their childhoods as happy can perhaps be explained by social conditions, the national psyche, or other causes. However, the manner in which they chose to express this perception and the consistency with which they did so can be explained only by recourse to the literary tradition. Indeed, I believe that the only response one can have after reading a number of gentry autobiographies is a Tolstoyan paraphrase: All gentry childhoods are happy in the same way.[16]

The programmatic statement at the beginning of chapter 15 of *Childhood* ("Happy, happy time of childhood . . .") was an extremely influential model for the expression of the myth of the happy childhood. Gentry autobiographers not only repeated Tolstoy's interpretation of childhood but also borrowed typically Tolstoyan situations, cadences, and turns of phrase. The following excerpt uses the myth of the happy childhood, the iterative present-tense narrative style, and even many of Tolstoy's words: "My childhood was happy, joyous; it was passed in an atmosphere of deep motherly love, and was filled with the most tender attention. . . . It would often happen that you'd run your fill, breathed in the pure air of the steppes, and toward evening you'd want nothing more than to sleep and sleep." [17]

Although Tolstoy's depiction of childhood as a time of unadulterated happiness was important for many Russian autobiographers, a less well known statement from the end of *Childhood* was equally significant. In chapter 28, the narrator recalls the situation after the death of his mother as follows: "With the death of my mother the happy period of childhood ended and a new epoch began—the epoch of boyhood." It is precisely at this kind of critical moment that many gentry autobiographers tend to characterize childhood as a whole.

This, for example, is how P. P. Semenov-Tian-Shansky describes his family's move from the country to Moscow: "Thus our family fell apart. My happy childhood came to a distinct end: I moved on to boyhood." [18] Although Semenov-Tian-Shansky's epitaph to childhood is the most obvious example of direct borrowing from Tolstoy, he was by no means alone in doing so. For A. K. Lelong, childhood also ends with her departure for Moscow: "That is how my nice, quite childhood in the countryside ended." [19] For another autobiographer, happy childhood ends with the departure of her beloved French governess: "My dear, irretrievable childhood ends with her departure." [20]

While some autobiographers contented themselves with mere variations on themes of Tolstoy, others strove to develop the myth of childhood as a golden age even further. In addition to perceiving childhood as a marvelously happy time, they maintained that there was some qualitative difference separating the world in which they grew up from that in which they lived as adults. S. V. Mengden expressed this feeling in the course of describing the night sky: "It seemed to me that nowhere in the whole world were there such big, caressingly flickering stars as the ones that lit up my happy childhood."[21] For O. I. Kornilova, everything about the world of childhood was magical: "I have retained the most joyous memories of my childhood. It still seems to me that the sun was never as warm, that I never breathed more easily or lived more freely than in my native nest, where everything was marked by simplicity, care, and love."[22]

Of course, gentry autobiography was not the only form of literature to reflect the myths of Tolstoy and Aksakov in pre-revolutionary Russia. Dostoevsky's vaguely pseudo-autobiographical novel, *The Insulted and the Injured*, made use of these same myths as early as 1861. Parts of the narrator's later life in Petersburg roughly parallel Dostoevsky's own. However, the recollections of childhood in the novel have nothing to do with Dostoevsky's. Rather, they represent a distillation, probably parodic, of the myths of Tolstoy and Aksakov: "Oh, my dear childhood! How silly it is to yearn for you and to want you back at the age of twenty-five and, while dying, to recall only you among all with exaltation and thanks! Such a clear sun shone in the heavens then, not like the one in Petersburg. And our young hearts beat so quickly, joyously. There were fields and forests all around. . . . A golden, wonderful time."[23]

In all of the works quoted above, the influence of Tolstoy's *Childhood* is obvious, both in the location of references to happy childhood within the autobiographical texts and in the specific words used to describe it. However, in the absence of direct evidence that these writers realized what they were doing, it is impossible to prove whether or not Tolstoyan reminiscences were used consciously. There are, however, other instances in which the choice of Tolstoy's model was clearly conscious. Perhaps the best example is the autobiography of A. K. Chertkova. She was the wife of Tolstoy's secretary and companion, V. G. Chertkov. Considering her husband's relation to Tolstoy, it is not surprising that her description of childhood should have been heavily influenced by that of the master. However, just to ensure that readers would not miss the connection, she decided to begin the first chapter with an epigraph from *Childhood*. She chose, almost inevitably, the opening lines of chapter 15: "Happy, happy time of childhood . . . ."

For some gentry writers, an old-fashioned happy childhood became a synecdoche for Russia itself. Prince E. N. Trubetskoy uses this trope quite consciously. In the introduction to his memoirs, dated March 1, 1917, he adumbrates the reasons for writing about childhood: "And this is why I wish to remember the past in which I had the good fortune to experience so much joy and goodness. For that goodness does not belong to me alone. It is thoroughly native—Russian."[24] A description of childhood is perceived as being the way to preserve all that is truly worth preserving about Russia in the face of a revolution that would eventually remake the country.

Unhappy Childhoods

Paradoxically, the extent to which the myth of the happy childhood permeated Russian thinking in the nineteenth century can best be appreciated by examining those exceptional works that describe an unhappy childhood. Unhappy childhoods can be divided into two main categories: autobiographies and pseudo-autobiographies by members of the gentry who, later in life, became disenchanted with their class; and narratives by writers of nongentry origin. Writers from both of these groups had clear ideological reasons for opposing the old order. And, since a happy childhood quickly became a badge of the conservative aristocracy, the "progressive" aristocrats and the *raznochintsy* soon realized that one way to dramatize their ideological opposition was to attack the gentry myths of childhood. Aristocrats who had broken with their class wanted to show that the entire system in which they had grown up was rotten. A realization of systemic inadequacy had either made their childhood miserable (if they came to this realization when they were still children) or, at least, it poisoned their adult recollections. Nongentry writers had experienced a different type of childhood altogether, and, by depicting their early years in negative tones, they sought to show that what gentry writers saw as attributes of childhood in general were true only for children of a certain class. What both groups of unhappy childhood narratives shared was an acute and often painful awareness of the myths of gentry childhood as set down by Tolstoy and Aksakov and canonized by gentry autobiographers. As opposed to typical gentry autobiographers, whose references to Tolstoy and Aksakov could have been unconscious, these writers consciously referred to the gentry's childhood myths in order to oppose them. However, although they resolutely rejected the gentry myths, they failed to create an alternative model for childhood. A true alternative model for the interpretation of childhood was not to appear until the twentieth century.

In A. I. Levitov's "My Family" (1863), the narrator begins his story with the following observation: "How deeply I envy those people who, with radiant joy on their time-creased faces, have the right to speak of their childhood as a *golden, unforgettable* time."[25] The italics on the last two words indicate that they are meant to be seen as a quotation or paraphrase; evidently, a mere decade after the publication of *Childhood*, the gentry model was so well known that a pair of words was thought sufficient to recall it to the Russian reader. Yet, although Levitov portrays a deprived childhood, his story does not represent a full-scale attempt to overturn the gentry myths: no alternate model for childhood is proposed. Indeed, Levitov's narrator is perfectly willing to admit that childhood should be a golden age; he wishes that it had been so for him as well. Levitov calls the universality of the gentry myths into question without disputing their reality or desirability.

The tendency of nongentry writers to accept gentry myths of childhood as the truth (albeit only for members of the gentry class) is even more obvious in N. G. Pomialovsky's "Bourgeois Happiness" (1861). His story, which is narrated in the third person, begins as follows: "Egor Ivanych Molotov was thinking about how nice life in the wide world was for the landowner Arkadii Ivanych: to live in the same village in which he, the landowner, was born, to live by the same river, in the same house, and beneath the same lindens where his childhood had been passed."[26] That the non-gentry character envies the life of the landowner is not surprising. What is unexpected, however, is that he desires neither the landowner's material goods nor his power. Instead he yearns for the happy memories of childhood that he is sure the landowner possesses. Once again, an unhappy childhood is portrayed through its absence, through the contemplation of an aristocrat's happy childhood.

It has often been claimed that it is easier to give a convincing depiction of hell than of heaven. This was definitely not the case in nineteenth-century Russia. Whereas the arcadian pseudo-autobiographies of Tolstoy and Aksakov spawned a host of imitators and left a lasting impression on the Russian cultural mind, the hells depicted by nongentry writers disappeared from the literary scene leaving barely a trace, after having enjoyed a brief vogue in the early 1860's. Of course it could be argued that this was because nongentry writers of pseudo-autobiographical works were not as talented as Tolstoy or Aksakov. This may be true, but it is equally significant that, implicitly or explicitly, nongentry writers accepted the gentry's myths of childhood. Their narratives are expressions of envy at not having shared in the golden age, rather than proposals for an alternative conception of the role of childhood. In a literary culture that demanded positive models of how to think or act, purely negative counterexamples were not sufficient.[27] It was not until the appearance of Gorky's trilogy that a nongentry writer created an alternate model of childhood that successfully challenged the gentry myths.

Although the gentry model of childhood faced little serious competition from the outside in the nineteenth century, it was confronted by dissenting opinions by members of the gentry class itself. These works were by noblemen and women who were in sympathy with or themselves became Socialists, Communists, or Anarchists. It is not clear whether they became disaffected from their class as the result of an unhappy childhood or whether, having become disaffected, they recalled the world of their childhood in a negative light.[28] What is clear, however, is that despite having experienced a gentry childhood (or because of it), these writers were not willing to structure their reminiscences along the lines required by the prevailing myths. This made their attacks far more ideologically dangerous than those of nongentry writers. Nongentry writers came from a different world entirely and could be ignored. It was not nearly so easy to dismiss different interpretations of the same childhood experiences by members of one's own class. Even so, negative accounts had less of an impact on contemporary thinking about childhood than might have been expected.[29] For the most part, this was because even the most highly negative portrayals of childhood continued to take the gentry myths into account instead of ignoring them or creating an entirely new vision of childhood.

This is certainly true of the autobiography of T. P. Passek. She was a cousin of Herzen's, and although she was not an active social democrat, she was at least in sympathy with his criticism of the old regime. In her description of childhood she seems to have avoided the typical gentry myths insofar as possible. She declines to characterize her childhood as happy or unhappy, but her disclaimer shows that she was well aware of the prevailing mythology: "It is said that childhood is the happiest age. Enough already! Happiness depends on very many circumstances."[30]

Even the most thoroughgoing refutation of the gentry myths of childhood, Saltykov-Shchedrin's pseudo-autobiographical *Old Times in Poshekhonie* (1887–89), is characterized by an often painful awareness of the strength of those myths. Saltykov-Shchedrin realized that portrayals of happy childhood were, in many cases, ideologically motivated attempts to glorify the old way of life as a whole. In fact, it appears that the work was written in direct response to the growing number of happy gentry childhoods that were appearing in various Russian journals. In answer to Chernyshevsky's query as to why Saltykov-Shchedrin was wasting his time on the musty days of serfdom, L. F. Panteleev (who knew the satirist well) wrote: "The times have changed noticeably: that which was considered buried and sealed with the mark of Cain has suddenly become an object of rehabilitation, even of idealization. *Old Times in Poshekhonie* is a response to this trend."[31]

In the sixth chapter of his pseudo-autobiography, Saltykov-Shchedrin takes on the myth of the happy childhood. As opposed to the writers of nongentry unhappy childhoods, Saltykov-Shchedrin does not merely show that his own childhood was an unfortunate one. Rather, he attempts to prove that childhood as such is a disastrous period of life. He begins his dissenting opinion by paying tribute to the myth: "If one is to believe the generally accepted opinion, then there is no happier age than childhood."[32] The rest of the chapter is devoted to proving this statement false. He concludes by saying: "I continue to assert that, in the absolute sense, no age is more ill-fated than childhood and that general opinion is deeply wrong in supporting the reverse view. I think that this is a dangerous error because it confuses society and prevents it from looking soberly at the question of childhood."[33]

While *Old Times in Poshekhonie* presents a strongly dissident view of gentry childhood, its very structure betrays the strength of the models it was attacking. The debate is carried on entirely in terms of the myths that Tolstoy and Aksakov had created. In the end, in spite of the narrator's attempts to generalize from his unhappy childhood, his experiences read more like the plaint of one who was not able to share in the golden age, rather than a new view of the subject. The life described in *Old Times in Poshekhonie* simply did not correspond to the Russian gentry perception of childhood. The idylls of Aksakov and Tolstoy continued to be read by generations of Russians (and to be a source of inspiration for autobiographers and novelists), whereas Saltykov-Shchedrin's dissident view was almost completely forgotten.

The Myth of the Perfect Mother

Next in importance after the myth of the happy childhood is the myth of the perfect mother. Of course, the two were usually related. Childhood was often happy precisely because of the love and affection that the child received from his mother. As with the myth of the happy childhood, the myth of the mother was derived mainly from *Childhood*. In this case, however, gentry autobiographers did not borrow specific words and phrases from Tolstoy. Instead, in descriptions of their own mothers, they chose to reproduce the nebulous aura of goodness and beauty that radiates from Irten'ev's mother throughout *Childhood*.[34] Consequently, descriptions of mothers in Russian autobiography lack definition. It is as if autobiographers are portraying bundles of abstract qualities, rather than people of flesh and blood. Not surprisingly, the image of Bagrov's mother was not widely imitated by gentry autobiographers. Although there could be no doubt that Bagrov loved her and that she played a crucial role in his upbringing, Aksakov's description was too realistic, too filled with contradictions to serve as a general model.

Most gentry autobiographers remember the mother as the center of their childhood universe;[35] mothers are seen as a fount of goodness, influencing the course of the child's moral development: "The most outstanding place in my first memories belongs to my mother. According to all who knew her, she was an especially original and strong personality."[36] After introducing the mother, the anonymous author of this autobiographical sketch goes on to describe all of her wonderful qualities. The list sounds like a general catalog of virtues, some of which were always attributed to Russian gentry mothers:

The sacred fire of fantasy lived in her soul . . . she enjoyed the love and trust of the young . . . she could sympathize with other peoples' sorrow like no one else . . . a feeling for beauty lay at the root of her soul. She was especially sensitive to the beauty of nature. . . . One of her wonderful character traits was a love of truth. . . . Her relations with her servants were very caring, she entered into their family affairs, advised, helped, and defended the aggrieved.

Although I am not prepared to deny that the particular mother described above may have possessed all of these virtues, the fact that they are seen as belonging to practically every Russian gentry mother leads one to suspect the existence of a mythological "mother" figure. Indeed, it is their very perfection that lends these portraits a degree of unbelievability and makes them seem rather one-dimensional.

One of the most important functions that mothers fulfill, especially in families with spendthrift fathers, is keeping the family finances in order. In addition to financial prudence (but never stinginess), mothers are praised for their housekeeping ability (in the sense of organization and management, because, given the number of servants, they never had to do any physical labor). Fet's mother combined these two traditional abilities: "[She] concentrated all her efforts to avoid spending money, getting by insofar as possible with home-made things." [37] Benois recalls that "it was frail little mamma who regulated our budget." [38] This is certainly the role played by the mothers of Tolstoy's Irten'ev and Bunin's Arsen'ev. Each of these literary mothers tries to restrain her husband's spendthrift tendencies and to keep the household financially afloat.

An account that takes the holy mother theme to its (unintentionally) comic extreme is Kornilova's *A True Story from the Time of Serfdom*. This little book of "reminiscences" is actually a work of hagiography. The mother is presented as an omniscient provider for all the local peasants: "She found out about every want and had a kind word for every grief." [39] When her daughter (the work's author) falls ill, the mother has a vision telling her to go to a distant monastery, where the local saint will give her something with which to heal the little girl. Upon arriving at the monastery she kneels at the grave of the saint and a little pearl falls, by itself, from the reliquary. When she returns home with the pearl she places it on her daughter. The girl promptly gets better, although all hope for her recovery had been lost long before. The author claims: "Everyone felt that Alexandra Ivanovna [the mother] had been, as it were, chosen by the Lord to work a miracle." [40] An icon is made incorporating the pearl, and, during a cholera epidemic, the icon cures all whom it touches. Finally, like most true Orthodox saints, the mother feels that she is going to die (although she is in seemingly excellent health). She takes to her bed and passes away, just as predicted, leaving her grieving children with memories of her perfection. If the work had been published as hagiography, a mother figure of this sort would not be surprising. However, the fact that it could be written, published, and read as an autobiography illustrates the extent to which the cult of the perfect mother had permeated gentry culture.

One can only imagine the difficulties of growing up female in Russia in the second half of the nineteenth century. A young woman was expected to act like the strong-willed heroine of a Turgenev novel before her marriage. Afterwards she was expected to be the saintly self-abnegating type of woman described in the autobiographical and, to some extent, the literary traditions. That some women actually did act in such ways is a tribute both to their strength and to the power of literary and social mythology.

Father Figures

There is more variety in portraits of gentry fathers than in those of gentry mothers, a fact that leads one to the conclusion that the father was a less-frequently mythologized figure in gentry autobiography. Nevertheless, most fathers in the gentry tradition fall into two basic categories: the "stern but fair" man who works hard to manage his estate, or the extravagant father who is unable to deal with the realities of life, is self-indulgent, and has a passion for cards and/or a certain eccentric bent. Interestingly enough, the serious father is typical for autobiographies, while the impractical one predominates in pseudo-autobiographies. Both types are affectionate to their children when they see them, but they are frequently remembered as having been somewhat distant. Certainly, fathers in this patriarchal society did not take as active a role in bringing up children as did mothers.

The two types of fathers had an identical background. Almost all of them had grown up on the family estate and had then served in the army or, more rarely, in the civil bureaucracy. Upon the death of their fathers, they retired from the service, returned to the family estates, and devoted the remainder of their lives to the estates and their families. The memoirs of N. P. Grot summarize the typical background for the child's father: "At that time a gentry landowner who had served 10–15 years, usually in the military or, less frequently, in civil service, considered it his duty to return to his patrimonial estate and to settle there, to establish a good family life." [41]

Another example of this canonized type is the father of Iu. Karpinskaia. [42] After the death of her grandfather, her father returned home, at the age of 36, to find the family estate in ruins. "But despite all the unfavorable conditions, unstinting labors and irrepressible energy won out. The estate gradually began to flourish." [43] This kind of landowner was usually characterized as stern but fair: "He was deeply respected and feared on the estate and in the surrounding district, although in his whole life he never so much as raised his voice against anyone." [44]

After more than half a century of autobiographies, the stern, somewhat cold father became so expected that writers felt special explanations to be necessary if their fathers did not fit the pattern. Thus, M. Osorgin begins his description saying: "In all the memoirs of childhood that I have read, everyone has a gentle mother and a stern, intelligent father: the brain from the father, the heart from the mother. That, I guess, is how it's supposed to be. My mother was also gentle . . . but there was not an ounce of sternness in my father." [45]

In opposition to the serious, stern father is the carefree and slightly eccentric one. He is constitutionally unable to hold onto his money and, ultimately, often brings the family to bankruptcy. The classic literary example is Count Il'ia Rostov in *War and Peace*, but the type appears constantly in pseudo-autobiographies and novels. This is, of course, the father figure in Tolstoy's *Childhood*. His major flaw is an insatiable desire to gamble; to the despair of his wife, he constantly wins and loses huge sums of money at the card tables. She exacts a promise that he will not gamble away his children's inheritance, but he clearly cannot keep his word.

Gambling fever seems to have been endemic among the Russian gentry: "I don't know where or how my father served. . . . I only know that he always lived in Moscow, where he gambled at cards frightfully, both during my mother's life and after her death. He always lost";[46] "My father . . . could have lived comfortably, had it not been for the debts (caused by a passion for cards) that remained after his military service."[47] Indeed, the consistency with which the authors' fathers lost makes one suspect that the card players who won were all bachelors. In any case, if they had families, their children never wrote autobiographies.

Even if the father failed to gamble away massive sums, he managed to find other ways to waste the family fortune. Thus, when Arsen'ev says that his father had "an unquenchable passion to squander everything" (Bunin, 6: 85), he is only describing a pattern that was repeated, with variations, all over Russia, especially after 1861. Emancipation may have changed the economic rules of life in principle, but the patterns of daily existence and thought that had grown up over the years, both in landowners and in serfs, changed slowly. Although a complete collapse of the rural economy was averted through the purchase of land by merchants and peasant cooperatives, the position of the gentry worsened considerably (due mostly to overspending and an inability to adjust to new economic conditions) as did that of the majority of the peasantry (who were locked in a cycle of poverty, population increase, and burdensome debt).[48] B. B. Glinsky sums up the immediate post-emancipation period as follows: "Somehow the following question did not occur to anyone then: What will happen in a few years when the credit funds and reserves dry up and we have to look the 'rainy day' in the face? Neither the inhabitants of the main part of the manor house nor those of the backrooms, the stables or the servants' quarters thought about it."[49] It is precisely this carefree attitude on the part of "the fathers" that Arsen'ev/Bunin would blame for the Russian Revolution.

Whether or not this kind of father can be justifiably blamed for the Revolution, the type was certainly widespread and caused the

man's wife and children (if the latter were old enough to understand
the family finances) many anxious moments. Alexandre Benois,
describing his father, gives another fine example of the type: "Father, on the other hand, was filled with an energy that knew no
moment of gloom. . . . I remember him always gay and brim-
ming over with vitality, never troubling about what would happen
next. He had the haziest ideas about economizing."[50] Even though
the Benois family had only been in Russia for two generations, it
seems that they had caught the true Russian gentry spirit. The
same inability to economize, coupled with a tendency to gaiety
and leniency toward the children (which practically all of these literary and nonliterary extravagant fathers share), is described by
Aleksei Tolstoy in his autobiographical novel *Nikita's Childhood*.

Interesting echoes of the nonpractical father type can be found
in two works that are slightly beyond the pale of the gentry autobiography. In Belyi's *Kotik Letaev*, the father fits the mold by being an
absent-minded professor of mathematics who has no contact with
the real world and who, much to the distress of his wife, has no
ability at or interest in providing for the economic or social well-
being of his family. Finally, in Nabokov's semi-autobiographical
novel *The Gift*, the father is an eccentric butterfly collector who
leaves his family for years at a time to go off collecting. This incarnation is particularly interesting because Nabokov's actual
father was not at all this type; instead, he was a rather serious
and respectable politician. However, the literary tradition demanded a less staid father, and this could well have been one of the
reasons that Godunov-Cherdyntsev was given a father quite unlike
Nabokov's own.

Dead Parents

For a number of medical and social reasons, death was likely to
intrude on the life of a young child in the nineteenth century. Since
it was not uncommon for husbands to be twenty or thirty years
older than their wives, it was inevitable that a certain number of
them would die when their children (especially later children) were

still quite young. In addition, as a result of poor prenatal and postnatal care and of a lack of birth-control methods (which ensured the wife's giving birth almost once a year throughout her childbearing years), there was a high incidence of death in connection with childbirth. Finally, because families tended to be of the extended type, there were always some aged relatives present, and their deaths could throw the whole house into a frenzy of funeral preparations at any moment. The Russian Orthodox custom of laying the body out for three days in an open casket, along with numerous final kissings of the lately departed, ensured that the image of the dead person would sear itself on the memory of those whom that death touched. In Russian gentry autobiography the death of a close relative is often described in detail, and it often plays a major structural role (placed at either the beginning or the end of the narrative).

One might imagine that the death of a parent or loved one should mark a natural and, consequently, a fairly common ending to childhood. Surprisingly enough, however, in her chapter on perceptions of death in French literature and autobiography, Chombart de Lauwe does not note a single case in which a novelist or autobiographer describes a death as marking the end of childhood.[51] This may well indicate that, while death itself is not unusual, its frequent presence as a structural element in Russian gentry autobiography has a mythological basis. As with so many other situations, I believe that gentry autobiographers projected their own memories of the death of a parent onto Irten'ev's depiction of his mother's death in *Childhood*.

The first important scene connected with death is the last view of the still alive but unquestionably dying parent. Tolstoy relates the scene graphically in *Childhood*, although he was not working from his own experience: "Mother's eyes were open but she saw nothing... Oh, I will never forget that terrible gaze. It expressed so much suffering" (Tolstoy, 1: 83). For others, however, the experience was as real as it was unforgettable: "Then I remember his death. How he lay on his deathbed and how he blessed me. That sad picture etched itself in my memory and I look at it as if it were today."[52]

After the parent's death, a truly frightful scene for a young child was the final parting with the corpse on the day of the funeral. Time and again adult autobiographers speak of the fear and revulsion they felt at this sight. Perhaps the most powerful of these descriptions is from an anonymously published memoir. The author's father had been a general in the Imperial Army:

> The general lifted me over the coffin and suddenly I saw my father, dead, white as a sheet, with his eyes closed and his lower lip quite distended.
> My strength returned.
> I began to yell despairingly, to hit and kick.[53]

Before the death of a parent, the child had lived an isolated existence, protected from unwanted and unexplained contact with the outside world by a lovingly erected screen. In the wake of death, however, that screen broke down, leaving the child or children exposed as never before. This was especially true in the case of a father's death. Often, during his lifetime a man could fend off his creditors and keep his family in the dark as to the true state of his financial affairs. After his death all the creditors came knocking, and the poor widow and children found themselves in a precarious position. In the case of a mother's death, it was the emotional center of gravity that was lost. Either way, the new situation stimulated the child's powers of observation and judgment, which, having been less necessary previously, had lain dormant. A number of writers seem to notice the hypocrisy surrounding them for the first time: "Many of our neighbors arrived with expressions of sympathy or to ask questions; they oohed and aahed and pitied the poor children, but they pitied and patted us so dully, officially, with words only, that I found their sympathy and caresses disgusting."[54] This is, of course, the same feeling experienced by Irten'ev at his mother's funeral. In fact, Kornilova's description above sounds as if it came straight out of Tolstoy: "I found all of the outsiders at the funeral intolerable. . . . The comforting comments they made to my father . . . evoked a kind of annoyance in me. What right did they have to grieve and cry over her?" (Tolstoy, 1: 87).

For some writers, the moment of a death is the first conscious memory and marks the beginning of their life story. Thus, Gorky begins his *Childhood* with the death of the narrator's father. For others, death marks the end of the period defined as childhood: this is the case in Tolstoy's *Childhood*. It is also the case in a number of the autobiographies. For example, Grot, describing the death of her father, remarks: "It was as if all the happiness of our house suddenly collapsed, and our young hearts, which tightened painfully, felt all that."[55] The family is forced to move to Moscow and "a completely new life began for us in Moscow."[56]

The Wet Nurse

Although in *War and Peace* Tolstoy portrayed Natasha Rostova nursing her own babies, such a practice was the exception rather than the rule. Usually the child was given over to a wet nurse immediately after birth. Before emancipation, wet nurses were chosen from among serf women; later they were hired. Not surprisingly, adult writers rarely have direct recollections of the time they were nursing; however, in *Childhood Years* Aksakov provided a model for memories of the wet nurse: "I remember myself at night, either lying in my little bed or in my mother's arms, crying bitterly; weeping and howling, I repeated one and the same word, calling someone. And that someone appeared in the murk of my poorly lit room, took me in her arms, laid me on her breast... and I began to feel good" (1: 268).

Although Bagrov's recollection of nursing is unusual, memories of his wet nurse's visits when he was already an older child conform to an accepted tradition. Many autobiographers recall visits from their former wet nurses. These poor peasant women would bring sweets or various little presents to their former "children." Lelong's description of her wet nurse illustrates both the lasting tie and the potential tragedy inherent in the relationship. After commenting that her wet nurse loved her dearly, she continues: "I am amazed that she was able to love me when feeding me with her milk had cost her the life of her only son." [57]

The Nanny

After having been weaned, the child was usually given over to the care of a nanny (*niania*). Nannies left an indelible positive mark on the life of almost every Russian gentry child. [58] As opposed to their prim and proper counterparts in nineteenth-century England, Russian nannies were invariably of peasant origin and were seen as sources of folk wisdom and wholesome goodness. Nannies, who were always female, looked after both male and female children. Except in quite wealthy families, it was generally the practice to have a single nanny for all the young children, so that, in many cases, nannies looked after two or three children at once. The nanny's job was to wake, wash, and dress the children in the morning and to supervise their play during the day. In the summer this meant taking them on walks around the estate and teaching them such things as how to gather berries and mushrooms. In the winter she had to devise various ways of keeping the children amused, the most popular being the recitation of fairy tales. At night she had to undress the children and put them to bed.

The tie between child and nanny seems to have been extremely strong on both sides. In fact, it was not at all uncommon for grown men and women to remain in frequent contact with these peasant women: the famous story of Pushkin's attachment to his nanny is typical in this regard. Traditionally, the nanny protected her children from the discipline of parents and tutors. The following passage from the memoirs of A. V. Vereshchagin gives some idea of her role. Here the children are supposed to be sleeping (which they are not) when the mother comes to check up on them:

"Well, nanny, are the children sleeping?" she asked sternly.
"Yes, ma'am, they're sleeping. . . ."
"All right Anna, remember, if the children don't obey, tell me."

And then she would walk away with the same measured tread, accompanied by low curtsies.

Nanny, in her turn, was madly in love with us and tried, in various ways, to hide all our pranks and mischief.[59]

The necessity of parting from one's nanny was seen both as a catastrophic event and as a milestone, a rite of passage from one stage of life to the next: "In two years it came time to send me off to Petersburg. I found this out well in advance, and the thought of separation from my nanny frightened me most of all. It seemed so incredibly scary that I would wake up in the night, cry, call my nanny and say to her: "Nanny, my dear friend, you won't really leave me, will you?"[60]

In addition to their other good qualities, nannies were often credited with awakening or strengthening religious feeling in those children who remained believers later in life. The nannies' religion tended to be of the Russian peasant superstitious type, in which good and evil spirits and fortune-telling mixed freely with Orthodox teaching, but their belief was always fervent: "How wonderful was our nanny! Intelligent, always serious, very devout; I would often wake up in the nursery at night and see nanny praying by the door of our room, from where she could see the votive lamp."[61]

In fact, for many Russian adults, the image of the nanny and that of childhood itself were inextricably linked. The peasant nanny came to be identified with all that was positive in the old patriarchal way of life. Memories of one's nanny could serve as a direct bridge to the lost idyll of childhood:

It may seem strange, but 40 years have passed since then and our nanny remains alive in my memory. The closer I get to old age, the more sharply and clearly pictures of childhood arise in my memory, and I relive them so vividly that the past becomes the present... and everything connected in my heart to the memory of my dear, good little nanny becomes all the more valuable.[62]

The extent to which the nanny was felt to be the common property of the whole gentry class can be sensed in the memoirs of Ariadna Tyrkova-Vil'iams: "Simply and unthinkingly I gathered the life-giving fluids of love from my nanny, and they keep me going even now. How many loyal, loving, and wise Russian nan-

nies guarded and inspired the childhood life of their charges, affix-
ing on them an unnoticeable but indelible stamp." [63]

In addition to influencing the minds of gentry children by
bringing them up, nannies also served as the link between the
manor house and the servants' quarters. Although parents might
have preferred to keep their children segregated from serf children
of the same age, given the reality of their isolated existence and the
nannies' close ties to the rest of the peasants, this was impossible;
inevitably, gentry children played with peasant children of their
own age. Later, after the emancipation, when it became fashionable to understand "the people," this early contact became a
source of some pride to the authors of memoirs: "I have most
joyful and pleasant memories of my nanny. I feel that I am indebted to her for the first seeds of 'democratism' in my character. . . . To the credit of my parents, they did not oppose this
tendency; on the contrary, they always showed us the way and
strengthened us in this regard." [64]

Not all parents were equally liberal, however: "We played with
the children of the house and field serfs under the supervision of our
nanny, but it seems our parents did not know this, since, on our
way home, she would say: 'Don't tell mommy too much about how
you played with the other kids because she doesn't like it.'" [65]

When they themselves became parents, those autobiographers
who felt that contact with peasant children had been a healthy element in their upbringing systematically embraced such contacts
for their own children: "I always gave my children complete freedom to associate and to play with peasant kids, and I never noticed
anything but great physical and moral benefit from this system." [66]

The Serf World

In addition to the full-time attentions of the nanny and frequent
contact with the children of house and field serfs, the young gentry
child was surrounded and spoiled by a veritable army of adult house
serfs. Before and even after emancipation, the number of house
serfs or servants (that is, those serfs or, later, hired help who did no

field work) was disproportionately large. This anonymous description is typical:

Our domestics were serfs and, as was typical at that time, they were remarkable for their quantity, their slovenliness, and their incompetence. There were two coachmen for two teams of horses, four laundresses (for whom extra help was sometimes acquired), a cook, a dishwasher, a manservant, two maids—this whole group served us, that is, my mother, us two little girls, our governess, and our old nanny.[67]

This description indicates that those who marvel at the Soviet tendency to employ three workers for every job are witnessing a reenactment of a traditional situation.

The servant world surrounded the child constantly and provided much of his society and entertainment. In times of stress, especially after private lessons began, usually under the direction of French or German live-in tutors (although the tutor could also be a Russian imported from outside the estate), the house servants could usually be counted on for support against the "alien" invasion. N. I. Shatilov's memoirs give a taste of the composition of the typical warring factions. His tutor, Shemiakin, would lock him in his room for not studying: "In those difficult days of the 'Shemiakin yoke,' my true friends were my old nanny, our cook Stepan, and the old laundress Aleksandra Nikolaevna. Marfa Nikanorovna sweetened my imprisonment with various treats, the cook Stepan . . . told me the news of the city . . . and I found out what was going on in the house from the domestics."[68] This feeling of camaraderie between gentry children and serf (or later, servant) adults was shared by almost all writers of autobiographies and, certainly, by most of the Russian gentry. Thus, the scenes in *Childhood* describing Irten'ev's close relationship with Natal'ia Savishna and those in *Childhood Years* describing Bagrov's friendship with Evseich must have struck an emotional chord in contemporary readers.

The servant world also provided material to pique and to satisfy the early sexual yearnings of slightly older male children. Although by no means all landowners had sexual relations with female serfs, the practice was common enough to be mentioned with some frequency in both literature and autobiography.[69] Of course, children always know what their elders are up to, and they often realized what was going on, even at a relatively early age. L. E. Obolensky's memoirs present an especially vivid description of the awakening of the child's sexual feelings:

> Once I accidentally went into the nursery where the wet nurse of my new-born sister was ironing. Her name was Nastasia and she was a very pretty woman. . . . She was standing and, next to her, I saw one of my uncles, who was visiting us. He was embracing her, but quickly jumped away when I entered. . . . And right there, for the first time in my life, a kind of anxious feeling of curiosity, almost of pain, vaguely flickered within me... From then on I could never look at the wet nurse just like that.[70]

Similar emotions are described by Irten'ev when he talks about having observed his older brother's attentions to one of the maids. At first he is confused by the situation, then he is intrigued. Later he spends much of his time hiding near the maids' room trying to catch a glimpse of his brother with the maid in order to participate, at least vicariously, in Volodia's adventure. As he puts it, no greater change occurred in adolescence than that whereby he "stopped seeing a servant of the female sex and began to see a *woman*, on whom, to some extent, might rest my tranquility and happiness" (2: 19). Arsen'ev's first consummated love affair is with a maid in his brother's house in post-emancipation Russia, showing that the tradition continued into the late nineteenth century. Indeed, the theme was clearly an important one for Bunin; it is treated a number of times in the cycle of stories called "Darkened Paths."

The autobiographical and literary record is silent on the subject of sexual awakening and/or contacts between female members of the gentry class and their serfs or servants. Given the double sexual standard that prevailed in Russia, one expects that such contacts were less common, although they certainly must have occurred. Moreover, they were limited by the practice of marrying off daughters in their mid-teens and keeping a fairly close watch on them beforehand.

1 The family of V. A. Ostrogradsky on a boating expedition on their estate near Poltava, ca. 1914.

2 (*top left and right*). Vvedenskoe, an estate south of Moscow. This picture gives an excellent feeling for the estate as a whole. Note the arcades connecting the two wings of the main house to the center.

3 (*bottom right*). Kopenki, an estate near Orel. Note the covered porch on the second floor.

4 (*top*). Petrovskoe, the manor house that belonged to Pushkin's maternal grandfather. Constructed in the second half of the eighteenth century. A fine example of a typical middle-rank gentry landowner's house.

5 (*bottom*). Petrovskoe seen from the pond. Note how close the pond is to the main house and how the garden (which is planted in an orderly fashion in front of the house) is left in a more or less natural state.

6 "Family Portrait (On the Balcony)," by Fedor Mikhailovich Slaviansky, 1851. Both parents are present, as is the nanny. The profusion of vegetation allows the balcony to seem to be outdoors.

7 (*top left*). "Portrait of Evgeniia and Ekaterina Zaitsev," by Platon Semenovich Tiurin, 1847. The two girls are characteristically depicted outdoors, linked to each other and to their surroundings by a daisy chain.

8 (*bottom right*). Bereza, an estate in Kursk province. This is a fine example of a modest but elegant gentry house from the first half of the nineteenth century.

9 (*top right*). The quintessential Russian nanny.

10 (*top left*). Plan for the layout of a Russian estate by A. T. Bolotov (late eighteenth century). Note the formal garden (directly in front of the house) flanked on the right by an English-style park.

11 (*top right*). Tolstoy's house at Iasnaia Poliana. This house is significantly grander than that of Pushkin's grandfather. The photograph was taken by Tolstoy's wife, Sophia Andreevna.

12 (*bottom right*). Panoramic view of Iasnaia Poliana. The estate is seen as a productive whole, with haying going on in the foreground, outbuildings to the sides, and the manor house in the center.

13 (*top*). Muranovo, the estate that belonged first to the poet Baratynsky and then to the poet Tiutchev. Note the two architecturally unrelated additions that were evidently tacked onto the cental house when more space was needed.

14 (*bottom*). "The Nursery," by Varvara Aleksandrovna Chikhacheva, from the first half of the nineteenth century. The two children seem to have the run of the house, while their nanny sits quietly in the background.

The Myth of the Contented Peasant

The Russian estate was characterized, it would seem, by a degree of informality that did not exist in other European countries in the mid-nineteenth century. The Russian gentry child of moderately well-off parents grew up in the country and knew neither the stifling oppression and relatively strict class separation typical of urban centers nor the cold formality of, for example, English aristocratic estate life as we know it from literary descriptions of this period. Patriarchal mores were still observed on many estates and the *barin* (master) was the symbolic father of all his chattel. The child's position was on the plane where the life of the gentry family and that of its numerous retainers intersected; indeed, to a certain extent the child could be said to have belonged to both worlds.

Perhaps the only place in the nineteenth century where childhood resembled that of the Russian gentry was the antebellum South in the United States. However, the violent change brought about by the Civil War prevented most Southern aristocrats from idealizing their childhood in the same way. In Russia, emancipation was realized with far less bitterness, allowing adult Russians in the latter half of the nineteenth century to recall nostalgically the patriarchal way of life typical of the first half of the century.[71] Nevertheless, given the undeniable fact of serfdom in pre-emancipation Russia, it would have been difficult for autobiographers to idealize their childhood had they perceived that the cost of this happiness had been the serfs' misery. As a result, those who chose to remember childhood nostalgically could not and did not simply dismiss the fact of serfdom; instead, by appealing to an idealized model of patriarchal society, they tried to make a virtue of the old system.[72] To do so they appealed to what might be called the myth of the happy peasant; standard topoi of Russian childhood accounts became the contentment of the serfs belonging to the child's family and the great efforts made by the child's parents on their behalf. Claims of this sort are so universal that one begins to wonder why serfdom was abolished at all if life was so wonderful in pre-emancipation times. Since the condition of the serfs in Russia as a whole was, by all historical accounts, clearly not ideal, the "happy peasant" must be considered yet another social and literary convention of the gentry autobiographical tradition.[73]

A few excerpts from various autobiographies will show just how widespread nostalgia for the old way of life was in post-emancipation Russia. That desire is expressed indirectly, through descriptions of the care and attention lavished on the family's serfs:

One could say that the more than ten years my father stayed on his estate, from his marriage to his death (1821–32), were filled with deeds of Christian love and mercy. He tried to improve the lot not only of his dependents, but of all the surrounding rural folk. He concerned himself with the needs of the peasants and small farmers, arbitrated their disagreements, gave them advice, went into town to petition on their behalf.[74]

Despite his European education, my father was, both by upbringing and by nature, a real Russian landowner nevertheless. Any economy other than a serf economy was unthinkable for him. But this believer in serfdom did more for his peasants than many enlightened humanists and progressives.[75]

After her household chores, Alexandra Ivanovna [the author's mother] devoted all her free time to the needs of the peasants: she wove, knitted, and sewed for them; she taught their kids to read and write. She never kept any money, but whatever she could, she shared with the peasants and made their life easier.[76]

Although floggings or other punishments of servants and serfs are sometimes mentioned, they are depicted as having been fair and deserved. Abuses that occurred in the past and those committed by other families are not ignored, but almost every autobiographer sees his own parents as model serfowners. This is true even for those autobiographers who decry the existence of serfdom in general.[77] In short, based on the accounts available, one might be tempted to say about the father of every autobiographer what Vereshchagin says about his own: "My father was one of the kindest landowners in the district and it seems that the peasants loved him, although they feared him too."[78]

The combination of the "ideal landlord" and "happy peasant"

myths entered a new phase in the 1860's. Describing this period, authors concentrated on the cheerful readiness with which their parents freed the serfs. Although there was, historically speaking, a fair amount of grumbling from some landowners over the emancipation, one would never guess it from gentry autobiographies:

He freed the peasants willingly, allotted them enough land, and, in the presence of his former serfs, held a public prayer in his courtyard on the occasion of the manifesto of February 19.[79]

Our peasants . . . were given their freedom three or four years before the general emancipation of the peasants. Neither my father nor my grandfather was in favor of serfdom and they did not exploit their peasants.[80]

Our relations with our former serfs remained excellent. They came from all over for help and advice.[81]

It is possible, of course, that some families did indeed have ideal relationships with their serfs. Nevertheless, with all the old institutions of Russia under fire in the liberal press, it must have been difficult to express nostalgic feelings toward the old order unless the patriarchal way of life as a whole could be shown to be morally defensible. The literary/autobiographical myths of the contented peasant and the good landlord were necessary both for a positive evaluation of the entire childhood experience and as a political statement. They were meant to be seen as alternatives to the criticisms of reformers and socialists of various shades whose views were characteristic of the nongentry strand of Russian social thought. Gentry autobiographies and pseudo-autobiographies can be seen as an instinctive response to the attacks of the "progressives." When Tolstoy's and Aksakov's works appeared in the 1850's, the battle lines were still being drawn. Both writers were sympathetic to the old way of life (Tolstoy, in fact, managed to live it, for all intents and purposes, until 1910) and, having sensed that change was in the air, they produced fictional elegies (implicit celebrations of the old patriarchal society) even before the disappearance of the traditions they commemorated. By the 1870's the results of the changes that Tolstoy and Aksakov had anticipated were clear, and gentry autobiographers felt the need to emphasize the advantages of the old way of life explicitly. Grot states the case and the political ideas of the autobiographers forcefully:

I have also gone on about this because embittered attacks against the old ways in the literature of the 60's and 70's have inculcated in our times a feeling that there was something wild and savage about pre-emancipation estate life. I was born and spent the years of my early childhood in the country and I returned to estate life as a young woman. I brought many impressions away from that way of life which prove that it was not all bad. . . . I cannot recall the patriarchal and truly Christian family principles characteristic for the mores of our home without a feeling of deep emotion.[82]

Since many gentry children seem actually to have had close and friendly relations with serfs, it was probably not difficult for them to believe that the same had been true of their parents, and to interpret the entire pre-emancipation system through the rose-colored glasses of nostalgia.

After the Revolution this line of thought naturally disappeared in works published in the Soviet Union, but it continued among the émigrés, especially in the works of those writers who considered themselves heirs to the gentry literary tradition. The most obvious example is Bunin, who even before the Revolution had styled himself as the last in the line of the great gentry writers. In his notebooks Bunin praised his gentry literary ancestors (Pushkin, Lermontov, Tolstoy), saying of them: "They knew the common people. They couldn't not know them, having lived their whole lives with them in familial closeness." He then goes on to rail against the *raznochintsy* who broke that tradition, particularly for their invention of "so many legends about the cruelties of serfdom."[83]

The Estate

While the people who surround the happy child in a gentry autobiography can be of varying types and their relative importance can change, the child's physical surroundings and the way they are interpreted remain amazingly consistent. I have already mentioned that the gentry childhood always takes place in the country. As with so many aspects of gentry life, the estate was mythologized by gentry autobiographers; but before turning to gentry myths of the estate, let us try to get some idea of what the typical estate actually looked like. The center of the child's world was, of course, the manor house. These houses were rarely the classically proportioned stuccoed pleasure palaces that Intourist delights in showing foreign visitors today. Instead, they were one- or two-story rambling wooden affairs that had grown by accretion over the years; that is, whenever more space was needed, the master called his serf carpenters and simply had them tack more rooms onto the back and sides.[84] Upon entering the front door, guests found themselves in a foyer that led directly into the main *zala* (often a combined living and dining room). From that *zala* a number of doors led to servants', maids', and butlers' pantries and often to the owner's study. The second floor or mezzanine contained bedrooms, a nursery, and, almost always, a spacious covered porch overlooking the garden. The house of a friend of Fet's was typical:

From the big foyer a single door led into a large reception room which also served as the dining room. From that room there were doors to the right, which led to the mistress' office, and to the left, into the formal living room. In addition, from the same reception room there was a left-hand door to the servants' section. . . . On the right side of the reception room there was one more door, which opened into the corner office of the master.[85]

Sometimes, as in the house in which Lelong grew up, the center hall was two stories high, flanked by rooms of one story over which other rooms, called "entre-sols," were constructed.

For children the most intriguing part of the house tended to be the back stairways and corridors (the places where the house serfs spent their time) and the second-floor porch: "The lower floor, with its staircases and corridors, produced the impression of some kind of fairy-tale world on us children."[86] This type of internal landscape plays a role in Tolstoy's *Childhood*. It is through one of the innumerable corridors created by frequent reconstructions that the children spy on Grisha when he is praying in his attic room. In addition, Irten'ev uses a hidden spot under the stairway to observe his brother's attentions to one of the maids.

The porch was fondly remembered, because it offered shelter from sun and rain and a venue for tea drinking: "On the level of the belle-étage there was a wide porch round the whole house. We could run around on it in raw or rainy weather and you could find shade there at any hour of the day in the summer. Two wide staircases, surrounded by lilacs, came down from it on the main facades; one led into the garden, the other into the courtyard."[87]

Guest quarters, servants' quarters, stables, and the kitchen were located in separate outbuildings that might or might not be attached to the main house by covered passages. This arrangement was prompted both by fear of fires (in the case of the kitchen) and to give the guests and family a break from each other. As Kropotkin puts it: "In addition to the main house that my father had just finished building, there were several outbuildings in the big courtyard. They allowed those living within them a great degree of freedom without destroying the close ties governing family life."[88]

Stretching out from the manor house was always a garden. Usually the part closest to the house was more or less formal, with flower beds, paths, and hedges. Slightly farther away were geometrical alleys planted on both sides with lindens, birches, or other deciduous trees. In accordance with the sentimental and romantic tastes of the late eighteenth and early nineteenth centuries, these alleys generally led to a less organized, forest-like park. Behind the house there was often a vegetable garden or a fruit orchard of some kind. No two gardens were exactly alike. Their extent depended on the whim of the estate's owner, the condition of the soil, and the age of the estate. One thing almost all gardens did have in common, however, was a pond—unless, of course, the estate was on a river bank. Somewhere in the park there was sure to be a gazebo, where the secret assignations of Russian novels were inevitably held. It was in these gardens that gentry children ran, played, and communed with nature in their earliest childhood, and this oasis of greenery was what many remembered for their entire adult lives, especially if they passed their later years amid the granite of Petersburg or in exile.[89]

Beyond the immediate estate garden were the fields, forests, and pasture land owned by the landlord. After the emancipation (under the terms of which the peasants effectively had to buy their own land), the amount of property belonging to the former serfowner became smaller and smaller as most sold land to meet expenses. By the 1880's their situation often resembled that of Arsen'ev's family. They had sold all of their land and had only the manor house and the immediate garden left. Still, none of the surrounding land was fenced off and fields were not enclosed, so the feeling of endless space remained.

The final structure that could be found on some estates was a church. Since the landowner had to build the church from his own funds and had to see to the upkeep of the priest and his family, many estates did not have their own church. Instead, the inhabitants went to one on a neighboring, richer estate or to the nearest town. Still, because it was a sign of prestige to have one's own church, many status-conscious landlords, as well as very pious ones, built their own.

The Myth of the Estate as a Garden of Earthly Delights

As they had with the "happy peasant" and the "good landowner," Russian autobiographers developed a set of conventions relating to the estate; it was always seen positively, a "natural" realm in opposition to the "unnatural" city. Like so many other ideas, arcadian idealizations of the estate seem to have crossed the Russian border from France in the age of Catherine the Great. Aided by huge grants of land, serfs, and money, Catherine's favorites vied with each other in the construction of pleasure palaces. These elegant homes and parks were built just beyond the capital cities (Moscow and Petersburg) and, in their opulence, were not at all similar to the middle-level gentry estates that produced most Russian authors. On the other hand, the literary ideal of country life that was developed on the grand eighteenth-century estate was preserved in nineteenth-century descriptions of a far humbler reality. The philosophical impulse underlying eighteenth-century estate culture was, in the words of a Soviet specialist, "the idea, quite utopian at base, that it is possible to create a sublime world, where a man could feel himself at ease and happy."[90]

This Enlightenment-inspired dream saw the countryside as a place of escape from the "artificial" cares of the city and society.[91] Such is the position expressed by poetasters such as I. Dolgoruky in a number of laudatory eclogues:

Tortured by evil yearning
And the falsity of man,
Hiding from my friends, I strode,
Moaning, on a path obscure,
And I suddenly awoke
In a land enchanted;
Rubbed my eyes and crossed myself,
Is this all not but a dream...[92]

The delights that one might behold on such a walk and their healing powers are described quite elegantly by J. Delille:

On entering the garden what should you marvel at,
The bosquet calls you here, the pleasant meadow there,
Luxurious waters rush here, all around,
While there are Young and Fenelon, and crosses, a cemetery far,
Remind us of our home eternal
And teach us to unloose the bonds of life,
A bit, not breaking them withal.[93]

Thus, in the eighteenth and early nineteenth centuries the country estate was idealized as an oasis of tranquility amidst the cares of life. Sentimentalism, which flowered in Russia in the 1790's, provided a competing model for rural paradise. Nature was still idealized, but the ideal became the less formal English park, in place of the perfectly geometrical French garden. In literary works, authors such as N. M. Karamzin began to extol the beauties of "real" nature, and, although their descriptions certainly were not very realistic, they did depict a less stylized natural environment than that of classicism.[94] The sentimentalist preference for nature provided the bridge that linked the real world of the Russian estate with the pastoral ideals of the Enlightenment.

By the 1820's and 1830's, most of the great estates had been broken up (through a combination of the French invasion, spendthrift heirs, and the lack of primogeniture in Russia). The typical estate was, perhaps, smaller and less profitable, but the metaphor that compared the estate to a bucolic paradise became even stronger. In part this was because the new generation of writers had grown up on the estate and, instead of seeing it as a temporary escape from social life, knew it as a way of life. When their conservative, basically Slavophile ideals combined with Rousseauian ideas of childhood as a golden age, an idea complex that equated childhood on a rural estate with time in paradise was born.

This component of the Russian myths of childhood was in place even before the appearance of *Childhood*. It can be found in Goncharov's fragment "Oblomov's Dream." Eventually the "Dream" was incorporated into the novel *Oblomov* (1859), but it had first been published separately ten years earlier. It played a crucial role in defining the themes that were to be important for both autobiographical and pseudo-autobiographical literature in the next 70 years. In the novel, Oblomov's dream of the rural paradise where he spent his childhood is contrasted with the city where he slogs through his adult life. Even without the rest of the novel as contrast, however, the reader understands that he has been magically transferred to a different world by the vaguely Gogolian narrator of the "Dream."

"Where are we? To what blessed little corner of the earth has Oblomov's dream transported us? What a marvelous place!"[95] The enchanted nature of the place is enhanced by its lack of anything that could cause destruction or distraction: no mountains, no seas, no spectacular landscapes. Nature, anthropomorphized, is given parental qualities: "On the contrary, it seems that the sky presses closer to the earth there . . . in order to embrace her more strongly, lovingly: it stretches out, not very high above your head, like the haven of your parents' roof" (104). Like the ideal estates of the Age of Enlightenment, this spot of earth soothes the spirit: "A heart that has been worn by emotions, or even one unacquainted with them, simply begs to hide itself away in this forgotten little corner and to live in unimaginable happiness" (105). The estate described is, however, unlike its eighteenth-century counterparts in that its owners (Oblomov's family) live on it year-round. It is not a rich "weekend" home, but a productive agricultural enterprise.

The area is a bucolic paradise filled with images of the golden age. There are no dread diseases, no dangerous wild beasts, and winters are short (for Russia, anyway). It is populated by happy peasants, who grow their crops with little effort, and by contented cows, sheep, and chickens. The peace and quiet of the area are said to be uncongenial to the poet (that is, to the stormy Romantic imagination of the previous literary generation). There is no theft or murder, nor are there any unpleasant accidents. Like any utopia, the region is completely isolated, and this allows for the continuation of a simple patriarchal way of life with no interference from the outside world. The population of this ideal world is practically immortal as well: "Over the last five years, out of several hundred people, no one had died at all, neither of natural causes nor, certainly, of violent ones" (p. 110).

Having first set the physical background of the region, the narrator reveals that Oblomov spent an idyllic childhood there. Although "Oblomov's Dream" is a third-person narrative, Goncharov's treatment of childhood clearly anticipates the myths that would later be canonized for the autobiographical tradition by Tolstoy and Aksakov. The "Dream" takes Oblomov back to the time when he was the center of the universe, spoiled by his nanny and his mother. It is interesting that within this utopian world, a world that provided autobiographers with a mine of golden-age images, Oblomov's nanny told him fairy tales about an even more perfect world, where rivers flow with milk and honey and no one does anything. Despite the fact that the narrator relates Oblomov's dream with a certain amount of irony, the ideal of a tranquil gentry childhood on the Russian estate became common property of an entire class.

In the years after the publication of *Oblomov*, descriptions of the Russian country estate in terms of the golden age became widespread. This is particularly true when the estate is described in conjunction with a childhood that was spent on it. They turn up in surprising places: for example, one would hardly expect to find arcadian moments in Herzen's "realist" prose. Nevertheless, he characterizes life on his family's estate, Vasilevskoe, in the following terms: "The shepherd swishes his long whip and plays his birch-bark flute . . . over here one hears the songs of peasant women returning from the fields . . . children play on the street, by the riverbank." [96]

The most remarkable golden-age portrait of all is in Glinsky's autobiography. His depiction of summer life is so luscious it makes one want to abandon everything and head straight for the country:

To quench your thirst you drink milk to your heart's content, the gardener gives you fresh pea and bean pods, cucumbers, and tiny carrots, in the servants' dining room you slurp their hearty cabbage soup; you run around until you are exhausted and then you collapse under currant, gooseberry, or raspberry bushes and pull off berry after berry until sleep closes your eyes and, right there, to the hum of bees, mosquitoes, and midges, you fall off in a young and carefree sleep. [97]

An understanding of the importance of nature and the ability to commune with it is mentioned as the legacy of a rural childhood by almost all autobiographers. [98] Adult narrators consistently see nature as an antidote to society and the disappointments of life. Nature's intimate connection to childhood, the period before such disappointments begin, only strengthens its role: "Those who passed their early childhood in the country are very fortunate. It is only in the country that a person can learn to love nature with all her heart, and that love for mother nature remains with you for your whole life." [99]

For many an adult looking back on childhood, it was the isolation of the estate, the vast expanse of forest or fields surrounding it, that made the greatest impression: "My childhood was spent in close contact with nature. I always recall the summer, the hot, dry summer of central Russia... Beyond the meadow, on the horizon, the forest began; it stretched for tens, maybe hundreds of miles. For me, during childhood in any case, it seemed to be a kind of mysterious end of the world, beyond which there was nothing." [100] This feeling of isolation and endless expanse is characteristic for the perception of Arsen'ev: "I was born and bred, I repeat, in the kind of completely open spaces that a European cannot even imagine. I was surrounded by a huge space, without barriers or boundaries: where, in fact, did our estate end, and where did the endless field with which it merged begin?" (Bunin, 6: 40). The European countryside was, of course, dominated by small, enclosed fields. Russians felt the difference between country and city more acutely than their European counterparts precisely because they were used to the vast expanses of the Russian countryside.

For some, the natural world of the Russian estate stands for childhood as a whole:

Everyone enjoys recalling the places he grew up in—that is why I, personally, am writing about them.

And how could one not love them! The clear brook flowing over a white sandy bottom; the green meadows stretching far and wide. . . . Oh! I remember these sublime pictures, even as I remember the very haven of my homeland. They have often come to life in my memories and their appearance has joyously soothed my soul. [101]

The even, unspectacular Russian landscape corresponds to happy memories of childhood, unbroken, as a rule, by high peaks or deep valleys of emotion. Some adult writers even go so far as to endow nature with the power to form whole lives: "The rivers, the groves, the village paths on which we rode with our parents left such deep impressions on me that my entire moral nature has been woven of them, as if from threads. It is clear to me that my attachment to my homeland, to its people, and to the church grew from this foundation; those threads and impressions of childhood gave a direction to the whole contents of my life." [102] This quotation, more directly, perhaps, than any other, expresses the decisive importance of childhood in the Russian gentry mind. Childhood sets the tone for one's entire life, and the experiences of childhood, shared as they were by a large proportion of gentry children, defined many of their adult attitudes. This is in sharp contrast to the need, so commonly present in English and French culture, to overcome one's childhood. In European realist literature, one of the most common plots involves the poor boy from the provinces who tries to make good in the big city. Of Russian writers only Dostoevsky, whose relatively unstable and unhappy childhood set him apart, uses the European model with any frequency. In Russian gentry literature, on the other hand, the main character's early years are generally a source of joy, a time to which the hero would like to return, not one that must be escaped at all costs.

The rural places in which gentry autobiographers grew up are often contrasted to the cities in which they spent the latter part of their youth. Exile to the city (usually for the purposes of schooling) produces a feeling of "paradise lost" in relation to the estate and, during vacation time, of "paradise regained." This is how Vereshchagin describes his return to the family estate after a year in Petersburg: "I don't know with what you can compare the joy you feel when you approach your dear native places after a long separation. It seems to me that such moments are indescribable." [103] After a horrible year spent at boarding school, Glinsky returned home for summer vacation and "the country air dissipated all my nightmares, soothed my heartaches, and calmed my nerves." [104]

Of course, these constant descriptions of paradise lost lend a nostalgic and elegiac accent to gentry autobiographies. Instead of the historicist ideal of gradual improvement through the course of one's life, the Russian model is based on a gradual falling away from the perfection of childhood. The fact that most of the estates described had been broken up by the time these accounts were written meant that the authors could not, as a rule, revisit the places they described. Instead they had to depend on distant memories and on the literary tradition. Moreover, many authors first experienced nature through the medium of literature. Thus, for example, in a chapter called "A Winter Evening," Chertkova tells of seeing a winter storm through Pushkin's poem and of not understanding either of them completely:

> Storm with mist the heavens covers,
> Snowy whirlwinds twisting;
> Now like a wild beast falls roaring,
> Now falls crying like a child...

(I remember that, for a long time, I said "howls" instead of "with mist," because, I guess, I didn't understand the words.)[105]

This same technique is used masterfully in Bunin's *The Life of Arsen'ev*, where Arsen'ev characterizes entire periods of his life and his views of the world and nature through Russian poetry.

The Russian gentry myth of happy childhood in the midst of nature is an unusual combination of fact and literary tradition. Russian gentry children had been growing up in patriarchal environments at least since the age of Catherine the Great. One imagines that they may have had happy childhoods then, as well. However, they did not learn to express their joyous memories until Goncharov, Tolstoy, and Aksakov had given literary form to childhood in a concrete historical situation. Simultaneously, the changed social and political circumstances in the countryside after 1861 made their memories more valuable. The emancipation of the serfs convinced many people that the type of childhood they had experienced would never again be possible. Personal desire for a recreation (albeit literary) of paradise lost joined with a certain class consciousness induced by the psychological jolt of emancipation, and the result was a flood of idealized autobiographies.

As it turned out, however, reports of the death of an entire mode of existence were premature. There was no more serf labor and the economic realities of life had changed, but the ideal of the estate and, particularly, of the estate childhood lived on through the nineteenth and into the twentieth centuries. Just as it had survived despite the transition from the wealthy "weekend" estate of the eighteenth century to the full-time gentleman's farm of the early nineteenth century, this ideal was flexible enough to be suitable even in post-emancipation conditions. In fact, there was quite a revival of interest in the Russian estate in the years just before the Revolution. A fascination with the old gentry lifestyle and the attempts to revive it were chronicled on the pages of the opulent magazines *Bygone Years* (1907–16) and *The Capital and the Estate* (1913–17). In addition to the latest society information and gossip, the latter magazine included articles on many historic Russian estates. The nostalgic feelings of readers and their love for traditional Russian literary culture were constantly played upon in attempts to rehabilitate the gentry way of life:

Pushkin, Lermontov, Turgenev, Pisemsky, Aleksei and Lev Tolstoy: all were fledglings of Russian estates. From there they brought into literature something ineffably tender, virginally chaste, magically dreamy, something endlessly noble and holy.[106]

The Russian estate—gentry landowners—it sounds like an anachronism. We look at pictures from estate life with a condescending smile, as if they represented the distant and amusing, but still somehow cherished past. Why? . . . What a surprise, therefore, to find family estates that have been passed down from generation to generation.[107]

Such passages were by no means unusual. Practically every issue described a different estate, some in not very good condition, others restored or preserved rather well.

However, the ultimate expression of the connection between an idealized picture of estate life and gentry childhood belongs to a contributing editor of *Bygone Years*, Baron N. Vrangel':

And how could one not love and not wish to recreate that naive artlessness of earlier life. It was an epoch of childish, almost funny (but at the same time serious) belief in everything that now seems to us like youthful fancy. . . . And that is why we see each even trivial object from that irrevocable past not simply as a curious amusement for an antiquarian, but as a precious relic of cherished times, as a kind of talisman about which we still dream with childhood memories.[108]

Education

Until the child was about eight or nine, he or she was free to roam the little kingdom of the estate pretty much at will, although always under the watchful eye of the nanny. In these early years children were generally not burdened with lessons. However, many autobiographers remember having been taught to read and write by their parents well before the appearance of teachers. Chertkova's memories of learning to write with a set of alphabet blocks capture the pleasure with which young children can learn before the advent of formal schooling: "I remember how I put together the words 'shchi' and 'zhuk.' They seemed so serious and important. And I always called the letter 'zh' 'zhuk,' because its shape reminded me of a beetle's." [109]

When the child reached eight or nine years of age, a more formal program of education was usually devised. In some cases parents continued to teach their own children. More frequently, however, the child was given over to a tutor, male for the boys and female for the girls. (The tutor's qualifications and abilities depended on the family's ability to pay and on some good luck.) In most cases this next step in the educational process did not involve leaving the countryside. Instead, like Irten'ev's tutor, Karl Ivanych, the *gouverneur* came to live on the estate. In a description of the circumstances surrounding the arrival of her father's tutor, Karpinskaia illustrates perfectly the untranslatable ideal of *barstvo* (that is, acting as befits a true *barin*, or master) that was the key to the whole gentry ideal:

One time he hired a teacher for the boys. The teacher turned out to be married with children. They built him a little outbuilding next to the manor house (the house was already full). Soon the teacher's mother-in-law came, and seeing that life here was very pleasant, she moved in permanently. Her widowed daughter and the daughter's grown children joined her. Pavel Mikhailovich was told that the teacher's family had grown so much that the outbuilding was crowded; he ordered another, bigger one to be built. [110]

The general impression one gets from reading Russian literature is that tutors were most often French, sometimes German or English, and only rarely Russian. According to the autobiographical record, however, this is not entirely true. The great age of the French tutor was from the late eighteenth century (many French aristocrats and pseudo-aristocrats fled to Russia after 1789) through the 1820's (after which most of the flotsam and jetsam remaining from La Grande Armée had left). In the 1830's and 1840's there were fewer Frenchmen available and, in addition, Russian became more fashionable than it had been previously, so families began hiring Russians. Lelong recalls: "I remember that from the time I was eight years old a Russian teacher, Ol'ga Sergeevna Tkacheva, lived with us: she was a tall, dried-out old maid. . . . She had completed a course of study at the 'House of Industriousness' in Riazan', knew her subject well, and taught soundly." [111] Although Russian alone was good enough for the first few years, when the children had grown up a bit something more was demanded of the governess, even if she was, again, a home-grown product: "When I was eleven a new governess arrived; Pelageia Alekseevna Syreishchikova knew French and German and some music." [112]

Of course, a real French tutor (even a bad one) still conferred a sort of status on the household that no Russian, no matter how well qualified, could match. Describing the Frenchwoman who was forced on her by the will of her father (and against the wishes of her mother and grandmother), Kornilova says: "It is strange but true that our house gained much in the eyes of our neighbors with governesses when we got ourselves a mademoiselle. It was as if we became people too, of the same status as the others, who had, albeit poorly, Frenchified." [113]

In the houses of the rich, French and German tutors remained *de rigueur* even for relatively young children. This ensured that only the wealthy would be able to speak French and German with a perfect accent. As Irten'ev notes in *Youth*, a perfect French accent was one of the necessary qualifications for being *comme il faut*. Whatever the tutor's nationality, however, he or she usually brought something of the outside world into the family circle and widened the children's horizons. Indeed, Russians owed more than they could tell to these peripatetic teachers. Kropotkin's experience is typical. By the time he was in his early teens, he had already had a French tutor named Poulain, followed by a German: "They took on a teacher, Karl Ivanovich, who turned out to be one of those idealists one finds quite commonly among Germans. I especially remember the way he read Schiller; his naive declamation sent me into ecstasy." [114]

By the second half of the nineteenth century, the fashion seems to have switched to English nurses and tutors in the houses of the wealthy. S. V. Kovalevskaia was brought up by an English governess on English principles. In fact, one of the main reasons that her childhood was unhappy was that it was, for all intents and purposes, English and not Russian. The changing situation is also reflected in *Anna Karenina*: Vronsky organizes his estate and the upbringing of his and Anna's daughter along English lines. Anglophilism continued into the twentieth century. Irina Skariatina speaks of her English nanny, and Nabokov claims that he wrote English before Russian.

A form of education that became more and more popular for male children throughout the nineteenth century was the gymnasium. [115] In his discussion of gentry life in the 1810's and 1820's, Iu. M. Lotman does not mention the gymnasium as an educational option. [116] Even in the 1840's the gymnasium had not yet become popular: "In my day the gymnasium was not abundantly stocked with pupils, because the gentry sent their children to the gentry institute and not to the gymnasium." [117] By mid-century, however, many young boys began to attend these more organized schools, which certainly had the potential to provide a better education than that afforded by a single tutor. [118] In many cases boys were trained at home first and entered the school in one of the middle courses. Most boys who had been tutored at home had few problems passing the entrance exam.

The decision to send one's child to the gymnasium was a difficult one for parents in many respects. It meant that the family had to move to the city in which the school was located or that the child had to board at the school or with relatives or friends in the city. In any case it meant a severe change in the family's hitherto stable way of life: either a parting from the estate or separation from a child. Still, as education became more important in Russia (it became difficult for a nobleman with social or cultural ambitions to do anything without a university degree, and graduation from a gymnasium was an automatic ticket to higher education), parents became inured to the idea.

For the child, the gymnasium meant the beginning of a new life, away from the rural surroundings that had defined his world. In all the autobiographies and pseudo-autobiographies, the start of regular school is a crucial and often traumatic moment. If, as I have noted previously, the death of a parent often put an abrupt and unnatural end to a gentry childhood, the departure from the estate to begin studying at a school in the city marked a more natural conclusion:

So the years passed. And when I was ten they brought me to the gymnasium for my exam. . . . That was in 1893. From that point began a new, eight-year period of my life—the gymnasium period.[119]

When I was ten my mother announced: "All right, my dear, you've had enough sitting around doing nothing! We're off to Penza where I'm going to get you into the gymnasium."[120]

If there is one area of solid agreement among the writers of autobiographies and pseudo-autobiographies, it is an intense dislike of the gymnasium.[121] Over and over again one reads of poor conditions and uninspired teaching; the gymnasium was perhaps best summed up as "a world of dead languages and people."[122] Kropotkin describes the experience as follows: "They put me in the third grade. I was all of eleven and had to deal with a whole series of subjects beyond a child's comprehension. They taught all subjects in the most senseless way."[123] Aksakov talks of the terrible trauma that the gymnasium caused him as a young child, and Arsen'ev leaves school before graduation with no love lost.

Although many of the criticisms leveled at the gymnasium are probably justified, it should be borne in mind that there were specific reasons for gentry children to dislike it so much. In *Childhood*, Irten'ev professes amazement when he sees peasants who fail to doff their hats to his family because they do not know them. He had thought the Irten'evs were known and loved by the entire world and can hardly believe that this is not so. Most gentry children spent their childhoods (up to the age of ten or eleven) in more or less the same way: as the center of attention for an entire rural world. This was in strong contrast to their European counterparts and to the Russian *raznochinnaia* intelligentsia, who, by the age of ten, had had four or five years of formal schooling. All of a sudden these young aristocrats left the security of their familiar world and were thrust into a new one where no one cared who they were. This must have been a major shock, and it is a primary reason that the gymnasium was usually the first sustained negative impression for a gentry child. He was shut up inside all day long and forced to work on things that were no fun. In contrast, the rural paradise in which childhood had been passed began to seem even rosier. The city meant imprisonment and isolation, the countryside, freedom and attention. In the psychological conflict of country and city, the city never really had a chance. From now on it would always be associated with the wrench from childhood and would always suffer in comparison to the estate. The myth of the happy childhood is confirmed and strengthened by that of unhappy adolescence. The pattern was given powerful literary form by Tolstoy in *Childhood* and *Boyhood*, but it was a pattern that conformed to the idiosyncrasies of the gentry lifestyle and one that is repeated, with variations, in numerous autobiographical accounts.

Chapter Four

இலை

M. Gorky: Anti-*Childhood*

From the 1860's to the turn of the century, there were numerous attempts to dislodge the myths of childhood that Tolstoy and Aksakov had proposed from their canonized position in the Russian cultural mind. These attempts failed, in part because of the strength of the original models, but also because the cultural/literary opposition was unable or unwilling to create countermyths of its own. The best the "dissidents" could do was to chip away at the gentry myths by showing that they were not universally true. Still, the Russian conception of childhood continued to be dominated by Tolstoy's contention that it was a "happy, happy time."

The first Russian literary work to attempt to overthrow the gentry conception of childhood and to replace it with an entirely new model was M. Gorky's *Childhood* (1913). For Gorky, a difficult and unhappy childhood was the "proper" kind, because adversity early in life was thought to lead to a desire to change the world for the better. In order to attack the gentry myths more effectively, Gorky decided to describe his childhood using the same literary form, the pseudo-autobiography, that had been created by Tolstoy more than 60 years earlier. But Gorky radically altered the pseudo-auto-biography's ideological function: instead of affirming the gentry's conservative *Weltanschauung*, his version expressed a forward-looking socialist ideal.

The literary paths of Tolstoy and Gorky had, of course, crossed long before Gorky began work on *Childhood*. In fact, of all the writers of the previous generation, Tolstoy was the one with whose reputation Gorky had to contend most frequently. He was often compared with or set in opposition to Tolstoy during his lifetime, and the multifaceted relationship between the two has continued to interest critics to this day.[1] Gorky himself quite obviously felt anxiety about Tolstoy's influence; during his career he wrote a number of works in which he tried to come to terms with Tolstoy's literary heritage and social/historical persona.

In 1908 Gorky published a first-person story called "A Confession," which is, in many respects, a response to Tolstoy's eponymous autobiographical work. While Gorky's "Confession" is based primarily on stories related to him by others (although it evidently does contain at least some autobiographical material),[2] the strivings of the main character to "find himself" often parallel and sometimes stand in opposition to those of Tolstoy. Tolstoy's work describes an aristocrat who has lived easily, happily, and productively before his inability to answer important metaphysical questions leads him to a crisis. He resolves the crisis after tortured self-analysis, an analysis that brings him to a very personal belief in God and to his own version of Christianity. Gorky's narrator, on the other hand, is a poor abandoned child who leads an exceptionally difficult early life. In the course of the story, by dint of observing other people and the external world, he moves away from a search for a personal God (which had both sustained and tortured him in his youth) and toward a belief in the possibility of the creation of the kingdom of heaven on earth. This is to be achieved through the rational organization of "the people."

Although Gorky and Tolstoy come at the epistemological problem from different directions and reach different conclusions,[3] they are similar in their rejection of organized religion and in their use of religious terminology to define their own positions. Near the end of the novel, for example, Gorky states: "And so I began my humble preaching, calling people to a new service, in the name of new life, but still without knowing the name of my new god" (9: 384). Both Tolstoy and Gorky saw "the people" as the repository of future hope for mankind, but both felt that "the people" needed guidance from some outside source before they could realize their potential. The major difference, of course, is that Tolstoy ultimately saw himself as the source of guidance, whereas Gorky preached a version of the tenets of Marxism. While the ideological purpose of Gorky's "Confession" is clear without reference to Tolstoy, the earlier work exerts a constant, if indirect, intertextual presence.

In the memoir "L. N. Tolstoy," on the other hand, Gorky tried a more direct approach in order to establish his position both as the heir to the Tolstoyan tradition and as its modifier. One of the central literary/ideological purposes of the essay is to chronicle the physical contacts between the two writers and to characterize their differing views of literature. The fact that Tolstoy is seen criticizing and appreciating the early works of his literary "son" makes the "son's" inheritance of the literary mantle seem a more natural process. By the same token, by including scenes in which he successfully disagrees with his spiritual "father," Gorky emphasizes his right to carve out his own path while still remaining true to the legacy. A typical passage describes Tolstoy's criticism and Gorky's rebuttal:

> I read him my story "The Bull." He laughed a lot and praised me for knowing "the tricks of language."
> "But you handle words awkwardly,—all your peasants speak very intelligently. In real life they speak stupidly, absurdly. . . . And they're always speaking in aphorisms. That's not right either,—aphorisms don't belong in the Russian language."
> "But what about proverbs, sayings?"
> "That's different. They weren't made up today."
> "But you yourself often speak in aphorisms."
> "Never! And then you overembellish everything." (16: 268–69)

The passage first shows Tolstoy praising Gorky's work. Then follows a criticism of a particular aspect of the "son's" story. This criticism is partially rebutted by the "son" (to the obvious discomfort of the "father"), thereby underscoring Gorky's right to make his own path in the world.

Finally, and even more important for the present purposes, Gorky relates an episode in which Tolstoy supposedly requested him to produce the very work through which he assimilated, and to some extent overcame, the influence of his "father": "Come now, tell me something, you're a good talker. Something about a little boy, about yourself. It's hard to believe you too were once little, you're so—strange. As if you were born grown-up" (16: 310). This conversation is supposed to have taken place in 1902, before Gorky had written *Childhood*. Gorky, as it were, hints that Tolstoy had encouraged him to write a generalized childhood that was, simultaneously, his own ("Something about a little boy, about yourself"). That is, Tolstoy is shown inviting Gorky to use the very form that he had used 50 years earlier. Yet by the time Gorky published the essay (1919), he had already finished his *Childhood* and knew very well just how distant his work was from the Tolstoyan model.[4]

Thus, Gorky's *Childhood* should be seen not solely as an attempt to overturn the gentry myths of childhood, but also as the work in which Gorky tried to come to terms with the legacy of Tolstoy. The means that Gorky used to overcome Tolstoy's cultural and literary presence can be defined in terms of parody. In the Russian critical tradition, parody has been described as the classic method by which literary "sons" overcome the influence of their "fathers."[5] To do so, they use the literary material characteristic for writers of the previous generation, but they use it in their own way, changing its valuation: positive becomes negative and vice versa. In *Childhood*, Gorky parodies the form and content of Tolstoy's *Childhood* on a number of levels.

That Gorky meant his work as a kind of challenge to Tolstoy and to the tradition he had spawned can be seen from the work's very title.[6] In the 60 years separating the publication of Tolstoy's *Childhood* and Gorky's, no one had had the temerity to reuse Tolstoy's title (although many autobiographies contained a section called "Chilhood").[7] In terms of genre, Gorky's intent becomes apparent very early as well. One of the crucial characteristics of pseudo-autobiography is the disjunction between the author and the narrator. Thus, Tolstoy's *Childhood* is narrated by Nikolai Irten'ev and Aksakov's *Childhood Years* is narrated by Sergei Bagrov. In Gorky's *Childhood* the familiar situation is subtly varied. The author is called M. Gorky and the narrator is Aleksei Peshkov. The disjunction seems to be preserved, but the narrator's name is, in fact, Gorky's real name, while the author's name is his pseudonym. The formal separation of narrator and author is retained, but the resulting work takes on the illusion of being even more autobiographical than it would have been had the reader been presented with the autobiography of M. Gorky. Because this formal sleight of hand makes the work a pseudo-autobiographical novel and an autobiography simultaneously, I will not always make a definite distinction between author and narrator when discussing the trilogy (as I am careful to do when discussing other pseudo-autobiographies). Gorky has different ways to make the reader perceive that the trilogy pertains to many as opposed to one—that is, to show the story of *a* child, not *the* child.

To some extent the differences between Gorky's childhood and those described in the gentry tradition are simply a function of his having grown up under extremely different circumstances. On the level of fact, for instance, the contrast between the countryside, where gentry autobiographers lived as children, and the city, in which Gorky struggled to survive, has nothing to do with literary parody. However, the way in which Gorky chooses to structure his autobiography, the scenes he chooses to include, and the interpretations he gives them reveal that his work is oriented specifically against the gentry autobiographical tradition and, in particular, against Tolstoy. Thus, to cite only one example, although the city/country opposition itself is factually based, it is the literary myth of the happy childhood (which takes place on an estate that is connected, by a whole series of indicators, to paradise or heaven) that Gorky is attacking when he has his mother call the city environment "this hell" (15: 30).

Variations in the construction of the work also point towards parody. The event that effectively ends Irten'ev's childhood is the death of his mother. Tolstoy's choice of ending point was purely literary, since his own mother died when he was less than two years old and he had no memories of her at all. In addition, as I have shown in the previous chapter, the death of a parent marked the end of childhood in many autobiographies. Gorky, on the other hand, chooses to *begin* his childhood with the death of his father. While it is true that Gorky's father did indeed die when Gorky was three years old (that is, unlike Tolstoy's purely literary choice of an ending, Gorky's choice of a beginning was, on some level, autobiographically motivated), it should not be forgotten that there were any number of possible ways for Gorky to have started his work. By choosing to begin with a death, Gorky immediately emphasizes that his childhood is going to differ from the happy two-parent childhoods typical of the gentry model.

If Gorky's choice of a starting point reveals, in part, his desire to turn the structure of Tolstoy's *Childhood* upside down, his treatment of the ending makes his intent even more obvious. Like Tolstoy, Gorky ends his first volume with the death of the mother. However, whereas the mother's death evokes a highly emotional and introspective reaction from Irten'ev, Gorky's narrator describes the scene in a startlingly detached manner:

> I stood, with a cup in my hand, for an immeasurably long time next to my mother's bed watching her face harden and turn gray.
> Grandpa came in and I said to him: "Mother has died . . ."
> He glanced at the bed. "What are you lying for?"
> He went over to the oven and started to take out a pie, making a deafening clatter with the rack and the baking tin. I looked at him, knowing that mother had died, waiting for him to comprehend. (15: 209)

While the death of his mother leads to important changes in Irten'ev's life (most important to the loss of the final link with childhood paradise and the beginning of his generally unhappy boyhood), the death of Aleksei's mother produces no major changes in his life. He is, it is true, sent away from the home of his grandparents, but for all intents and purposes he had already left of his own accord and, what is more, the banishment proves only temporary.

In part, Aleksei's extreme detachment at his mother's death is connected with Gorky's diminution of the myth of the perfect mother.[8] In the gentry tradition, the mother is the repository of all good qualities and forms a very strong bond with her children. Although Aleksei remembers his attachment to (and even admiration for) his mother at certain periods of his childhood, there was no real bond between them because she more or less abandoned him to the care of his grandparents. To some extent, in fact, Aleksei's grandmother plays the role normally assigned to the mother in the gentry tradition, although she also has the "mother earth" traits that were the property of nannies. However, Aleksei's detachment at his mother's death is not due only to his emotional distance from her. It is also related to the fact that the child is, by this time, inured to death.[9] Life in his world is "nasty, brutish, and short," and so death does not produce the kind of emotional self-analysis typical of a gentry narrator. In this respect it is instructive to compare Gorky's trilogy with Bunin's *The Life of Arsen'ev*. Arsen'ev witnesses almost as many deaths as young Peshkov, but each one causes him deep emotional trauma. Death becomes one of the main themes of the novel. For Gorky, death is a natural condition of life, not a source of material for philosophizing or self-analysis.

There is one more important aspect to Aleksei's detachment at his mother's death. His lack of soul-searching is symptomatic not only of a natural reaction to the specific situation described, but of a more general eschewal of self-analysis characteristic for the work as a whole. For Tolstoy in particular, and for gentry autobiography in general, the past is explored in order to achieve self-understanding. Childhood is seen as the time when the self is formed, and therefore the events of childhood are subject to intensive commentary from the adult narrator. This lends gentry pseudo-autobiography and autobiography a distinctive style in which an event, narrated by the voice of the child, is immediately dissected by the adult narrator. Gorky is not concerned with motivated psychology in order to analyze childhood. If Tolstoy and his followers tend to "tell" a great deal, then Gorky mostly wants to "show."[10]

In his attack on the gentry autobiographical tradition, Gorky refuses to use the Tolstoyan "dialectic of the soul," even when it would seem that self-analysis is required. This is the case with the famous suicide scene near the end of *My Universities*. With absolutely nothing to prepare the reader for such a resolution, the narrator says: "In December I decided to kill myself." He then explains that he tried to adumbrate the motives for this action (unsuccessfully, according to him) in a different story. Instead of following this digression with a more successful analysis of his action (as the reader expects), he continues as follows: "Having purchased a revolver loaded with four cartridges at the bazaar, I shot myself in the chest expecting to hit the heart, but I only pierced a lung; a month later, quite embarrassed and feeling impossibly stupid, I was working in the bakery again" (16: 84). And that, to the reader's amazement (especially if he is used to the conventions of Tolstoyan psychological realism), is all. Thus, Gorky's parody works, at times, through the omission of a Tolstoyan literary device at points in the narrative where it is "required."

Another way in which Gorky orients his work against Tolstoy's is by including certain scenes that seem to have been chosen to clash with similar scenes from Tolstoy. For example, a characteristic passage in the earlier *Childhood* comes when the narrator recalls the emotions he felt while listening to his mother play the piano. When she plays the Second Concerto of Field he remembers having felt "some kind of light, shining, and transparent memories" (Tolstoy, 1: 31). When she plays the "Pathetique" Sonata he recalls something "sad, heavy, and gloomy." His overall recollection of his mother's playing, however, is that it "resembled memories; but memories of what? It seemed you were recalling things that never happened." Significantly, even at an early age, Irten'ev does not have a direct emotional response; he reacts by analyzing his reaction, by reminiscing. In Tolstoy's work the act of reminiscing is generally a positive one that serves to bring the soul back to an earlier, more innocent stage. Moreover, the responses produced by the music are rather muted. This is primarily due to their lack of a direct referent. If you are remembering things that never happened, you cannot, after all, be expected to have a strong emotional reaction to them. For Irten'ev, music belongs to the magical world of childhood, and his nebulous response to it corresponds to his hazy memories of his "angel" mother.

When Gorky's narrator describes his childhood emotions on listening to Uncle Iakov's guitar, one can immediately feel a sharp contrast to the scene presented by Tolstoy. As opposed to the calm induced by Irten'ev's mother's playing, Uncle Iakov's music produces direct, strong emotion, tension, and anxiety. It is hypnotically unpleasant. Whereas Irten'ev only notices the effect that the music had on him, Aleksei carefully watches the response of the others in the room (such as his cousin and the "gypsy"). The music has an irresistible effect on them. In fact, his cousin becomes so involved in the performance that he literally falls off his chair. The gypsy begins to dance uncontrollably, like a dervish: "It seemed that if someone opened the door to the outside he would go on dancing like that along the street, through the city, who knows where" (15: 39). Only Aleksei's grandmother is able to control her reactions. She dances also, but her dance is a joyous one. It makes her seem younger, slimmer, and "wildly beautiful." Aleksei does not try to analyze his observations; he merely notes: "It was all horribly interesting. It all made me tense, and a kind of quiet insatiable sadness oozed into my heart from it all. Sadness and joy lived side by side in people; they were almost inseparable and they alternated with elusive incomprehensible speed." He adds that the music caused him to weep "in unbearable anguish" (15: 38).

Gorky also attacks the gentry myth concerning the close bond that is supposed to exist between the child and his environment. In contemplating the natural world, the child is able to merge his still-innocent self with nature. Later in life, memories of such moments fill the adult's (no longer innocent) soul with joy. Gentry autobiographers see such moments as a universal component of childhood.[11] Gorky's childhood takes place in an urban milieu, and he exploits the different setting to show that the gentry model of the "ideal" relationship between the child and nature is classbound. It is not that nature plays no role in the child's life; it is present even in the city, but the emotions it evokes are specific and unexpected. A characteristic passage describes the narrator's feelings while watching the autumn twilight: "At such moments particularly clear, light thoughts are born, but they are fragile, transparent, like spiderwebs, and they cannot be caught in words. They flare up and disappear quickly, like shooting stars, and searing the soul with grief over something they caress it, disturb it. This is when it boils, melts, takes on its shape for life, this is where its image is formed" (15: 108).[12] The sight of the natural world produces a certain sadness (at another point in the novel Gorky characterizes the emotion evoked by nature as "pleasant boredom" [15: 27]). This sadness (probably caused by the disjunction between the natural world's quiet and the dirtiness and noise of the urban landscape) is remembered for one's whole life.

At first glance it might seem that Gorky's lack of enthusiasm for memories of the natural world is a result of his urban milieu. This is true in part, but even when he moves to the countryside in *My Universities* his relations with nature fail to change for the better. Instead, this move allows him to explode one more gentry myth: the myth of the happy peasant.[13] The main reason that the peasants were presumed to be happy was that they lived a simple life in the midst of nature and were not subject to the corruptions of urban society. In describing rural life, Gorky specifically refers to the myth of the happy peasant and then proceeds to dismiss it:

Village life rises before me joylessly. I had often heard and read that in the countryside people live healthier and heartier lives than in the city. But—I see peasants in continual back-breaking labor. There are many unhealthy ones who have been torn up by their work and there are hardly any happy people among them. The artisans and workers in the city, who work no less, live more joyfully. . . . All the people in the village live by groping, like blind men. They are all afraid of something, they don't trust each other. There is something wolflike in them. (16: 102–3)

The ideology of the gentry autobiographers is conservative patriarchal. They look back to an ideal society in which master and man live in harmonious contact close to the land: nature (the world of the estate as opposed to the city), the peasant (as opposed to the industrial or semi-industrial proletarian), and the landowner (as opposed to the merchant or capitalist) form the central pillars of their worldview. Gorky, on the other hand, has a Marxist distaste

for "the idiocy of rural life" and markedly favors the urban proletariat. Coupled with this is a preference for city over country and
a diminished role for the natural world in the formation of personality. Of course, none of these ideological positions would have
been interesting from the literary point of view had they appeared
in a tract on child-rearing. However, by choosing to express them
in a pseudo-autobiography, Gorky invaded a bastion that had been
the exclusive property of the gentry literary tradition. Gorky's trilogy did not merely express the experience of a writer from a different socioeconomic background; it challenged the Russian notion of
childhood as such. By orienting his work against the trilogy of
Tolstoy, Gorky could both satisfy his personal desire to write an
account of his own childhood and dispute the implicit claim of the
gentry that their model of childhood was universal.[14]

Even as he attacks gentry autobiographical and pseudo-autobiographical models, Gorky is careful not to reject the Russian literary
tradition entirely. He wanted to overcome one aspect of it, yet he
also wanted his account to take its place in the overall pantheon.
His childhood was not to be merely an exception to the rule; it was
supposed to be the "true" Russian childhood. To succeed he had to
explode the gentry childhood myths and simultaneously demon-
strate his organic connection to selected aspects of the literary tradition. As did many gentry autobiographers, Gorky speaks of the
roles that folk poetry, Pushkin, and Lermontov played in his development. This is a common feature of all early-twentieth-century
pseudo-autobiographies. Each writer (Gorky, Belyi, Bunin, and
Mandel'shtam) takes pains to connect his text with some aspects of
the nineteenth-century tradition (no matter how innovative his
text may be in other respects) in an attempt to trace his lineage
back to that tradition.

Aleksei's first exposure to the power of literature is through his
grandmother's recitations of fairy and folk tales. Ever since Pushkin had praised the story-telling ability of his nanny, the necessity
of oral literature for the development of "serious" writers in Russia
had become almost a cliché. Aksakov's narrator, for example, includes a long prose fairy tale as an appendix to *Childhood Years*.

These tales were always told to the gentry writer by the nanny or some other peasant woman. Gorky includes two verse tales told by his grandmother (15: 103–5, 156–58). Both are moralizing tales whose content resonates with his own experience, but, more important, their presence allows Gorky to emphasize that his connection to the oral tradition is stronger and more organic than that of gentry writers. They heard such things told by their servants, while Gorky had a blood tie to "the people" who produce folk tales. He thus wrests back a part of the tradition that gentry writers had reserved for themselves.[15]

In addition, while rejecting much gentry writing, Gorky makes it clear that he admired and learned from such aristocrats/writers as Pushkin and Lermontov. It was not uncommon for gentry autobiographers to define the world through the prism of Pushkin's poetry. Later, as an émigré in the 1920's, Bunin would assert his claim to be the inheritor of the great Russian literary tradition, in part by evoking Pushkin. Gorky also takes pains to mention the role that Pushkin played in his development. Not surprisingly, it is Pushkin's fairy tales (the works with the most pronounced "folk" character and, thus, the natural link between the oral poetry of Aleksei's grandmother and the written tradition) that most affect the young Peshkov: "The simplicity and music of Pushkin's verse so amazed me that prose seemed unnatural for a long time and I found it awkward to read. The prologue to 'Ruslan' reminded me of my grandmother's best fairy tales" (15: 363–64).

Slightly later, when the young narrator reads Lermontov's long poem "The Demon" to the workers in the icon-painting shop where he is apprenticed, he notices that the emotion the poem generates in him is strengthened by the effect it has on his audience: "The fire chief once gave me a volume of Lermontov and that's when I felt the strength of poetry, its powerful influence on people. . . . The poem affected me, agonizingly and sweetly, tears welled up in my eyes. But I was even more affected by the muffled careful motion in the workshop. The whole place was slowly moving, it was as if a magnet were pulling people towards me" (15: 434).

Through Lermontov, through the Russian literary tradition, Gorky discovers the power that literature has to change the lives of those who read or hear it. In his trilogy Gorky rejects the gentry's claim to have discovered a universal model for Russian childhood based on the supposedly natural relationship between the happy gentry child, the environment (i.e., the estate), and the literary tradition. Instead, he demonstrates that an entirely different kind of childhood in different circumstances can still produce a writer who is in sympathy with the greatest achievements of the Russian literary tradition but who assimilates these achievements into a new kind of text, a text that has little in common stylistically, structurally, or ideologically with its immediate predecessors. As Iu. N. Tynianov might have said, he asserts his connection with the generation of his literary grandfathers in his battle with that of his fathers.

This leads to the central question surrounding the entire pseudo-autobiographical enterprise: the reasons for writing such a book in the first place. Although each work in the genre has specific features, the Russian pseudo-autobiography usually answers the general question, What is childhood? and provides a developmental "portrait of the artist." In the case of Tolstoy's trilogy there are only hints indicating that Irten'ev might become a writer. By the 1920's, in Bunin's *The Life of Arsen'ev*, the problem of becoming a writer is central to the narrator's concerns. There are indications scattered throughout Gorky's trilogy that the narrator will grow up to be a writer; I have already noted his appreciation of the power of poetry to influence the actions of others. Even as a small child, he understands that there is creative power locked within him. For one thing, he is unable to remember poetry properly; instead, he rearranges the verses, leaves some out or creates his own. Significantly, the creative impulse is connected to his grandmother: "At night, lying in my grandmother's bunk, I pestered her, repeating everything that I remembered from books and everything that I had created myself" (15: 141). Slightly later he describes retelling fairy tales for his school friends (15: 190). In some sense, this activity is paradigmatic for the narration of the trilogy as a whole.

Throughout the three volumes, Gorky takes fairy tales (the myths about childhood typical for nineteenth-century Russia) and retells them in his own way, modifying them to fit his own situation and creative needs.

However, although problems of creativity and personal literary development play a significant role in the trilogy, the development of the writer is not Gorky's central concern. What is central is his attempt to redefine the nature of Russian childhood. For the gentry tradition, childhood is the time when a person comes to understand his or her self through contact with a strictly limited outside world and through self-analysis. The process of growing up is complete when the narrator becomes fully conscious of the spatial and temporal distance separating him from his past incarnation. This distance can be bridged only through memory and is always expressed in terms of a nostalgic longing for the period of childhood innocence that preceded the development of self-consciousness.

Gorky, on the other hand, has a radically different view of the purpose of childhood and the reasons for writing about it. He begins the ninth chapter of *Childhood* saying: "In childhood I see myself as a beehive to which various people, like bees, brought the honey of their knowledge and thoughts about life. Each one generously enriched my soul with whatever he could. Often that honey was dirty or bitter, but every bit of knowledge is honey all the same" (15: 114). The natural-historical metaphor of the empty beehive focuses attention on the child's mind as a tabula rasa. It indicates that the most important forces for development are not inner psychological processes but contact with the outside world. Of course, observation is the means for any human being to broaden experience and to grow. However, the gentry child's field of observation tended to be extremely limited: almost all the honey collected in childhood was sweet, as it were. Self-analysis, the passage of time and space, and contact with the real world gradually threw up an almost insurmountable barrier between the adult and his earlier self. For Gorky, the process of nonanalytic observation allowed him to accept both the sweet and the bitter throughout his life and to conceive of life as an organic process that can improve through the accretion of knowledge over time. Rather than seeing a sharp break between the lives of the child and the adult, Gorky sees a continuum. Thus, toward the end of *My Universities*, the narrator approvingly quotes the words of a friend: "There is something childlike in every person,—and that's what you have to build on, on that childlike part!" (16: 119). For gentry autobiographers, childhood was a kind of sacred state that could only be reached by going into a kind of trance. For Gorky the positive aspects of childhood (that is, the malleability and optimism of the young) are potentially present at all times and need merely to be tapped rationally.

For the gentry, the estate was frequently connected to the garden of Eden. The end of childhood (often marked by physical departure from the estate) echoed the fall of man and the exile from paradise. This new fall and exile were occasioned by the acquisition of knowledge and self-consciousness; they are the true villains in the gentry childhood. For Gorky, the equation is reversed. It is only through the accumulation of knowledge and self-understanding (acquired through experience, not through self-analysis) that one can move forward, away from the ugly past and into the bright future.[16] This ideological conviction (which has its roots in historicist beliefs in the progressiveness of history) receives confirmation in Gorky's own life, which, through contact with good people and progressive forces, describes an ever-rising line, from the brutishness of his childhood environment to his adult position as a famous and influential writer.

The gulf between the almost exclusively happy memories of gentry children and those of Gorky is exemplified in the passage with which Gorky begins the second chapter of *Childhood*. He describes his early days in his grandfather's house as a "bleak fairy tale well told by a good but excruciatingly truthful genius." He then continues:

Now, when bringing the past to life, I sometimes have difficulty believing that everything was as it was, and I wish to dispute or deny many things—the dark life of the "unintelligent tribe" was overabundantly cruel.

But truth is higher than pity, and besides, I am not writing about myself, but about that crowded stuffy circle of horrible impressions within which simple Russians lived—and still live to this day. (15: 20)

The motif of doubt in the veracity of childhood memories is standard for the autobiographical tradition. Normally, however, the autobiographer wants to recover and to believe his earliest memories but, after a careful editing process, he must reject some details because they turn out to be either false or not really memories at all. Gorky, conversely, expresses a wish to forget certain things but is eventually forced to admit that they really were part of his life. The second paragraph quoted above deals with the reasons for writing such a work in the first place. In part, Tolstoy and Aksakov chose the pseudo-autobiographical form because they felt that it would allow them to depict a generalized childhood as opposed to the specificity required by autobiography. I have already discussed Tolstoy's annoyance when Nekrasov changed the title of *Childhood* to *The Story of My Childhood*. Like his predecessors, Gorky insists that his pseudo-autobiography is not merely the reflection of individual experience but, in addition, the description a typical Russian childhood. That is to say, he is proposing an opposition model for childhood, not claiming that his own experience was the exception to a rule.[17]

If childhood memories are so painful, then the question arises, Why should one write about them at all? In part the answer is that Gorky desired to wrest control of childhood from the gentry, to expose the myth of Russian childhood for what it was. However, there were also deeper, more personal reasons for writing the story of a childhood. After one particularly lurid scene of early memories, the narrator stops recalling the past and questions the purpose of his present endeavor:

Recalling the leaden vileness of savage Russian life, there are moments when I ask myself: Is it worth speaking about this? And, with my particular assurance, I answer myself—it is; for this is the living, vile truth, it hasn't died to this very day. It is a truth that must be

known to its roots so that it can be ripped out by those roots from the memory, from the soul, from all of our hard and shameful life. . . .
But our life is amazing not only because it has such a thick and fertile layer of swinish trash, but because, through that layer, in spite of everything, something shining, healthy, and creative will grow triumphantly, something good and human is growing, awakening indestructible hope for our rebirth into a bright and human life. (15: 193-94)

In the gentry tradition, knowing the past leads to nostalgically pleasant reminiscences; one "soothes the soul" by recalling childhood and returning, at least mentally, to a bygone idyllic period. For Gorky the result achieved by reminiscing is entirely different. The past must be known in order for it to be "ripped out . . . from the memory, from the soul." Autobiography is not a nostalgic attempt at eternal return but a means of overcoming the past, of leaving it behind. The organic "scientific" metaphor (reinforced by echoes of the parable of the flower growing from the dung heap) is a logical and effective expression of this theme. Like some gigantic plant, humankind is seen growing ever upward towards the sun, which provides the light for the "bright future."

As if to reinforce the purpose about which he spoke toward the end of *Childhood*, Gorky repeats practically the same question and gives a very similar answer to it in the last chapter of *Among the People*:

Why do I talk about such vileness? So that you will know, honored sirs,—this has still not passed, it has not passed. . . . We are all living a base and dirty life, that's the way it is.
I love people very much and I wouldn't want to torment anyone, but you can't be sentimental and you can't hide the terrible truth in the colorful little words of a beautiful lie. On to life, on to life! We must dissolve everything that is good and human in our hearts and brains into life. (15: 524)

Once again we see a belief that knowledge of the past is necessary in order to move into the future. The "honored sirs" who try to hide the truth by means of "a beautiful lie" are the same people who look at the past through rose-colored glasses; the gentry autobiographers and pseudo-autobiographers whom Gorky was specifically attacking are undoubtedly among them. The autobiographical call is a call to arms, away from the "beautiful lies" of the past and into the heady world of the future.

Like Tolstoy, Aksakov, and their gentry followers, Gorky wished to create his own model of Russian childhood. Although the trilogy was based on material from his own life, he clearly wanted it to represent the experience of a Russian "everyman." This was extremely difficult, however, because of the strength of the gentry model of childhood in the Russian tradition. The myths of childhood that had been formed and canonized during the previous 60 years were so entrenched and generally accepted that they could only be challenged by a full-scale assault. That is why Gorky chose to orient his work in such an obvious manner against Tolstoy's trilogy. By reusing structures, devices, and themes typical of the canonical gentry childhood, but by changing their evaluation, Gorky was able to create the first compelling alternative pattern for childhood in Russia. Ideologically, he opposed his faith in the socialist future to the past-oriented patriarchal conservatism of his gentry opponents. Of course, this general division in outlook between the conservative aristocracy and their progressive opponents had been present throughout the second half of the nineteenth century. Childhood, however, was a literary topos that had belonged almost exclusively to the aristocrats. Gorky's attack on the very foundations of the gentry's myth of self was a bold attempt to take the literary and social initiative in an area from which the "progressives" had traditionally been locked out. In rising to the challenge, Gorky produced (in *Childhood*) one of his greatest works. He reached deep into his past with the ostensible purpose of overcoming it, and he created a childhood model for the "have nots" worthy to stand in opposition to the great literary and social canon that had been produced by the "haves."

Under any circumstances, Gorky's childhood model would probably have posed a powerful challenge to the traditional Tolstoyan one in the Russian cultural mind. As it turned out, a purely cultural/literary battle between opposing models for the control of childhood never took place. Instead, political events intervened to obviate the necessity for a long ideological struggle. The Bolshevik Revolution of 1917 marked the triumph of the "have nots" and led to the liquidation of the Russian gentry as a class. In the newly formed Soviet Union, there was no place for the model of childhood that had been created by Tolstoy and Aksakov and nurtured by generations of gentry autobiographers.

As the importance of gentry models waned for Russian culture, Gorky's influence became ever greater; he rose from being simply a well-known writer to the "founder of Soviet literature," a literary demigod whose word in cultural matters was practically law. Thus, in the changing literary climate of the 1920's and 1930's, it was almost inevitable that Russians would turn to Gorky's *Childhood* for new, Soviet myths of childhood.

In fact, to some extent Gorky's model of childhood did attain mythical status, influencing the childhood memories of many Soviet literary figures and autobiographers. For this, Gorky himself must be given much of the credit. A letter to A. S. Makarenko, the founder of "colonies" for orphans and juvenile delinquents, illustrates that Russia's literary tsar was not at all bashful about proposing his myths of childhood as a model for others: "I would like it if your colonists would read my *Childhood* on autumn evenings; they would see that I am the same kind of person as they, only that I was persistent from youth on." [18]

Evidently, Makarenko did just what Gorky requested. The hero of A. Avdeenko's *I Love*, a later Soviet pseudo-autobiography clearly influenced by Gorky's *Childhood*, describes how he and his fellows were introduced to the life that became their personal and literary model: "It must have been Antonych who really brought me and the other colonists closer to Aleksei Maksimovich. Gradually, step by step, we went through all of Gorky's creative life, beginning from his earliest stories to his last works." [19] The extent to which Gorky's model of childhood became known in the Soviet Union can be seen in the responses he received to a letter he published in *Pravda* in 1933. He proposed establishing a special publishing house for children's literature, and he asked young people to tell him what should be published. One pioneer wrote: "I am twelve and I love books very much. I also know about your childhood. Well you know, Aleksei Maksimovich, mine isn't the same, it's better." For Gorky, one of whose avowed purposes in writing *Childhood* had been to remind people of the terrible past so that they would not repeat its mistakes in the future, such letters must have been heartwarming. Perhaps the most prescient letter of all, however, was sent by a five-year-old girl who had no trouble discerning the basic structure of the Gorkyan myth of childhood: "Best of all I like Gorky himself, because life itself was bitter for him, and then it became smarter and smarter." [20]

In Soviet literature, Gorky's myths of childhood became a standard component in works by such authors as K. Paustovsky, V. Kataev, and V. Smirnov. [21] However, there is one novel in particular, F. Gladkov's *Story About Childhood*, that shows how deeply Gorky's myths penetrated the memories of other writers. Gladkov makes no attempt to hide his indebtedness to Gorky: in the introduction, Gladkov reproduces a conversation about childhood with Gorky strikingly like the one Gorky claimed to have had with Tolstoy. Trying to get to know Gladkov better, Gorky is supposed to have said: "Well now, tell me about yourself—about your childhood, your youth." [22]

The novel that Gladkov was inspired to write by this conversation is quite similar to *Childhood*, not just in general outline, but in many details as well. There is, first of all, the question of why such a book should be written at all. Gladkov's discussion of this question preserves both the substance and the oratorical style of Gorky's reasoning:

And now, flipping through the book of my life, I am disturbed and I ask myself, Is it necessary to tell about these long-past days, is it necessary to depict the cursed tortures in which I passed in my childhood and then my youth? . . . But the inner voice of conscience and duty assures me constantly: you must tell, must show the torturous thickets through which the people of my generation had to pass . . . in order to escape from the hellish darkness onto today's open road. [23]

Were this the only instance of borrowing from Gorky, it could be put down to a completely conscious effort to follow the master's footsteps. This is not the case, however; from the dedication through the entire text, there is ample evidence of both conscious and unconscious borrowings of Gorky's childhood myths. In the novel's first scene, for example, the young boy sits uncomprehendingly watching his mother die. Although she eventually recovers, this opening almost exactly parallels that of *Childhood*, in which Aleksei observes his father's corpse. Gladkov's hero has the same grandfather as Gorky's, and he adopts a grandmother like Gorky's as well. Just as Gorky's narrator was shown the true path by idealists like the chemist he calls "khoroshee delo," Gladkov's autobiographical hero learns the truth of his situation from the tailor Volodimirovich. As for Gorky, childhood for Gladkov is a time of suffering, but that suffering is seen as necessary if the child is to grow up to become the right kind of person. In short, in almost every respect, Gladkov's *Story About Childhood* shows that Gorky's model was well on the road to being adopted as *the* new model for childhood.

It would seem, then, that the battle for childhood in Russia should have ended with a decisive victory for Gorky's model, but that is not exactly what happened. While the Russian Revolution put an end to the gentry way of life, it also eliminated the kind of world in which writers like Gorky, Paustovsky, and Gladkov spent their early years. The Tolstoyan myth was able to exert such a strong hold on the Russian cultural mind because it roughly corresponded to the actual conditions of gentry life over a period of more than 100 years. Similarly, Gorky's model of childhood could potentially have achieved the status of full-blown myth had it been written one or two generations earlier or had a socialist revolution not occurred in Russia.

As it was, however, Soviet writers whose childhood occurred after 1917 could not use Gorky as a model: his myths could be used only by writers more or less of his own generation. As far as Soviet propaganda and ideology were concerned, the "bright future" had arrived with the Revolution. For later Soviet writers and for the

Soviet cultural mind in general, a myth of childhood that saw it as a period of misery leading to gradual improvement and enlightenment was inappropriate. Instead, the myth of the happy childhood was fated to make a comeback, this time not in Tolstoyan terms but in a formula that every Soviet child of the 1930's and 1940's was expected to know by heart: "Thank you for our happy childhood, Comrade Stalin."

Chapter Five

࿐

The Modernist Childhood of
A. Belyi

While the battle for the control of childhood occupied realist writers and autobiographers on both sides of the political spectrum in the first decades of the twentieth century, there was one group of Russian writers, the modernists, for whom childhood played an entirely different role.[1] For some modernists, childhood seemed completely irrelevant. The early symbolists, for example, were far too concerned about finding the deeper reality beyond the phenomenal world to care about the details of an individual life.[2] However, some of the results of the "crisis of Symbolism" in 1910 were a partial rehabilitation of the individual and an increasing tendency to introspection on the part of the leaders of the symbolist movement. In the years before the Revolution, a number of important symbolists attempted to define what might be called "the modernist childhood."

Considering the symbolists' predilection for verse, one might have expected that the quintessential Russian modernist childhood would take the form of a narrative poem. In fact, the initial attempts did break with the pseudo-autobiographical prose tradition. In 1911, A. Blok recorded a plan for what was to eventually become his long poem, "Recompense": "A plan—4 parts—as follows: I—"The Demon"... II—Childhood, III—Death of the Father, IV—War and Revolution—Death of the Son."[3] Unfortunately, although Blok worked on this poem intermittently until his death, he was never able to finish it. Although he eventually completed substantial sections of "Recompense," he failed to get anywhere with part II, the portion of the poem that was to have dealt with his own childhood.

The next of the symbolists to try his hand at creating a model for the modernist childhood was V. I. Ivanov. In 1913 he began a poem entitled "Early Childhood." Evidently, he too found it difficult to deal with the subject, for he did not finish and publish the work until 1918. By that time, Belyi had already completed *Kotik Letaev*, a truly modernist childhood in pseudo-autobiographical prose. Before turning to *Kotik Letaev*, however, it is worth noting a number of details in "Early Childhood" that are characteristic of the Russian modernist conception of childhood.

Ivanov starts his poem with what he calls "An Introduction to a Poetic Biography": [4]

> Here is life's book of hours
> Memories' palimpsest,
> Life's sole idea—
> Amen to all lives—a cross in roses.

Ivanov's insistence on the connections between all childhoods and, consequently, his deemphasis of the importance of the individual child are particularly noteworthy. This is a radically new point of view for a Russian account of childhood. Of course, by reusing patterns taken from literature, gentry writers had, in effect, been undermining the notion of an individual childhood for a long time. However, they failed to realize the implications of their conscious or unconscious plagiarism: despite the existence of certain generally accepted myths of childhood, no autobiographer seems to have questioned the uniqueness of his own childhood. Ivanov, on the other hand, clearly sees childhood as a repetition of preexisting childhoods. [5] That the final ten lines of the introductory stanza are overwhelmingly concerned with the literary form in which childhood is to be described (as opposed to the content of the account) is only to be expected, considering the emphasis that the modernists placed on form in general.

Belyi's *Kotik Letaev*, finished in 1916, contains a number of important themes linking it with the modernist childhoods of Blok and Ivanov and differentiating it from the realist childhoods that had come before. At the same time, unlike the other modernist childhoods, Belyi's novel (and its sequel, *The Baptized Chinaman*) is also tied to the pseudo-autobiographical tradition.[6] Of course, the genre connections linking Belyi's pseudo-autobiographies to the tradition are not as clear or as direct as they were in Gorky's pseudo-autobiography or would be later in Bunin's. This is hardly surprising; within Belyi's system of thought, childhood played quite a different role and demanded techniques of expression unimagined by the writers who preceded or succeeded him. Other pseudo-autobiographical novels were written by authors who, both in perception and technique, can be called realists. Belyi had fought the assumptions of literary realism from his youth and never wished to embrace them, even in a genre so closely beloved by the realists. Nevertheless, Belyi was well aware that his childhood narratives could be seen within the Russian tradition even as they stood outside it. In his memoir *On the Border of Two Centuries*, he has this to say about *Kotik Letaev*:

Tolstoy and others took the later stages of a youngster's life; and they took it under different conditions; that is why they worked out a different language for memories; a linguistic tradition grew up; "Belyi" did not have a tradition for the notation of earlier events that were experienced in special conditions, about which we will speak later; thus "Belyi's" different language issues from different circumstances; thus, one shouldn't chide him for linguistic preciosity but instead ask the question, Is it necessary to study the different circumstances of "Belyi's" naturalism?[7]

Belyi's analysis of *Kotik Letaev* in this memoir has been all but dismissed by critics for its failure to mention any connection between the novel and anthroposophy.[8] Yet, considering the fact that Belyi is able to give a coherent, albeit limited, explication of his novel in the memoir, one should be careful about dismissing it out of hand.

I believe that Belyi's pseudo-autobiographies are based on a tension between cyclical and linear views of development.[9] The anthroposophic component is concerned with repetitive time; theories of reincarnation, the young child's ability to "read" the spiritual history of humankind, and the projection of an individual's life onto historical and mythological patterns drawn from various sources all fall into this category. In the other category are realizations of the forward march of time in an individual life; the place of specific incident, the facts of forgetting and of irreversible loss, and the development of a unique consciousness and a personal literary style are included here. The former group of concepts are most prominent in the opening chapters of *Kotik Letaev* and have been more than adequately studied.[10] The latter, which are present from the beginning of *Kotik Letaev* but become increasingly important toward the end, have been generally overlooked. It is through the latter group that the novel is connected to the pseudo-autobiographical tradition. The paradoxical attempt to reincarnate past events (in words, at least) while emphasizing their pastness had always been one of the central purposes of the pseudo-autobiography. Thus, although Belyi's mystical and anthroposophical searches severely bend the tradition, they do not distort it beyond recognition.

In typically cryptic fashion, Belyi points to his connections with the Russian literary tradition in the epigraph to *Kotik Letaev*: "'You know,' Natasha said in a whisper, 'I think that when you remember and remember, when you remember everything, you get so caught up in remembering that you recall things that occurred before I came into the world.'" This rather enigmatic statement taken from *War and Peace* becomes more significant when one realizes that it is actually a self-paraphrase from *Childhood*. In that work the young narrator sits and listens to his mother playing the piano (it is probably not accidental that this is also one of young Kotik's favorite activities). The flow of music elicits an inchoate sensation: "That feeling resembled memories; but memories of what? It seemed you were recalling things that never happened" (Tolstoy, 1: 31). The child's nebulous feeling is never explained by the older Irten'ev, but it certainly seems quite close to a central concept of *Kotik Letaev*: the "memory of memory."

Like Irten'ev, for whom the sensation was linked with music,

Kotik almost always describes "memory of memory" in musical terms. He speaks of early occult experience as:

> shinings within shinings, where the rhythm of the pulse of shinings is my own, beating in the land of the dance of rhythms and reflecting by means of an image, like—
> —a memory of memory! . . .
> The impressions of childhood years—are flights into the never having been; but—nevertheless existing. (pp. 111–12)

The intimate connection between music (particularly piano music) and the "memory of memory" is made even more clear in chapter 5: "Music is a dissolving of the helixes of memory and a free passage into another world . . . memory of memory is like that; it's a sweet rhythm; it got inside the piano" (pp. 184–85). Even before Belyi's acquaintance with the work of Steiner, he had viewed music as the most perfect of the arts because it stood outside the flow of space and time.[11] Thus, for him the association of music with worlds that existed outside of the "normal" space/time continuum was perfectly natural.

The link between Belyi's occult ideas and the tradition begun by Tolstoy becomes even stronger if we consider a passage from *Boyhood* that also seems to prefigure many of the concerns of *Kotik Letaev*. The narrator in the second part of Tolstoy's trilogy comments that, as a boy, he thought about things that were not appropriate for his age. Incidentally, the theme of the precocious (or even the too precocious) child is quite common in pseudo-autobiographies. In Belyi's novel it is closely connected to the "untimely development" that Kotik's mother so fears. After Tolstoy's narrator has characterized the thoughts of his younger incarnation, the author's voice enters with the following generalizing statement: "It seems to me that, in its development, in each separate individual, man's mind follows the same path along which it has been developing for whole generations, that thoughts which serve as the basis for various philosophical theories comprise inseparable parts of the mind; every person more or less clearly senses them even before he knows about the existence of philosophical theories" (Tolstoy, 2: 56). This, of course, sounds suspiciously like Belyi's contention that the child recapitulates all of the world's philosophical schools in the course of his early development. A Steinerian might say that Tolstoy and Belyi had, independently, reached the same occult insight. Since we are dealing with two works in the same subgenre, however, I am inclined to note once more that interpretations of *Kotik Letaev* that ascribe Belyi's entire novelistic conception to the influence of Steiner fail to notice the germ of some of the central concerns of the novel in the literary tradition within which the novel was written.

The classic narrative situation of the pseudo-autobiography involves the presence of the voice of an adult narrator (who is not supposed to be the author himself) and a child's voice. This structure is retained throughout *Kotik Letaev* and *The Baptized Chinaman*, and, considering the rapidity with which he cuts back and forth between the two points of view, Belyi can be said to develop this narrative technique to an extreme. He dramatizes the dual point of view and hence his connection with the pseudo-autobiographical tradition, in the introduction to *Kotik Letaev*:

> Here, on the sheer-cutting brink,—I hurl long, mute glances into the past . . .
> I am thirty-five years old: self-consciousness has torn up my brain and cast itself into childhood. (p. 9)

This is the voice of the adult narrator who will illuminate his past incarnation(s) in the course of the novel. The image of the narrator, who, at the age of 35, has reached the midpoint of his life amidst a mountain landscape, seems connected to that of Dante at the beginning of the *Inferno*. Both narrators find themselves temporarily lost and require some kind of guidance to find their way again. For Dante it comes as a religious revelation that leads to a journey through hell, purgatory, and heaven, whereas for Belyi it lies within the self and takes the form of a mental journey back to the world of childhood and to the occult worlds that the child experienced before birth. In both cases the narrator's visions produce the work of art that is presented to the reader.

In Belyi's oeuvre, this situation and its resolution are not unique to *Kotik Letaev*. The narrator is in an analogous position at the beginning of the autobiographical poem "The First Encounter." There, too, he is at a creative impasse from which he can escape only by recasting his memories in a work of art. In "The First Encounter" he returns to his student days, whereas in *Kotik Letaev* he harks back to earliest childhood. In both cases, however, the principle is the same. The artist can accept and, in some sense, overcome the weight of his past only by transforming memory into a work of art. Interestingly enough, Belyi had predicted this self-referential path as early as 1907: "Here is the answer for the artist: if he wishes to remain an artist without ceasing to be a person, he must become his own artistic form." [12] Of course, in *Kotik Letaev*, Belyi can be said to have taken on two forms: adult narrator and infant experiencer. The final lines of the introduction prepare the reader for their dialogue, which will be the formal basis of the entire novel: "Before me is the first consciousness of childhood; and we—embrace: 'Hello, strange one!'" (p. 14)

In *Kotik Letaev*, Belyi faced technical problems that had not confronted other writers of pseudo-autobiography. How could the inchoate memories of a child who did not yet know how to speak be presented in words? Throughout the novel (but especially in the first half) the adult narrator reminds the reader that the infant did not have the vocabulary to express what he felt instinctively. Instead, the adult narrator provides the idiom in which the child would have spoken had he been able to do so. The narrative process is clear from the child's initial utterance at the beginning of the first chapter. The child asks: "What's this?" and the narrator adds, "That is how I would condense the unspoken rising of my infant life in words" (p. 15). In earlier pseudo-autobiographies, the child's voice was generally quite simple, presenting the world as a conscious but not particularly sophisticated observer might have seen it. The adult narrator's voice provided more complicated commentary, fleshing out the child's point of view. The child's position was privileged only insofar as it was relatively happier than the adult's.

In Belyi's view, on the contrary, the child can see and experience things that adults cannot. He is privileged by an inner vision to which the adult narrator is not privy. In this respect Belyi obviously drew heavily on the thought of Rudolph Steiner. However, Steiner did not give Belyi any indication of how to express this philosophical/occult insight in a work of prose fiction. On the level of narrative, Belyi had to find his own resolution. He solved the problem by reversing the traditional relation between the experiencing child and the experienced narrator. His solution manifests itself in the greater complexity of the child's "voice" (translated into words by the narrator) vis-à-vis the narrator's simple commentary. This, for example, is how the child's first memories are described:

> Here is my image of the entrance into life: a corridor, an archway and darkness; crawling things are chasing after me...—
> —this image is related to the one of striding along temple-like corridors in the company of a man with a bull's head who was holding a scepter.
> ....
> The voice of my mother cut through all this:
>   —"He's burning as if he were on fire!"
> Later on they told me that I was continuously sick. (p. 28)

Two possible readings are given for this memory. The child is shown to have access to a world (the precise contents of which are not of primary importance) in which he is in touch with strange beings. It is a world filled with complicated imagery, often based on neologistic word use and alliterative or rhythmic connections between words. On the other hand, the adult narrator proposes a rather mundane physiological explanation for the mythological world: the child had a high fever and was merely hallucinating.[13] The latter explanation is not, however, sufficient; it does not explain, for example, how the child could have visualized images he had never seen or heard of. Thus, the adult's perspective never cancels out the child's occult perceptions. Instead it indicates that the adult narrator, although he can, with great effort, recall and verbalize the experiences he had as a young child, cannot return to that state; nevertheless, his literary intuition is able to recapture and transmit images that his conscious mind cannot adequately explain. Like the quests of almost all the narrators of pseudo-autobiography, the older Kotik's search is nostalgic. The time when he could actively read the record of previously existing worlds has passed; it can only be recreated by crystallizing previous experience in a literary text.

But just as memory can recreate a period when the child essentially existed outside of time and space, memory also forces the narrator to notice the changes that time brings in the course of an individual's biological life span. Nostalgia in *Kotik Letaev* is not only for the time of early childhood, when occult experiences occurred naturally, but also for places, things, and people that were dear to the child and have since disappeared from the physical world. What seems eternal to the child turns out not to be so in the real world, although, once again, it can be endowed with a kind of eternal life when it appears in a work of art.

Of course, one of the main tasks of the pseudo-autobiography had always been to represent the development of a child over time. Tolstoy begins his account when Irten'ev is ten, and so he does not deal with the earliest stages of development. Aksakov does include some of Bagrov's infantile memories and shows how the child's consciousness expanded in relation to early illness, the rhythm of the road, and the journey. His emphasis, however, is on the slightly older child. In *Kotik Letaev* it is precisely the earliest stages of life, when the child starts to understand the concreteness of the world around him and to be able to depict it in words, that form the core of the novel.

Both J. D. Elsworth and V. Alexandrov have noted that, in accordance with anthroposophical thought, Kotik recapitulates the historical development of humankind in the description of his early childhood. It could be added that before he does so he participates in the creation of the universe. At first the child is in complete chaos: all is darkness. Then he experiences the creation of light: "Barely noticeable points of light flared up: darkness began to fall away from me" (p. 20). His first conscious memory is "a point" (p. 25). In mathematical terms (which Belyi, the son of a mathematician, certainly knew),[14] a point exists in infinite space and has no mass; the firmament has evidently not yet been created out of the void and chaos still reigns: "At first there were no images, though there was a place for them in what hung in front of me" (p. 27). Soon the child begins to distinguish certain objects in the real world. His first remembered image is one of the animals that was created before mankind's existence: a lion.

At this early stage of development, images and the words used to describe them are not always connected. One could say that the child experiences ambiguity because of his inability to differentiate signified from signifier. He first sees the "lion" while he is playing in a sandbox. The section describing this encounter is written in an intentionally confusing manner that, for a number of pages, prevents the reader from realizing that the "lion" was actually a Saint Bernard. Presumably the child knew what a lion is because of some occult understanding of the concept "lion." However, the child's occult knowledge was not applicable in the real world, where a verbal lion turned out not to be one after all. As a child he never understood his mistake, and it was only twenty years later, according to the narrator, that an acquaintance told him that "Lion" was the name of a Saint Bernard that had lived in their neighborhood. Nevertheless, as was the case with the physiological explanation of the child's hallucinations, the narrator is not completely satisfied with a realistic decoding of his childhood vision. In the narrator's present tense (that is, at the time of writing the novel), he knows that the lion was a dog, but he continues to assert that it was a real lion insofar as the word has the power to create its own reality: "Clearly there was no dog. There were exclamations: 'Lion is coming!' and a lion came" (p. 48).

The child began his existence in total chaos and started to bring order to it. That is why his first definite image, the "lion," is important. Images by themselves, however, do not necessarily constitute an entry into the concrete world. After all, the occult record of humankind's existence is filled with images that the child's or initiate's soul can read into. But occult images lie outside of time and space. The child can begin to concretize the real world only within the confines of time and space and that is precisely what he does. He orders the jumbled images he has retained into a time/space continuum. In a subchapter entitled, significantly, "The Formation of Reality," the narrator describes his early universe:

> That membrane is the wallpaper; between it there were spaces. Papa, mama, and nanny appeared in those spaces. I
> > remember—
> > —I
> engendered rooms; I laid them out to my right and left; I placed myself in them: amidst times; times are the repetitions of patterns in the wallpaper. (p. 52)

The child is still able to create his own world (by adding "rooms" to his one-roomed universe), but he creates that world within a structure of space and time based on the regular repetition of units, "patterns." [15] That is, the child begins to make greater order from chaos. It is this tendency that the narrator has in mind when he ends the first chapter saying: "My life began in imagelessness [*bezòbrazii*]: and it continued in images [*obrazy*]" (p. 61).

The same contrast is repeated in chapter 2 in the problem of "swarm" (*roi*) and "form" (*stroi*). In this case, form flows from formlessness both on the level of perception and on the level of language. Here the etymological connection between these antonymic concepts is not primary (as was the case with "imagelessness" and "image"). Instead the most obvious link is aural—rhyme. Belyi emphasizes the acoustic connections by exploiting the Russian language's flexibility in the area of word formation. Quite literally he creates a "form" from a "swarm" of sonically related words: "My first moments are swarms; and swarm, swarm, everything swarms was my first philosophy; I swarmed in swarms. I described circles later, with the old lady: a circle and a sphere are the first forms: coming together in swarm" ("pervye moi migi—roi; 'i roi, roi,—vse roitsia'—pervaia moia filosofiia; v roiakh ia roilsia; kolesa opisyval—posle: uzhe so starukhoiu; koleso i shar, pervye formy: sroennosti v roe") (p. 64). In quoting this passage I do not mean to imply that the narrator (or Belyi himself) felt that "form" was somehow better or more advanced than "swarm." To some extent the two are locked in battle, a never-ending conflict that can have no conclusive end. Complete order leads to paralysis, to a positivistic limitation on the imagination. On the other hand, complete entropy makes it impossible to record and express the products of imagination. If I am concentrating on the process of reification, it is, first of all, because recent scholarship has focused on the occult side of the novel and, second, because I would argue that the overall structure of the work is marked by movement from greater disorder to greater order. That Belyi saw the relationship between "swarm" and "form" as one of conflict can be seen in the following passage: "I know that form; it is the opposite of swarm; form bound swarm; form is a stronghold in formlessness; everything else is fluid" (p. 86). Still, no matter how hard form struggled or struggles to conquer formlessness, there is no ultimate victor. *Kotik Letaev* itself is the best model for such a system. It is a highly structured, artistic form whose purpose, in part, is to express the disorder of "swarm." This paradox is what made the task of pseudo-autobiography particularly difficult for Belyi.

The first two chapters of the novel were primarily concerned with the way in which the child begins to create images out of formlessness. Since this activity occurred before the child had any verbal ability, all of the words describing the child's sensations and understandings are formulated by the narrator using, as he avers several times, the words the child would have spoken had he known how. In chapter 3 the child speaks his own first word. That word is "fire" (*ogon'*), which, if we remember that Kotik is in some sense reliving the creation of the world, is not far from the first words of God the Creator: "Let there be light." [16] From now on the child's creative impulses will be satisfied not simply through a reading of external images, but through his own words. The word is still an aural concept for young Kotik, but even at this early stage he has the ability to create a universe from words. He watches his father preparing for a lecture. The father draws x's (*iksiki*) on paper and, as an involuntary mark of self approval, says "that's it, that's it" (*tak-s, tak-s*). The child combines these sounds with others he has heard and makes a meaningful (for him) model of the universe: "And it came out 'dox.' The 'x's' reminded me of dachshunds [in Russian, *taksy*, A.W.]: they reminded me of doggies; dachshunds

(I thought) grow out of those doodles" (p. 97). Kotik's creative flow is essentially linguistic. It is not that the real world must be explained through language. Rather, a world is created by language, a world that may have but a tangential connection to the real one.

Chapter 3 is filled with examples of the child's gradually increasing curiosity about language and his realization of various ways in which sounds can be combined into words, words into sentences, and, finally, sentences into some kind of verbal approximation of a world. For example, the child tries to understand the meaning of the word "Kremlin" through its partial homonymic identity with "crème-brulée" (pp. 115–16). He finds his thesis provisionally confirmed when a model of the Kremlin, probably made of gingerbread, is pointed out in a bakery window. He then goes on to create a linguistic system wherein the sound "kre" combines with "m" or "ml'" in order to designate a class of tasty sweet objects.

His infatuation with the literal meaning of language makes him incapable of understanding metaphor. When he hears his mother say that a neighbor "is burning up with drink," he imagines the poor man literally consumed by fire. Upon seeing the neighbor again, he is extremely surprised and is forced to come up with a complicated explanation for the neighbor's seeming reincarnation. Such realized metaphors appear all through *Kotik Letaev*. In a perceptive comment about them, particularly in light of my emphasis on nostalgia as the driving force for pseudo-autobiography, A. Steinberg says: "Realization of the metaphor, which draws a smile from the adult, compels one to reflect on one's irretrievably lost childhood, when a word still held its primordial freshness and brightness." [17] In fact, this observation holds true for all of the devices Belyi uses to illustrate the child's attempts to grasp the real world through language. Indeed, for the young Kotik, the universe was as much a verbal construct as an experiential one, so it is not surprising that the narrator's nostalgic return is to the words of childhood as much as to its people and places. Whereas Kotik's memories in the earlier chapters were connected to images and scenes of other worlds, by the end of chapter 3 he says: "The impressions of words are my memories" (p. 117). Gradually the world is beginning to crystallize into the word.

Chapter 4, which is entitled "Gropings of Cosmoses," demonstrates the broadening of the child's horizons that comes with age. It starts with the general statement, "Impressions are the records of Eternity." The narrator continues: "If I were able to link my conception of the world at that time into a whole, then the result would be a cosmogony" (p. 142). Then the child's perception of the world is presented: "Kosiakov's house, my papa, and all conceivable Lev Tolstoys—they all seem eternal to me." The child is sure that all the people who enter his world have always been a part of the world. Even the nameplate on the door of the neighbor, Pompul, seems to be "like a memory of the time of antediluvian existence, from which Pompul was dragged into our world" (p. 143). By the end of the first subchapter, the older narrator's voice returns to remind the reader of the ineluctable passage of time, which, at least on the physical plane, proves the child's vision of the world to have been incorrect, and which serves as the source of the adult narrator's nostalgia: "Lev Tolstoy is no more. Nor is the academician Pompul . . . for twelve years now snowflakes have been falling over a grave marker with the inscription—Mikhail Vasil'evich Letaev" (p. 145). Still, although the people may be physically dead, impressions of them remain in the mind of the narrator. These impressions form the "traces of the eternal" that were mentioned in the first line of the subchapter. Once again we have a case in which the child's perceptions are modified or corrected by the narrator. Nevertheless, at the same time, the narrator's truth is not all-encompassing, nor does it nullify the child's point of view.

According to Steiner, the child loses his ability to travel freely into preexisting worlds sometime between his second and third years of life. In *Kotik Letaev* the loss of free access to previous incarnations is marked, and made up for to some extent, by the four-year-old's increasing ability to perceive new experiences in the physical world. In this regard the sections describing young Kotik's first memories of the countryside are illuminating. For the young child the entire universe had, at first, encompassed only his nursery. It gradually expanded to include the apartment with the view onto the street and then to all of Moscow. When the child is transported from the safe haven of his known universe into the countryside, he feels as if his whole world has collapsed. It should not be forgotten that in the gentry autobiographical tradition (wherein the childhood years are almost always spent on an estate in the countryside), arrival in the city put an end to many of the child's previous assumptions about life. Young Kotik's disorientation is the result of a journey in the opposite direction, but it is equally strong. He thinks of "the loss of old masses" and "the collapsed cosmos."

Gradually he begins to explore the world around him, conversing with a chicken, discovering mushrooms in the grass and so forth. When he was very young, Kotik's understanding of self was fluid and abstract. Now his expanding consciousness even allows him to comprehend his own image, when he sees his reflection in a pond. At first he does not recognize himself and thinks he is seeing another "little boy," but, a moment later when a surfacing fish breaks up the mirror image, he remarks: "Ach, the fishy destroyed him: I am the 'little boy'; it's me, ach, me that she has destroyed" (p. 157). Thus, very gradually, the child's identification of himself with various preexisting figures and worlds weakens, and the idea of a unique self, which emerges both from those previous selves and from the specific situation of Kotik, takes form.

At the beginning of chapter 5, the narrator compares the evolution of his perception of the world with the development of Italian art. On the one hand, this section can be seen as still another example (influenced by Steiner) of the individual recapitulating the history of humankind. On the other, it can be read as a portrait by analogy of the budding artist's growing ability to order the world around him. Particularly important is a grasp of perspective (said to come sometime in his fourth year) that allows for the portrayal of the world in three dimensions. The five-year-old child scrunches up his eyes and the world seems to be completely chaotic. Now, however, he knows how to reorder his surroundings. He blinks and "all the walls fly back into place; and they are solid there. Reality standing all around me is like that: it solidifies; I sharpen myself in experiences" (p. 171). Kotik's growing awareness of reality goes hand in hand with his new-found ability to describe it verbally.

In the real world, the child sees the battle between chaos and order, timelessness with measured time, symbolized in the conflict between his parents. His mother is associated with music (pure motion out of time and space), and she is constantly trying to prevent Kotik from developing (i.e., from leaving a timeless infantile state). His father is associated with mathematics, has no appreciation for music, and tries to force Kotik to exercise his mind, to move forward in time. In Aksakov's *Childhood Years*, the young Bagrov was also caught between the conflicting impulses of his parents. But he was able to overcome their differences, to synthesize them in a way. The trauma of the child torn between the opposing poles of parental desire becomes a crucial theme for the latter part of *Kotik Letaev* and for all of *The Baptized Chinaman*. It is stated succinctly, in the child's plaintive voice, in the subchapter called "Neither Papa's nor Mama's": "I am a sinner. I sin with mommy against poppy; I sin with poppy against mommy. How can I win: not to sin?" (p. 209).[18]

By this point in his life the child is already cut off from free access to the spirit world. His only path to it is the same as that open to the narrator: creative memory. As the child becomes more and more adept at crystallizing the world around him into words, the words into images, and the images into patterns, he realizes the power that the word has to describe (create) worlds that do not correspond to the real world. In the creative act all worlds are equally valuable. Thus, although he is cut off from direct access to the spirit world, the narrator can recreate it:[19] "I begin to relate this image; and my little story is a little fairy tale; my little fairy tales are, in fact, scientific exercises in the description and observation of impressions that fade away in grown-ups" (p. 204). As was the case in both pseudo-autobiography and gentry autobiography, the return to the past is an attempt to bring back, in verbal form, that which was lost in the process of growing up. The use of the words "fairy tales" to describe the narrator's works is significant. What better way to recreate the child's world than through the fairy tale, the quintessential genre of childhood? As is typical for the pseudo-autobiography in the twentieth century, the work at hand is shown to be the autobiography of a writer, one who will eventually grow up to produce the text we are reading.

One of the most important concepts for gentry childhood was that it was a kind of golden age. The estate was seen as paradise, and departure from it corresponded to the fall. Closely connected with the golden-age theme was that of the nanny. She was a required component of childhood paradise, and separation from her was linked with the whole constellation of themes connected to paradist lost. In *Kotik Letaev* the theme of paradise and that of the nanny are transformed, but they remain inseparable. As a result of his father's recitations of Biblical stories, the young Kotik identifies closely with various figures from the Old and New Testaments. He puts himself in a number of Biblical situations: "Memories of paradise lost oppress; I too was in heaven. Where is it?" (p. 250). He then proceeds to describe a fantastic Garden of Eden in which he sees himself as Adam and his nanny as Eve.[20] Her connection to paradise is emphasized by phonetic and etymological correspondence (her name, Raisa, is linked to the root meaning heaven, *rai*). The child fears that they will be exiled from paradise. In fact, this is precisely what happens: "I lived in the expectation of a catastrophe; and it happened one day; Raisa Ivanovna and I, we were exiled; I—from the light-filled worlds, she—onto Arbat, beyond Arbat" (p. 252). The child is exiled from the worlds in which he traveled before birth by the inexorable flow of time. The nanny is exiled because of Kotik's mother's jealousy.[21] The gentry autobiographical paradigm that connected nannies with childhood paradise and their loss with the end of the golden age is preserved. The nanny had, to some extent, shielded Kotik from his parents. When she leaves, Kotik feels that his entire world has collapsed: "—all that there was was linked with her, with Raisa Ivanovna" (p. 252).

The child's gradual loss of his occult abilities is reflected in his understanding that he is becoming more like his father. He thinks he is turning into "a second mathematician" (p. 259). In *Kotik Letaev* this movement is incomplete. The child retains (and the adult desires to regain) the occasional ability to enter preexisting worlds and to reexperience the "music of the spheres." However, the only mythological world into which the older child enters continually in the latter part of the novel and in *The Baptized Chinaman* is the Biblical. It is significant that, although Steiner sets the recapitulation of Jesus' life as the goal of man's strivings,[22] the world of the Bible also enters Kotik's consciousness through his father's reading aloud. Thus, the Biblical world can be seen not simply as another, higher, Steinerian intuition, but as the father's substitute for the mythological realms in which the child once roamed.

The child continues to have occult experiences right up until the end of the novel. One of them involves his feeling that he was entered and filled by the Holy Spirit. For Belyi the Holy Spirit was perhaps the most important member of the Trinity. It was linked, both religiously and personally, to the idea of poetic creation. The festivals Pentecost and Dukhov Den' (The Day of the Holy Spirit, which is the Monday after Pentecost) are connected to the gift of tongues to the apostles through the agency of the Holy Spirit. According to Acts 2:

3 And there appeared unto them cloven tongues like as of fire, and it sat upon each of them.
4 And they were all filled with the Holy Ghost, and began to speak with other tongues, as the Spirit gave them utterance.

For Belyi the days had immense personal significance as well. Much of his first published work, *The Second Symphony*, was written on Dukhov Den' in 1901. The novel *The Silver Dove* begins on Dukhov Den' (which was, incidentally, the most important holiday of the year for those Russian sects that believed in glossolalia, or speaking in tongues; this was a subject that fascinated Belyi). Belyi's long poem "The First Encounter" begins on Dukhov Den' as well, with the poet's prayer for heavenly inspiration. Thus, when the narrator says, "I saw the spirit: it is—shining; birayedness emanates from it" (pp. 274–75), he is probably describing an early experience of this same phenomenon. The connection of the Spirit to specifically poetic inspiration and to the poet's mission is strengthened by a four-line quotation from Pushkin's lyric, "The Prophet." Through this quotation Belyi not only allies himself with the Russian literary tradition but also raises Kotik to the level of a divinely inspired prophet. Like Pushkin's narrator, Kotik takes on a certain responsibility. Even as a child he realized the creative power of the word and also the difficulties of expression: "Words are bricks; to express myself I must work in the sweat of my brow on the composition of stone-heavy words; grown-up people are able to construct their words deftly" (p. 277). Of course, the ease with which grown-ups can express themselves is illusory, as Belyi and his narrator know but the young Kotik does not. In fact, all of Belyi's career was a never-ending struggle to put the unyielding stones of words into meaningful units. For the future writer Kotik, the struggle begins in childhood.

The epilogue is constructed on the opposition of forward-moving time and space with a Steinerian-influenced mythical belief in eternal return. The narrator repeats the stages in which the world opened out before him: "My eyes widen; and with an unseeing glance I look into space; events spring up like a village or the seasons of the year; the noises of time await me" (p. 290). The widening of consciousness leads ultimately to death (crucifixion in this case). After death, however, the narrator sees the promise of resurrection into the world he knew as an infant.

In the Russian pseudo-autobiographical and gentry autobiographical traditions (and in European traditions as well), the lost world of childhood, the happiest time of life, could be reentered only through memory. For Belyi there are two roads to childhood: one backward through the creative force of memory, the other forward through death, which will physically bring him back to the world of "memory of memory." The myth of childhood (in this case earliest childhood) as a kind of earthly paradise is still present in *Kotik Letaev*. But the content of childhood paradise is radically modified in accordance with the teachings of Steiner and with Belyi's private mythology. The way in which the narrator shows the child creating his own world, by concretizing eternal stimuli in a highly personal idiom, makes *Kotik Letaev* the spiritual history of a modernist. Whereas realist writers accepted the existence of the phenomenal world and strove to show their younger incarnation's development in that world, Belyi's narrator both grows within the real world and creates (or rediscovers) other worlds in the process of writing. Belyi's experimentation bends the Russian pseudo-autobiographical tradition almost to the breaking point, but *Kotik Letaev* remains a recognizable member of its genre.

For those critics who see *Kotik Letaev* as a work whose primary purpose is to translate Belyi's occult beliefs into a novel, *The Baptized Chinaman* presents an interpretive problem. Clearly the latter work is a sequel to the former, yet the occult element is almost completely absent.[23]

If, however, one sees the general progression in *Kotik Letaev* as being from the child's almost complete immersion in the occult world to greater and greater contact with the real world, then the logic of narrative presentation in *The Baptized Chinaman* becomes clear. The older child in the latter work does not have, for all intents and purposes, occult experiences and, therefore, the narrator cannot vicariously enter the realm of "memory of memory" as he could when he recalled his earliest memories.[24] The nostalgia that informs *The Baptized Chinaman* is not for lost occult worlds but for the lost real world that the fully conscious six-year-old Kotik inhabited. That is why detail takes on more and more importance. The world being recreated is not one of "swarm" (which could best be relived through a stream of jumbled images) but of "form" (which cries out for exact descriptions of things, places, and people).

One opportunity that arises in the sequel is to depict some of the same scenes that had appeared in *Kotik Letaev* from the perspective of the older child. In some sense this device lends a triple point of view to the description: young child, older child, and narrator. Within the framework of *Childhood Years*, Aksakov used the juxtaposition of such scenes quite effectively to show the development of the child over time. The most noticeable instance in *Kotik Letaev* and in *The Baptized Chinaman* is the story of how Kotik's father set the curtains on fire and then put out the flames himself. In the earlier novel, the memory of the fire is elicited by a still older memory. The child recalls being scared by his father, whom he perceived as being "fire-breathing." This image connects the father with various other members of mythological worlds [25] and, simultaneously, it reminds the narrator of an event that took place when he was older: "Memories of my fire-breathing papa merge with memories of later stories" (p. 55). The narrator then proceeds to relate, in quite simple prose (remember that in *Kotik Letaev* the narrator's voice is simpler than the child's), the story of how his father lit the curtains on fire.

In *The Baptized Chinaman*, the order of memory is reversed. The older child sees his father standing with a nail in his hand. This sight causes him (not the narrator) to move further back into his memory: "The picture that I saw—papa with a nail, brings up a huge fragment of the past—Oh, I remembered!" (p. 157). Then the child begins to relate almost the same story about his father and the curtains. In its turn this story elicits even earlier memories:

I felt that beyond that event of memory another event, an ancient, an ancient one, was lurking: in the frenzy of flame—
—even greater frenzies—
—were recalled: wild, Scythian ones.
(p. 157)

The older child is not capable of reentering the occult worlds and has only a vague sensation that they must have existed. The narrator could, as he did in *Kotik Letaev*, find the words that would open up preexisting worlds, but such a procedure is no longer appropriate. Of course, the reader through his recollection of the scene in *Kotik Letaev* does have a kind of vicarious access to the occult world in which the father was incarnated as a kind of fire-breathing monster. Thus, by using the same memory in *Kotik Letaev* and *The Baptized Chinaman*, Belyi is able to show both the development of the child over time and to allow the reader to make connections that the older child is no longer capable of making.

As Kotik develops further, he begins to grasp the concept of cause and effect. If his younger incarnation could blithely create worlds in which dachshunds grew out of pencil marks on a page and the Kremlin was a kind of dessert, the older Kotik checks his linguistic intuitions against the real world. His changing perspective can be discerned in the scenes when he first begins to understand something about the sexual relations of men and women. He overhears his mother saying that their servant Duniasha is uncontrollable because she is always "going out." He realizes that he too "goes out" with his nurse. Formerly that would have been enough for Kotik to equate himself with Duniasha. Now, however, he realizes that something more complicated is going on:

> Duniasha goes out with the salesman: that's not important; While going out Duniasha drops in on the salesman: they do something and that's more important.—
> —The cook has her "own": Petrovich's appearance in the kitchen is permitted; and they do something; they really did something;—
> —later on little "Kotiks" appear; How that happens—I don't know. (p. 46)

Kotik is not quite sure how the system works, but he knows that some kind of cause and effect is at work and that a purely linguistic explanation is not sufficient.

One could choose many more scenes to illustrate the child's increasingly rationalistic relation to the real world, but it is probably unnecessary to do so. It is more important to discuss the scenes based on Biblical imagery that appear toward the end of the novel. They can simply be read as recapitulations of the same occult memories present at the end of *Kotik Letaev*. However, it is clear throughout *The Baptized Chinaman* that Kotik has lost access to the world of "memory of memory." He has, on the other hand, shown a precocious ability to reason. It seems more logical to assume that he has projected himself (the innocent victim) onto the remembered story of Christ rather than to posit an occult experience that has brought him to this identification. An anthroposophist might say that the very fact of the connection proves Steiner correct. That is a theological argument which cannot be resolved here. On the level of the text, however, there seems no reason to assume that the young Kotik's Biblical reminiscences are the result of occult insight.

Like all the other Russian writers of pseudo-autobiography (with the possible exception of Gorky), Belyi used autobiographical material frequently. There are Belyi incarnations present in his writing as early as *The Second Symphony* (1901). However, the figure who was to turn into the writer Andrei Belyi does not appear at the center of a work until *Kotik Letaev* (1922). Thus, one line of his literary development (although not the only one) can be seen to trace a curve from lesser to greater autobiographicalism. Belyi moves from highly encoded depictions of self in *The Second Symphony* and the early novels, through the two pseudo-autobiographical novels, to the directly autobiographical poem "The First Encounter" and the trio of prose autobiographies that he produced toward the end of his life. This analysis sees the pseudo-autobiographical genre as being of crucial importance to him. *Kotik Letaev* and *The Baptized Chinaman* allowed Belyi the chance to be both himself and not himself simultaneously. He could express his increasing interest in a unique self without having to acknowledge that it was his *own* self at the center of the work of art. Having shown how the child develops in the real world, Belyi was then able to acknowledge that he was that child in "The First Encounter" and in the autobiographies.

Belyi's pseudo-autobiographies provided Russian culture with a new model of childhood. The myths and countermyths that had concerned Tolstoy, Aksakov, Gorky, and their followers were largely irrelevant for Belyi, even though he was well aware of the tradition in which he was working. Instead, he found childhood to be a crucial period for two new reasons. The first, derived from his interpretation of Steiner, was connected with the young child's ability to enter preexisting worlds. Because few Russians were interested in the details of anthroposophy, this line of childhood mythology produced no literary successors. The second reason for writing about childhood was to show how, through the acquisition of language, the child constructs a world and a self from the perceptual and linguistic fragments that surround him.[26] In this sense, the child's situation is analogous to that of the adult writer, and childhood experience becomes a metaphor for or prefiguration of the creative process in general. As opposed to Belyi's anthroposophical myths, his myth of the child as creator played a significant role in later Russian literary conceptions of childhood. It was important both for authors whose aesthetic was clearly modernist (Mandel'shtam and Pasternak, for example) and for those who wrote in a more traditional style (such as Nabokov and Bunin). For all of these authors, the child is not so much the father to the man as he is the father to the writer.

Chapter Six

⟲

I. A. Bunin:
Preserving the Tradition in Exile

By the 1920's the gentry autobiographical tradition should have
been as dead as the class whose myths it had once expressed. Paradoxically, however, the myths of gentry childhood thrived and
even became stronger in Russian émigré culture. In their haste to
depart after the Revolution, the émigrés left many of their most
precious possessions behind. Among the few things almost all of
them carried into exile were rose-colored memories of the days
before the Bolshevik takeover. As the reality of pre-revolutionary
Russia gradually faded farther into the mists of time, the myth
of the happy childhood lost none of its luster. In fact, in post-
revolutionary émigré autobiographies, a Tolstoyan childhood became almost an article of faith, the badge of a true aristocratic
background.

The introductory section of A. V. Bolotov's memoirs affords an
excellent example of the kind of mythological baggage that so
many Russians took to places like Berlin, Paris, Prague, Riga, and
Constantinople:

Starting work on an edition of my memoirs . . . these lines, imbued
with sadness for pleasant, irretrievable, past time . . . [I think] about
my dear dead friends, and, most of all, about the gentry way of life
that has completely disappeared, sunk into the waters of Lethe; a life
that was lived on rich manors and humble but comfortable little estates, where, in rural tranquility, on the boundless steppes, among
the open, fertile fields, and in the untouched forests, the mighty Russian spirit that transformed the Kingdom of Muscovy into the Great
Russian Empire was gradually formed and forged.[1]

It comes as no surprise that Bolotov has recourse to every one of the canonized modifiers when describing his own childhood: "All of this is dear, but distant legend; an irretrievable, good, old, care-free time, insouciant childhood."[2] This quote is particularly revealing, because Bolotov recognizes the legendary status of the happy childhood, even as he claims to have had one himself. These same themes continue to echo in works written by Russian émigrés as late as the 1940's. Thus, when in *Speak, Memory* Nabokov says, "The nostalgia I have been cherishing all these years is a hypertrophied sense of lost childhood," he is merely one of the last and greatest writers in a 100-year-old tradition.[3]

In this rich lode of émigré works, fictional and nonfictional, Bunin's novel *The Life of Arsen'ev* stands out both as the most persuasive attempt to keep the Russian gentry conception of childhood alive and as the crowning achievement of the traditional pseudo-autobiography. Building on the rich legacy of the nineteenth century, Bunin captured the poignancy of an individual life and, at the same time, he continued the cultural and historical traditions of the entire gentry line of Russian literature. The familiar characteristics of the Russian pseudo-autobiography—idealization of life on a country estate, bittersweet nostalgia for lost time and space, an idealized mother figure, an eccentric father, and the sensitive central figure of the experiencing child—are all present and receive an unprecedentedly satisfying treatment in *The Life of Arsen'ev.*[4]

In part Bunin succeeded in summarizing the results of more than a century of cultural, literary, and social development because he quite consciously built on the work of those who had come before him. At the same time, the new circumstances of post-revolutionary Russia and his place as an émigré writer lent Bunin's nostalgia a depth that was rarely possible for nineteenth-century writers (with the possible exception of Herzen). For Tolstoy, Aksakov, and their gentry followers, nostalgia was primarily for lost time. The innocence of youth was gone forever, but the basic surroundings (even if threatened by change) remained. In addition to the inevitable displacement in time, Bunin was fated to experience an irrevocable displacement in space; not only was youth spent, but the Russia he had known, along with the social structures that had been characteristic of it for more than 150 years, had been destroyed. What is more, the line of Russian gentry culture that had produced Pushkin, Turgenev, Tolstoy, Aksakov, and Bunin himself had been severed by the social upheavals that accompanied the Revolution. Bunin felt himself to be the last of his race, the end of a historical line, and his literary expression of this feeling deepened the interplay between personal and general that is typical for the genre as a whole.

The extent to which Bunin felt himself to be continuing the work of Tolstoy, and the fact that he was quite conscious of the genre in which he was working, can be seen both in the text of the novel and in Bunin's statements about it. The notebooks of Bunin's wife contain the following entry for May 27, 1928: "In the evening Jan spoke about 'The Life of Arsen'ev' for a long time. He's saddened that he gave it that title; he should have called it 'At the Wellspring of Days' and have written it like 'dear old Tolstoy, who wrote *Childhood, Boyhood, and Youth* and then stopped short.'" [5] The almost identical connection is made by the narrator late in the novel when, as a struggling young writer, he searches for a theme: "Well then, I thought, maybe I should just start a story about myself. But how? Something like *Childhood, Boyhood?* Or even simpler? 'I was born in such and such a place at such and such a time...'" (6: 236–37). In addition to emphasizing the place of the novel in the Russian literary tradition, this passage is recognizable to the reader as the embryonic draft of the novel's second paragraph, which consists of the sentence, "I was born half a century ago, in central Russia, in the countryside, on the estate of my fathers" (6: 7). The device of allowing the reader to see the author (in this case, the putative author Arsen'ev) actually creating the work whose final result is the finished novel is common for various types of first-person narration. As we will see when we examine the dynamics of the novel's beginning, however, the way in which Arsen'ev actually starts his novel shows a great deal more sophistication than the beginning he first proposes. Thus, as in Tolstoy's

Childhood, there is a constant and complicated overlapping of time frames in *The Life of Arsen'ev*. We see events both through the eyes of the narrator looking back from his vantage point in time and from the unmediated point of view of the child. The result is that an event that happened later in life can appear to have occurred in the distant past, whereas events from early childhood often seem to be depicted in the present.

The first chapter is one of the most evocative in Russian literature and introduces all of the novel's basic themes and compositional methods. It begins with a quotation that imitates the diction of a Russian saint's life, although its provenance is not revealed: "Things and deeds, if they be not written down, are veiled in darkness and given over to the grave of forgetting, but written down, they are as if animated." Through the sentence's archaic form, one feels the weight of the Russian literary tradition, the crucial, almost mystical importance of the act of writing itself, and the written word's ability, at least figuratively, to cheat death. While fear of death and oblivion has always been a powerful stimulus to writing, an explicit connection between writing down one's life and the literary vocation of the narrator had not been a part of the Russian pseudo-autobiographical tradition. Neither Tolstoy nor Aksakov makes his narrator a professional writer, and the question of why Irten'ev and Bagrov chose to write or recite their autobiography is left open. In *The Life of Arsen'ev*, on the other hand, we are dealing with the modernist phenomenon of the "(self) portrait of the artist as a young man." Arsen'ev is an artist, and what we are reading is a consciously literary work.

The next sentence, "I was born half a century ago, in central Russia, in the country, on the estate of my fathers," both does and does not give specific information about the writer. It places him in time and space and identifies him as a member of a certain class, but leaves much room for generalization. It certainly is a more open-ended beginning than the one proposed by the fledgling writer Arsen'ev later in the novel. As yet we have no name and no specific characteristics to attach to the narrator. The very vagueness of his temporal and spatial designations has a generalizing, depersonalizing effect. As he comes from the "center" of Russia, the narrator, it can be inferred, is a typical representative of his nation. The reader's desire for autobiographical detail is frustrated for the moment by a longish philosophical passage that delves further into the realm of the abstract. It begins: "We have no feeling of our beginning or our end." Such an impersonal statement immediately following the personally oriented sentence quoted above is reminiscent of Tolstoy's technique of mixing a specific narrator's voice with that of a generalizing, authorial voice capable of rising above individual facts to grasp universal truths.

Naturally, the search for beginnings (the beginning of life and the dawn of consciousness) is often important for the autobiography. This is particularly the case because the idea of beginnings is closely connected to the problem of memory, for, as Arsen'ev says a bit later, "We know what we remember—we, who at times even have difficulty remembering yesterday!" (6: 13). Despite the inherent impossibility of the task, it is the writer's duty to search for that elusive beginning. The following passage from Bunin's posthumously published "Notes" illustrates the extent to which Arsen'ev echoes Bunin's feelings here: "As with everyone, my life is something having neither beginning nor end, it is a book doomed to decay and oblivion. . . . Birth is in no way my beginning. My beginning is in the impenetrable darkness in which I was surrounded from conception to birth and in my father, my mother, my grandfathers, great-grandfathers, and forefathers, for they are also me." [6] This latter sentence is strikingly similar to some of Belyi's statements in *Kotik Letaev* and elsewhere. [7] For Bunin, a partial solution to the problem of beginnings was the writing of his pseudo-autobiographical novel. *The Life of Arsen'ev* allowed Bunin to escape the personal problems of specificity. As he said in an interview: "I wished to show the life of one man in the narrow circle surrounding him." [8]

Like Belyi, Bunin wished to pierce the veil of personal consciousness, to allow his narrator to describe the world before he was born. But where the adult Kotik searched for occult memories of a world outside our world, Arsen'ev constitutes his "prenatal" world through an exploration of his historical and cultural roots. The history of Russia and of Russian culture is important to him because it provides the "beginning" that memory is incapable of giving. Thus, parallel to the autobiographical description of his life, the narrator places that life (a writer's life) in the context of Russian history and culture. His questions as to his personal origins are echoed by his lack of complete information about his family:

About the Arsen'ev family, about its origins, I know almost nothing. What do we know anyway? I know only that in the heraldic book our family is included with those "whose origins are lost in the mists of time." I know that our family is "distinguished though impoverished" and that I felt that distinction all my life, proud and happy that I was not one of those without family or tribe. (6: 7–8)

The narrator's story is inseparable from that of his ancestors.[9]

The next two paragraphs of the first chapter consist of a prayer for the dead and a commentary on that prayer. The use of a borrowed text (literary or ecclesiastical) followed by commentary is typical for Arsen'ev's narrative technique throughout the novel. The theme of death, treated on many levels from the intensely personal to the historically significant, complements the literary and personal concerns of the narrator. In particular, the loss caused by death is easily linked to the loss of a way of life and the loss of Russia, so that the personal, historical, and cosmic are never entirely separated. The section of the service reproduced here asks God to give peace to those of his servants "From Adam even unto today who have served thee chastely, our fathers and brothers, kith and kin!" (6: 8).

The narrator's commentary shows that he has grasped the historical implications of the prayer as well as the religious ones. He emphasizes the idea of community and the ability of the religious service, by virtue of its constant repetition, to escape the time frame of birth and death to which humans are subject: "And is it not a joy to feel your connection, participation 'with our fathers and brothers, kith and kin' who celebrated this service?" (6: 8). Religion was not a subject of great concern to the narrator of the nineteenth-century pseudo-autobiography. For Arsen'ev, however, the Orthodox liturgy, its ritual unchanged (or barely changed) by time or place, is an anchor, a last connection to a way of life that is forever gone.

The chapter ends with a paragraph that combines the themes of history and death and adds one more: that of exile. The narrator's position as an exiled writer in the south of France gives him a spatial distance from his childhood, which, together with the distance caused by time, encourages his mind to play freely over his past. Because Arsen'ev cannot physically experience Russia, his nostalgia for childhood paradise is given another dimension. This situation is, of course, typical for the exiled writer, and other exiles also make extensive use of the double nostalgic distance. [10]

On the level of autobiographical detail in *The Life of Arsen'ev*, there are remarkable parallels between the young lives of Arsen'ev, Bagrov, and Irten'ev. As has already been mentioned, all three of these fictional narrators depict the life of middle-rank gentry families on country estates. Given the resistance to change in Russia (especially in the countryside), the similarities among the three narrators and between their stories and those of other literary and nonliterary figures are not particularly surprising. As was the case with Tolstoy and Aksakov, the child is extremely attached to his mother. As Arsen'ev puts it: "The most bitter love of my whole life is linked to my mother. Everyone and everything that we love is our torment . . . from infancy I carried the great burden of my unchanging love for her" (6: 15). It is not merely the feelings of the narrator that are reminiscent of Tolstoy's text; the shift of voices from the very personal to the extremely general (a shift not entirely motivated by the specific information given) and back to the specific is typical for the pseudo-autobiography. In the first published draft of the novel, Arsen'ev's feelings for his mother were even more strongly expressed: "Thus she was the incarnation of love and self-sacrifice, the incarnation of motherhood" (6: 291).

Although such encomiums to the mother are not exceptional in pseudo-autobiography and gentry autobiography, they are usually seconded in the text by examples of the son's interplay with the mother. In *The Life of Arsen'ev* such scenes are noticeably absent.

Indeed, after speaking of his bitter love for his mother, the narrator almost never mentions her again. This is an excellent example of the degree of pressure that can be exerted by literary and social convention. Such a mother/son relationship was expected by reader and writer and, therefore, it was provided. But, as opposed to Tolstoy (who wished he had had such a relationship with his dead mother) and Aksakov (who seems truly to have been extremely close to his mother), Bunin seems not to have needed such a tie. His alter-ego Arsen'ev provides one for reasons of genre, but he is unable, unwilling, or uninterested in going into the subject any further. It is as if, having satisfied the genre requirement, he feels there is no need for elaboration.

While Arsen'ev's mother fills the central role as buttress of the family, the father (loved almost equally) is one more example of the unbusinesslike eccentric, incapable of holding onto the family's money. It is his fault that the family has fallen into poverty, but somehow their change in fortune does not seem to concern him. The narrator describes how, as a young boy, he tried to learn something about his father: "And so I found something out about him: that he had never done anything,—and in truth, he spent his days in that happy idleness which was so normal then, not just for the country gentry, but for Russians in general" (6: 13). Incidentally, this section shows how smoothly Arsen'ev is able to handle the transition from childhood memories to adult reminiscences. The first sentence, which merely states the fact that the father did nothing, is reported as the child might have done; the child sees his father only within the confines of a limited world. The next sentence, after "in truth," is the adult explanation of the child's perception; here the father's lack of activity is placed in a social and cultural context that is known to the adult narrator through his life experience.

Arsen'ev's father is the incarnation of the Russian provincial nobleman. He is always *comme il faut* when he has the money to be so, and he has no interest in or concern for such concepts as business and making money. Later in the novel, Arsen'ev characterizes his father as a person who had "an inexhaustible passion to squander everything" (6: 85). Nevertheless, Arsen'ev loves him, even though he believes that it is the personality type and way of life of his generation's fathers that led to the collapse of Russia and his own exile.

As was the case in Tolstoy's trilogy, the father's "society" manners and personality are inherited not by the sensitive narrator but by his older brother: in this case Georgi Arsen'ev. Arsen'ev's father's youth was spent romantically fighting for Russia in the Crimean War. By the time Georgi is growing up, however, there is no such patriotic outlet for youthful enthusiasm. Instead, he gets involved with a group of socialists and is eventually arrested. Analyzing his brother's involvement with this group, Arsen'ev wonders why his brother became so caught up by the personality of a local socialist named Dobrokhotov. He rejects any political reasons for his brother's concern and adds:

But what did my brother have in common with Dobrokhotov? . . . It was clearly only the strength of that eternal flippancy, enthusiasm that was so common in the gentry tribe and never left the Radishchevs, Chatskys, Rudins, Ogarevs, and Herzens even when they had gone quite gray: because the traits of Dobrokhotov were considered exalted, heroic, and, finally, for the simple reason that in remembering Dobrokhotov he remembered the entire happy holiday in which he had spent his youth. (6: 83)

This passage is noteworthy for a number of reasons. The most important, perhaps, is the realization of the historical continuum of Russian revolutionary thought and the identification of its cause not with conditions in Russia but with the character of a certain group of people. The fact that Arsen'ev does not distinguish between fictitious literary personages and actual historical figures illustrates the extent to which he perceives life and art as being intertwined. [11] He sees the same characteristics in Radishchev (an eighteenth-century author) and Herzen (author and publicist of the 1840's–60's) and in literary heroes like Chatsky (from Griboedov's *Woe from Wit*, 1820's) or Rudin (the hero of Turgenev's novel of the same name, 1856). Also added to the list by implication are Arsen'ev's father and brother. The double subtext of literary and historical roots is as important for Arsen'ev's explanation of his family as for his conception of the novel as a whole. The text is centered at the point where literary and historical lines of development cross.

Immediately after the description and analysis of his brother's "revolutionary" activity, the focus is broadened and the author's voice pronounces a universal judgment on Russia itself: "Ah, that eternal Russian need for holiday! . . . for was not the primordial dream of rivers of milk, of free will without constraint, of holiday, one of the most important reasons for Russian revolutionary activity? And, in general, what is the Russian protestor, rebel, revolutionary, who is always ridiculously aloof from reality and who despises it?" (6: 83). This is certainly not a very orthodox interpretation of the Russian revolutionary movement, but it shows Arsen'ev's concern with understanding all the phenomena that affected his life within their historical context. Of course, the narrator ignores the fact that his own life, complete with aimless wanderings around Russia and dreams of literary glory, is not oriented to concrete problems either. Indeed, Arsen'ev's pseudo-autobiographical quest to resurrect childhood in paradise is as much a utopian dream as that of his brother. In terms of self-analysis, Arsen'ev does not go nearly as far as Irten'ev, who would not have allowed himself such logical inconsistencies. But Arsen'ev is not merely telling the story of his life. He is recounting a story that was shared by generations of Russians; the historical context allows him to generalize. Tolstoy, with his supreme self-confidence, could shift from specific to general narrative voices with no mediating context. Bunin tries to motivate such passages by providing a historical context for them. Individual psychology is no longer the sole center in the pseudo-autobiography. The individual is important primarily because his reflections illuminate a larger historical and social context.

One part of Arsen'ev's personality was forged in relation to his family—that is, to his loving and emotional mother and to his light-headed and slightly eccentric father and his older brothers. This type of family was typical for the Russian country-dwelling gentry. There was only one other influence as strong as that of the family: the land itself. Arsen'ev, writing his autobiography in the south of France, feels compelled to point out the crucial importance of the physical surroundings of his childhood: "I was born and grew up, I repeat, in completely open field, the likes of which the European cannot even imagine. A gigantic space without fences or borders surrounded me" (6: 40). In this world, time is measured in the natural rhythms of the changing seasons, birth and death. Indeed, Arsen'ev's entire youthful existence is tied to this natural cycle. Describing the "beginning of youth" (like Irten'ev, Arsen'ev demarcates the periods of "childhood," "boyhood," and "youth" exactly), Arsen'ev characterizes himself through his ability to see distant stars, to hear the whistle of a groundhog from far away, or to be affected by the smell of the lily of the valley. He recalls his youthful vigor in terms of his ability to perceive and be in touch with the natural world (6: 92).

Perhaps the most remarkable scene describing Arsen'ev's bond with the natural world comes in his description of a moonlit night in the country:

The empty clearing in front of the house was bathed in a strong strange light. To the right above the garden, on a clear and empty horizon, shone the moon; the lightly shaded outline of its deathly pale face was filled from within by bright shining whiteness. And the two of us, well acquainted by now, looked at each other for a long time . . . and when I slowly walked on, along the pond to the right, again the moon floated alongside me, above the darkened crowns of the trees, which were motionless in their nocturnal simplicity.
And thus we walked around the entire garden. It seemed that we were even thinking together—always about one thing: about the mysterious exhausting loving happiness of life, about my mysterious future. (6: 120—21)

This passage is startlingly similar to one in Tolstoy's *Youth*. There, spending the summer at his father's estate, Irten'ev experiences the same feeling of communion with nature:

When there was a full moon I often spent whole nights on my mattress looking at the light and shadows, listening to the quiet and the sounds, *dreaming of various things, generally about poetic, voluptuous happiness* . . . at those moments it seemed to me that nature, the moon and I, we were all one and the same. (Tolstoy, 2: 178–80; italics mine)

The natural world is so much a part of the pseudo-autobiographical narrator that he can internalize external surroundings. The moon thinks both with Arsen'ev and about him. Such a relationship with nature could only make sense to a person who was raised in natural but poeticized surroundings; a peasant who grew up fighting for survival in the natural world is unlikely to perceive it in this way, nor is a city dweller.[12]

Bunin's work differs from Tolstoy's in the fact that, while the natural world is a part of Irten'ev, he does not always carry it with him. For Arsen'ev, on the other hand, recollections of the natural world form a lifelong theme. It is his ability to recall sights, smells, and sounds that transports him back into his past and allows him to compose his memoir. Looking back to early childhood, he says that the world around the cowshed had a special "appearance, color, smell, and taste" (6: 17). Such synesthetic associative patterns are one of the roots of his creativity. He speaks a bit later of how he fell in love with a girl whom he saw for the first time next to a fountain that was surrounded by a flower called "tabak." After setting the scene of youthful puppy love, Arsen'ev says: "From time to time, all my life whenever I sensed that smell I would remember her, and the coolness of the fountain, and the sounds of martial music" (6: 69). It is the associative power of Arsen'ev's memory that allows him to build up his self-portrait. Whereas Irten'ev constructed his narrative around the events of a number of typical days in his life, Arsen'ev takes a detail, a single event, and then gathers more and more material around it.

Arsen'ev uses associative memory chains to express his own personality and experience. Details that might have been trivial in any other life become the basis for a string of associations that have major significance for Arsen'ev. What makes the novel particularly rich, however, is that the same sorts of associative chains are used to show the ways in which Arsen'ev's experience is typical for that of Russia as a whole. For, if the task of a normal autobiography is to justify and explain an individual existence,[13] then the writer of a pseudo-autobiography should also try to generalize, to let the fictional narrator be both an individual and a symbol for his age. Were an autobiographer to do this, he would run grave risks of breaking the code of self-attention that is the basis of autobiography, not to mention the danger of seeming pretentious. One of Bunin's purposes in *The Life of Arsen'ev* is indeed to speak for an entire generation. Whenever asked, Bunin was careful to insist that his novel was not an autobiography: "I definitely do not want my work to be distorted, that is, described by the unfitting label autobiography; nor connected to my life, that is, discussed not as *The Life of Arsen'ev*, but as the life of Bunin. Perhaps there is much that is directly autobiographical in *The Life of Arsen'ev*. But to speak of that is not the business of *artistic* criticism."[14] Although he does not deny the use of autobiographical material (which would have been pointless), Bunin insists that its presence is unimportant on the aesthetic level. Arsen'ev's experience, the peculiar concatenation of time, space, and culture he describes, exists independently of Bunin. The facts of Bunin's life make up only one of the novel's subtexts.[15] The others are composed of material from other pseudo-autobiographies, from Russian literature in general, from Russian life in the last decades before the Revolution, and from the internal logic of the life of the fictitious narrator. The "artistry" of the novel lies in Bunin's ability to create, from these varied subtexts, a work so true to itself that readers could take it for an autobiography.

In some sense the novel can be read as an attempt to answer the question that Arsen'ev poses in the first chapter: "Anyway, why did what happened to Russia, which was destroyed before our very eyes in such a magically short period, happen?" (6: 41). Before Arsen'ev can address this question, however, he must first explain what gives him the right to do so. He must show his connection to the Russian past, must generalize his voice so that it can speak for the country as a whole.

After listening to his father's stories of bygone days, Arsen'ev begins to understand that he is not simply an individual with no ties to the outside world. For Irten'ev the knowledge that his family was not the center of the universe, that there were places where the peasants did not salute them and where people did not know them, came as an unpleasant shock. His childhood world, as well as his adult narrative, is far more centered on his own psychological processes and on family life. For Arsen'ev, on the other hand, this knowledge is thrilling: "Undoubtedly, it was just that evening when I became conscious of the fact that I was Russian and lived in Russia . . . and suddenly I sensed that Russia, sensed her past and present, her wild, frightening, and nevertheless somehow captivating particularities, and my blood relation to her" (6: 57). This passage is typical for the poetics of *The Life of Arsen'ev*, with its anaphoric verbs, parallel constructions, and balance between a simultaneous personalizing and generalizing tendency. Arsen'ev, writing, as he tells us, from France, far from his native country, speaks for all Russian émigrés.

At many points in the narrative, Arsen'ev's view of a thing is conditioned by its historical significance. He is particularly fascinated by anything that can be called "ancient," an adjective that appears with amazing frequency in the novel. Both the natural and the manufactured worlds are seen historically. Looking at a river, Arsen'ev thinks, "it flowed like this even at the time of the Pechenegs" (6: 92). Looking out at a barrow through the window of a train, Arsen'ev feels a nebulous but nevertheless strong connection between his world and the prehistoric Russian past: "It was something completely unusual in all its simplicity, so ancient that it seemed utterly foreign to everything living; current, yet, at the same time, it was somehow familiar, closely related" (6: 175). The dialectic of ancient/modern is typical for his perception. It is not clear from these historical and geographical musings how Arsen'ev finds a synthesis for this dialectic. However, when he describes his feelings upon seeing two paintings on the gates of a monastery, the source of the connection becomes more obvious. The paintings depict two saints holding parchment scrolls in their hands. Arsen'ev muses:

How many years have they been standing like that—and for how many centuries have they no longer been on earth? Everything will pass, everything passes, and there will come a time when we too will not be in the world . . . and these ancient Russian holy men with their wise and holy writings in their hands will stand at the gates, just as sadly and passionlessly. (6: 90)

The importance of "antiquity" in light of the novel's first sentence now becomes clear. These relics preserve the memory of a past that has otherwise died and left no record. Anything that does leave some record has, in effect, cheated death and prolonged the forces of life in the world. The saints, for example, have done so both through their painted presence on the gates (which implies the work of an unknown human artist) and through the parchments they hold, through the written word; that is, through the very medium Arsen'ev has chosen to cheat death and decay. The written word, by leaving a trace of the person who has written it, imparts immortality both to the writer and to the human race as a whole. In this conviction Arsen'ev is truly echoing Bunin's own voice: "In all times and ages, from childhood to the grave, each of us is tormented by an ever-present desire to speak about himself— in order, if only by means of the word and just in small measure, to fix the imprint of his life." [16] A comparison of these passages shows why Bunin did not want the novel taken as an autobiography even if it contained much autobiographical material. Whereas Bunin states his reasons for writing quite baldly, Arsen'ev voices the same feeling slowly, almost allegorically; he describes a series of situations whereby an individual or a race (or even God, since nature is taken to be God's creation) have immortalized themselves, and, in connection with the first sentence of the novel, he allows the reader to descry his reasons for writing an autobiography. History and the historical process are crucial to the novel because they hint that the creative process in humans and nature can overcome the finality of death.

Throughout the novel, Arsen'ev tries to orient himself in the flow of historical time. The work's original title, *The Wellspring of Days*, reflects this concern with beginnings or origins. In addition to history, however, there is another, parallel but not synchronized, process in which he must find a place. Since, as opposed to the previous narrators of Russian pseudo-autobiographies, Arsen'ev is a professional writer, it is only natural that he must define his place in the literary tradition. He measures his perceptions and his writing against the achievements of Russian literature, and his own autobiography, his crowning work, is an extended dialogue with the Russian literary past.

In this respect as well Arsen'ev closely resembles his creator. Bunin felt that he had a peculiar place as the last in a great series of Russian writers linked by upbringing, shared culture, and a unique feeling for Russia in general and the Russian language in particular. He expressed this sentiment in a number of places, but perhaps most strongly in an article on Tolstoy:

> I say this too, also Tolstoy's fellow-countryman, belonging to the same background as Tolstoy . . . a wonderful place, he has many glorious fellow-countrymen! Zhukovsky and Tolstoy—from near Tula; Tiutchev, Leskov, Turgenev, Fet, the brothers Kireevsky, and the brothers Zhemchuzhnikov—from near Orel; Anna Bunin and Polonsky—from near Riazan'; Kol'tsov, Nikitin, Garshin, and Pisarev—from near Voronezh... Even Pushkin and Lermontov are partially ours, since their relatives, the Voeikovs and the Arsen'evs are also from our area.[17]

In exile, after a revolution that had clearly swept away the tradition forever, it was up to Bunin and, specifically, to his creation Arsen'ev to keep the flame alive, to ensure that the traditions of the "gentry" line of Russian literature were not forgotten. Arsen'ev thinks in more or less the same terms, although, characteristically, he merely hints at the connection without expressly making it: "I heard that yesterday someone's hunting party together with that of the young Tolstoys passed by our place along the highroad on their way to the distant fields. How incredible—I am a contemporary and even a neighbor of *his*! Well, that's just as good as if I had lived next door to Pushkin at some time" (6: 159). Arsen'ev constantly measures himself against the heritage of the "gentry" line in Russian literature. He chooses to include the visits he made to the estate of Lermontov (6: 156) and to the estate that was supposed to be Turgenev's model for *A Nest of Gentryfolk* (6: 194). The conflation of a real person's estate with that of a fictional character is typical for Arsen'ev's worldview (cf. his interpretation of the Russian revolutionary tradition described above). Arsen'ev even goes so far as to place himself in consciously "literary" situations. The most obvious is when, young and temporarily disillusioned, he sits watching the peasants work and is invited to help them cut hay. At first he finds it impossibly difficult but then gets into the rhythm of the process. As he puts it: "Then I became so attached to my voluntary hard labor that I fell asleep with the blissful thought—tomorrow we'll mow again" (6: 132). It does not take much knowledge of Russian literature to recognize a repetition of the mowing scene in *Anna Karenina*. However, whereas the original scene had a definite ideological purpose (to show the wisdom of the peasants' way of life), Arsen'ev labors for different reasons. The first is to get over melancholy thoughts of an unsuccessful youthful love affair, and the second is a desire to connect himself to the Russian literary tradition (particularly to the autobiographically oriented literary tradition, since the connection between Levin and Tolstoy was clear by the 1920's).

Arsen'ev perceives the world through the mediation of the literary tradition from his earliest childhood. As he explains: "Gogol's 'Old World Landowners' and 'A Horrible Revenge' made a unique impression on me. What unforgettable lines! How they resonate within me to this very day. They entered me in childhood, never to depart, and they also became part of that most valuable kernel from which, in Gogol's words, my 'essential makeup' was formed" (6: 38).

Arsen'ev creates entire chapters of his novel—that is, he characterizes entire portions of his life—through a series of poetic quotations accompanied by short explanatory commentaries. As certain religious people find quotations from the Bible or the Koran to characterize their actions and feelings, so Arsen'ev uses Russian literature. He starts the chapter that describes the period when he was about fifteen years old with a simple statement: "At that time Pushkin was a genuine part of my life" (6: 126). The connection between life and poetry is so close that it is not clear whether life reproduces poetic situations or whether poetry allows those situations to exist:

So I wake up on a sunny frosty morning and I am doubly happy because I exclaim with him: "Frost and sun, amazing day,"—with him who not only spoke so amazingly about the morning, but who gave me, together with it, a certain miraculous image:
And you're still dozing, charming friend... (6: 126)[18]

The outside world recalls the poem in Arsen'ev's mind, but then the context of the poem begins to live its own life and to give him a special, poetically associative way of seeing the world. The remainder of this short chapter continues in the same way. The narrator describes a situation from life and then borrows a Pushkin quote that allows him to express the situation in language. Pushkin teaches him to crystallize the ephemeral world through art. Bunin has discovered an entirely new way of expressing the difference between the adult's perception and the child's. Whereas the adult Arsen'ev is now capable of choosing his own words to describe what he felt and saw at the time, the adolescent (though perhaps feeling the same thing) could express it only in another's words.

In addition to providing a vocabulary for describing the natural world, a world that Arsen'ev more or less understood by virtue of having grown up in it, the world of poetry provides details about a host of other, less directly familiar situations. In the natural world, the external situation calls up its poetic representation. In the area of human emotions, on the other hand, poetry speaks first and provides a pattern for existence. Describing an early love, Arsen'ev says:

My feelings for Liza Bibikova were the result not only of my childishness but also of my love for our way of life, with which, at one time, Russian poetry was so closely connected.

I was in love with Liza in an old-fashioned poetic way as with a being belonging to our milieu.

The spirit of that milieu, romanticized by my imagination, seemed even more beautiful because it was disappearing forever before my eyes. (6: 128)

This passage illustrates the relationship of life and art characteristic for the adult Arsen'ev's worldview. The girl is not merely a beloved but a symbol for a specific historical time and place and for a whole literary culture. All of Russian poetry was "at one time" tied to Russian life. Of course, from a position of exile it is obvious that the connection has been lost. Even so, the admission that the spirit of the gentry way of life was "disappearing before my eyes" indicates that it was not simply the experience of revolution and exile that destroyed the organic unity of the Russian social and literary tradition. Indeed, Bunin had held a nostalgic view of the Russian literary tradition and had searched for the reasons for the "fall of Russian literature" well before the Revolution. He blamed it on the *raznochintsy* (nongentry writers and intellectuals), who were "almost completely lacking tradition, thrown off the track by the eighties and nineties and, in addition, by that which had to go along with those years, European influences." [19] In Arsen'ev, Bunin created a narrator for whom no situation in life or nature exists as a thing in itself. Everything is refracted through the subtexts of Russian literature and a certain type of Russian life.

Nowhere is this clearer than in the chapter describing Arsen'ev's decision to travel through the Ukraine. He talks a bit about the wonders of the past and then says, "I went insane over *The Lay of Prince Igor*" (6: 180). This statement is followed by a series of quotes from the poem, all given as a background to and an explanation for the journey. To some extent Arsen'ev becomes Igor and sees the world through the medium of the Igor tale: "I was on those same banks of the Donets where the Prince once upon a time escaped imprisonment 'like an ermine in the rushes, like a white goose on the waters'; then I was on the Dnieper, just where it 'drove stone mountains through the Polovtsian land'" (6: 180). He enters Kiev to the sounds of the populace rejoicing at Igor's return. But, instead of ending his journey with a triumphant return from exile (as occurs in the original), he inverts the order and ends his modern-day "Lay" in the steppe, to the accompaniment of Iaroslavna's heart-wrenching lament. This is because the adult Arsen'ev, despite his verbal ability to discover *temps perdu*, realizes that the past has been destroyed and that the loss commemorated by Iaroslavna's lament is more appropriate to the situation than the triumphant return from exile, a return that, for Russian culture and the way of life Arsen'ev had known as a child, could never be. Once again it is clear why Bunin felt that the extent to which the work is autobiographical was unimportant from an artistic point of view. Certainly the loss suffered by Bunin and Arsen'ev is similar. Bunin expressed that loss in many ways, both directly and indirectly. Arsen'ev expresses it simply and elegantly by inverting a literary subtext, changing a triumphant return from exile to a lament for lost time and place.

For Arsen'ev, both history and literature, important as they are in and of themselves, are particularly crucial because they represent the poetization of loss, death, and destruction. The themes of death and decay and Arsen'ev's growing ability to come to terms with them, primarily through the act of writing (that is, preserving their memory so that they are not "covered by darkness and given over to the grave of forgetfulness"), become increasingly central in the course of the novel.

The theme of death is sounded on the first page: "Are we not born with a feeling of death?" (6: 7). In order to explain his heightened sensitivity to mortality, Arsen'ev invokes an authorial voice like that in Tolstoy's trilogy: "People are not at all equally sensitive to death. There are people who live under its banner all their days, who have a heightened feeling of death from childhood (this is often found together with an equally heightened feeling for life)" (6: 26). It is interesting to note that this hypersensitivity to death is not characteristic for Irten'ev's worldview, but it is crucial for Tolstoy's alter-ego Levin (a character with whom Arsen'ev has some affinity, as I have already noted). In addition, on the autobiographical level, the fear of death and love of life that characterized Tolstoy were present in Bunin as well.

In the course of Book One, Arsen'ev recounts his reminiscences of three deaths: that of a farm worker who drives a cart and horse over a cliff into a ravine; that of his younger sister; and that of his grandmother. Book Two closes with the death of Arsen'ev's brother-in-law. Book Three begins with a long description of the brother-in-law's funeral. Arsen'ev sees death as a type of parting and measures time by these partings. They do not always have to include a person's death to have an aura of finality about them. He starts Book Two, for example, with the line, "On that day when I left Kamenna, not knowing that I had left it forever . . ." (6: 56). Book Four begins: "My final days at Baturin were also the final days of our family's former life" (6: 147). Thus, Arsen'ev's life moves forward on a whole series of deaths, those of people close to him and those of entire ways of life.

There is one death in the novel, this time not of a member of Arsen'ev's family, that typifies the dual nature of the pseudo-autobiographical narrative. It confirms the existence of the narrator in two places and two times joined by the act of reminiscing. In addition, the parallel deaths described, those of Grand Duke Nikolai Nikolaevich, senior (the son of Nikolai I), and of his son, Nikolai Nikolaevich, junior, place the narration within the context of historical events. They provide the narrator with still another opportunity to muse on the meaning of death and to re-emphasize the destruction of Russia and his exile from it. When Arsen'ev is working in the offices of the Orel newspaper, he sees the funeral train of the Grand Duke on its way from the Crimea to Moscow. He watches in fascination as a gigantic young hussar (Nikolai Nikolaevich, junior, who was about 6′6″) steps out of the train to salute the crowd. Everything is solemn, elegant, regal. Up until this point the narrative has proceeded chronologically. The narrator has hinted at his position as an exile in France a number of times, but he has never described anything of his life there. Now, prodded by the reminiscences connected with this death and its symbolic implications, he moves 38 years into the future, almost to the actual time of writing the novel. Both Arsen'ev and Nikolai are living in exile in southern France. Arsen'ev reads about the Grand Duke's death in the newspaper. He thinks: "Should I go there? That is inscrutably strange—to meet twice in a lifetime and both times in the company of death" (6: 187). Even so, the pull is too strong for him to stay away. As always Arsen'ev must test himself, must see if he can create life from death as he has done so many times in the course of his life and his narrative. He looks at the dead man and listens to the beginning of the funeral service: "That soft harmonious singing, the measured clank of the censer, the sadly submissive, woefully tender exclamations and prayers that had already sounded a million times on the earth. Only the names change in these prayers and for every name a time will come" (6: 189). The Church Slavic of the funeral service is interspersed between Arsen'ev's musings on death, just as in earlier chapters Pushkin's poetry filled the gaps where unquoted words could not express the necessary feeling. The universal fact of death as expressed in the Orthodox burial service is linked to the specifics of Nikolai's life and Arsen'ev's own fate by the latter's associative memory: "I think about his spent life, so big and complicated, and I think about my own" (6: 190).

In adapting the pseudo-autobiography to the new literary and social conditions prevailing after the Revolution, Bunin was an archaist and an innovator simultaneously. In matters of style he is unquestionably an archaist; many of his sentences could easily have come directly from a novel by Tolstoy or Turgenev. He preserved the basic "epic situation" of the Tolstoyan model. Although he was less interested than Tolstoy in contrasting the voice positions of child, adult narrator, and authorial figure, all three voices are still present in the text. The family structures and childhood situation he depicts are very similar to the ones that Aksakov (writing about the 1790's) and Tolstoy (writing about the 1830's and 1840's) described. This was possible, in part, because of the remarkable continuity of Russian gentry life, but, in addition, it was the result of a conscious decision by Bunin. He wished to emphasize his connection to his predecessors and, therefore, arranged his text to include as much traditional childhood material as he could.

Yet there is much that is new in Bunin's work. He makes his central character a professional writer. This both fits with the general modernist trend to produce "a portrait of an artist" and helps to motivate the very existence of the pseudo-autobiographical text (a problem that Tolstoy ignored and Aksakov tried to solve with the age-old device of the author as editor). More important, Bunin weaves the historical and historico-literary situation of his narrator into the text in subtle and complicated ways. Arsen'ev feels his connection to real events in the real world far more strongly than do the narrators of nineteenth-century pseudo-autobiographies. In part, the actuality of the historical situation in the novel is a function of Bunin's reaction to the physical dislocation caused by the Revolution. Nineteenth-century pseudo-autobiographers, while often affected by personal shocks, were spared a "world-historical event" of such sweeping consequence. Bunin felt a need to explain the Revolution, and this necessity (which directs the novel away from the more personal orientation of its precursors) is reflected in Arsen'ev's constant concern with the historical situation.

In addition, Arsen'ev's profession allows him to fashion a much more consciously literary text. Whereas Belyi uses epigraphical quotations at the beginning of each chapter to emphasize his place in the tradition, Bunin's narrator weaves large portions of text around other works of literature. This technique of subtext with commentary has a literary effect similar to the historical effect produced by Arsen'ev's musings on "world-historical events": it places the narrative in a tradition and, most important, enforces the narrator's unspoken desire to show that the literature of emigration is the true continuation of Russian literature. Similar techniques are used by other émigré writers (particularly Nabokov) to emphasize their rightful place in a national literature that, in their homeland, had no use for them. Finally, the extraordinary concern with death, decay, and destruction balanced by the ability of art (primarily verbal art) to resurrect lost time and space is a theme that had not been typical for his nineteenth-century models. This is, of course, a common theme in modernist art, but it is lent new poignancy by the tragedy that Bunin (and his surrogate Arsen'ev) lived through. Even the final death in the novel (that of Lika, the woman with whom Arsen'ev lived for a number of years) is redeemed on the last page by two short paragraphs in the voice of the adult narrator: one describes the notebook given him by her and the words she wrote in it; the other depicts his vision of her in a dream. This final visual image, clearly resurrected in association with Lika's literary heritage (meager as that may be), is symbolic of the narrator's quest throughout the novel: to write down and thereby preserve the personal, literary, and historical world of his youth and the gentry tradition to which he belongs.

Conclusion

When one surveys the course of modern Russian intellectual history, from the battles over the shape of the literary language—which began in the middle of the eighteenth century and culminated in the first decades of the nineteenth century in the conflict between the "archaists" and the "innovators"—to the heated mid-nineteenth-century debates between the "Westernizers" and the "Slavophiles," from the controversy surrounding the "nihilists" in the 1860's to the bitter and sometimes deadly ideological struggles of the early Soviet period, it often seems that Russian society has been unable to define its ideological positions without recourse to works of art. After long polemical disputation, ideas that are initially advanced in linguistic, historical, or literary texts gradually become divorced from their original contexts and begin to be perceived as free-floating ideological positions.[1] The resulting ideologies take on a life of their own—a life that is often only tangentially related to the concerns of the artistic work or works that originated the process.

In his investigation of twentieth-century popular culture, Roland Barthes has described as "mythologization" the process whereby an object or idea is taken from its original context and turned into an ideological model:

Myth has the task of giving an historical intention a natural justification, and making contingency appear eternal. . . . In passing from history to nature, myth acts economically: it abolishes the complexity of human acts, it gives them the simplicity of essences, it does away with all dialectics, with any going back beyond what is immediately visible, it organizes a world which is without contradictions because it is without depth, a world wide open and wallowing in the evident, it establishes a blissful clarity: things appear to mean something by themselves.[2]

Standing back from the particular texts analyzed in this book and examining the overall development of Russian conceptions of childhood, we can see that it was precisely a mythologizing process that, in the Russian cultural mind, transformed the pseudo-autobiographies of Tolstoy and Aksakov from idiosyncratic works of fiction into iconic representations of childhood in general.

As is usual in such cases, the actual process of mythologization went on primarily outside of the high-cultural system that had produced the idea in the first place. Generations of Russian gentry children grew up reading Tolstoy and Aksakov, and later in life, when they recalled their own childhoods, they failed or chose not to differentiate between personal and literary reminiscences. Of course, the fact that *Childhood* and *Childhood Years* described experiences that were shared by many gentry children made identification fairly easy. But Russian gentry readers did more than simply note similarities between their own childhoods and that of Nikolai Irten'ev or Sergei Bagrov. They also accepted Tolstoy and Aksakov's interpretation of childhood as a golden age. The pseudo-autobiographies of Tolstoy and Aksakov became models not for living (since childhood could not, obviously, be relived) but for recalling and interpreting the past.[3]

This mythologizing process was by no means ideologically neutral. In the course of 60 years—from the late 1850's to the Revolution—members of the Russian gentry class used the works of Tolstoy and Aksakov to help legitimate their social and political preeminence, particularly as their way of life came under increasingly overt attack and as other groups challenged them for social, political, and cultural power.[4] Their own personal past—childhood—became inseparably intertwined with the past of their class, and the only way to recapture the latter was to remember a mythologized version of the former. A "proper" childhood provided the foundation for a good and productive life. Implicitly, at least, those who had grown up without such a childhood were incapable of leading such a life. After the Revolution, the situation changed. For many émigrés, memories became the only real tie to a world that had somehow slipped through their fingers. Childhood became a synecdoche for an entire way of life.

It will be noticed that the other sociocultural myths mentioned above always came in pairs; that is, every myth inevitably spawned its counter-myth. At first glance, childhood seems to form an exception. Of course, the gentry childhood myth did not go entirely unchallenged. There were attempts to discredit it both by discontented members of the gentry class itself and by members of other classes (most notably the non-noble intelligentsia). Nevertheless, no full-fledged counter-myth of childhood arose in Russia until the early twentieth century. Does this mean, therefore, that the nineteenth-century myth of childhood should be viewed as an exception to the generally bipolar system of sociocultural myth-making in Russia?[5]

I think not, but at this point I can only propose a hypothesis to account for this seeming anomaly. As I pointed out earlier, the Russian myth of childhood was connected to a much older tradition—the myth of the golden age. Descriptions of a lost golden age, of course, form a constant cultural/mythological pattern, from ancient Greece through the Renaissance and into the modern world. The Russian version of the golden-age myth is unusual only in that it places the golden age practically in historical time, as opposed to the "sometime" more typical of mythic chronology. I would suggest that, throughout the nineteenth century, instead of opposing the gentry model of childhood with a directly competing one (as Gorky was to do in the early twentieth century), the non-noble intelligentsia countered with a competing myth of the golden age. The ideological battle was, therefore, not between happy and unhappy childhood, but rather between a view that placed the golden age in the immediate past and one that set it in the immediate future.

Characteristically, the opposing myth of the golden age was also drawn from a literary text: Chernyshevsky's *What Is to Be Done?*

Like *Childhood* and *Childhood Years*, *What Is to Be Done?* was received by many Russians not as a work to be considered by the
canons of literary interpretation, but instead as a social and political program. Yet it was difficult to perceive all of *What Is to Be
Done?* as a blueprint for action. Whole sections of the novel—the
fourth dream of Vera Pavlovna is the most obvious example—are
obviously utopian projects for the creation of a future golden age.
But just as the gentry class ignored the contradictions of the past in
their mythologization of childhood, so the non-noble intelligentsia overlooked the utopian elements of Chernyshevsky's novel
in their mythologization of the future.[6]

Thus, *Childhood* and *Childhood Years* on the one hand, and *What
Is to Be Done?* on the other, provided Russia with two immensely
powerful—and mutually exclusive—cultural myths. Between the
1860's and the Revolution in 1917, myths derived from these
works became the ideological rallying points for Russia's "conser-
vatives" and "progressives." Indeed, it would not be an exaggeration to say that, to a great extent, these myths defined the poles of
cultural and social debate in Russia in this period. What both ideological positions have in common, of course, is that they derive
their vision of the golden age from a mythologized interpretation
of specific works of literature.

It has long been recognized that literature played (and continues
to play) a much more important social role in Russia than in any
Western country. Clearly, one of the primary reasons for this is the
peculiarly symbiotic relation between works of literature and ideological points of view. Indeed, one might say that in Russia literature has been a primary mechanism by which the inchoate strivings of social groups are transformed into full-blown ideological
positions. Often to the consternation of Western scholars, Russian
writers and readers refuse to see the realm of art as separated from
the real world. Readers constantly derive images of the self and
ideologically motivated programs of action from what would, in
other cultures, seem to be works of purely cultural significance. In
their turn, far from being outraged by this "improper" borrowing
of cultural material, Russian writers use social myths for the fur-

ther development of the literary system. The myths of childhood discussed in this book represent one instance of a much broader sociocultural phenomenon.

I believe that the best way to close this study is with a quote from a childhood description written not quite 100 years after the appearance of the pseudo-autobiographies of Tolstoy and Aksakov—a quote that illustrates, more concisely than any analysis could, the complex interaction of personal memories, literary models, and myth characteristic of the Russian gentry conception of childhood: [7]

Both then and now, I imagined all of my father's favorite places as scenes from the childhood years of Bagrov's grandson, familiar to me in every detail. Everyone creates his own paradise, and mine was created in total conformity with the pages of Aksakov. . . . I read *A Family Chronicle* so intensely that I could not always say whether something had happened to me or to that boy born in the age of Catherine the Great.

Reference Matter

Notes

Introduction

1. Indeed, a number of studies indicate that a "modern" conception of childhood had been developing in Russia since the time of Peter the Great. For a discussion of Russian conceptions of childhood in the eighteenth century, see Okenfuss. For a more general discussion of eighteenth-century gentry childhood, see chap. 4 of Raeff. Finally, for a study of the literature written specifically for children in the period before the appearance of Tolstoy's *Childhood*, see Pokrovskaia and Chekhov. In addition, there were two literary works that could be considered Tolstoy's predecessors in Russian: Karamzin's unfinished story, "A Knight of Our Time," and Goncharov's fragment, "Oblomov's Dream."

2. That is, what was lacking was a modern, secular conception of childhood in Russia. There had been an accepted pattern for a saint's childhood throughout the Middle Ages. It included such standard topoi as humility, precocious wisdom, and piety. Clearly, however, although the saintly childhood still appeared from time to time in works of literature (the early life of Alesha Karamazov, for example), it became an increasingly inappropriate model for general consumption in the aggressively secular nineteenth century.

3. See Ariès, particularly chap. 2, "La découverte de l'enfance."

4. The existence of such a substantial time lag points to a very interesting fact about Russian cultural development. Although it is generally felt that Russia had "caught up" with Europe by the 1830's, the process of catching up was, in fact, by no means uniform. There were large areas of European development that were assimilated far later or not at all in Russia.

5. Guillen uses the term "pseudo-autobiography" in *Literature as a System* (p. 81). However, he uses the term to include any fictional narrative that looks like an autobiography, regardless of whether or not it is based on autobiographical material. I will try to show that, at least in the Russian context, one of the crucial identifying characteristics of the genre was the presence of a real (or at least suspected) autobiographical connection. The term "pseudo-autobiography" will be discussed in more depth in Chapter 1.

6. The most influential reader of this type was Dostoevsky. In *Diary of a Writer*, he characterizes Irten'ev as "a rather unusual boy, but, at the same time, one who belongs to precisely that kind of upper-middle gentry-class family, whose poet and historian, completely and exclusively, was Lev Tolstoy" (Dostoevsky, 25: 32).

Chapter 1

1. Eikhenbaum shows that vague literary strivings of this kind were typical of young men of Tolstoy's age and position: "Why did literary projects appear in Tolstoy's programs for 1851? At that time, literature had become a typical occupation for a man of the world" (*Lev Tolstoy*, p. 30).

2. Eikhenbaum was among the first to point out the importance of Tolstoy's journal for his development as a writer. See *Lev Tolstoy*, pp. 33—37.

3. For a more complete account of the development of *Childhood*, see M. A. Tsiavlovsky, "Komentarii k 'Detstvu,'" Tolstoy, *Polnoe sobranie sochinenii*, vol. 1, pp. 303—28.

4. Describing this first version, Tsiavlovsky says: "The story of a family of the Tolstoys' close friends, the Islavins, forms the basis of the narrative" (ibid., p. 305). The final version is not, of course, completely autobiographical either, but it is more autobiographical than this initial version. For a more comprehensive discussion of the autobiographicalization of *Childhood*, see pp. 51—53 in this volume.

5. Tolstoy, *Polnoe sobranie sochinenii*, 1: 103. All further citations from the writings of Tolstoy will be made in the text by reference to volume and page number from this edition.

6. In this respect the trilogy differs from the diaries and "A History of Yesterday," even as it grows out of them. In the diaries Tolstoy speaks to himself. He is the implied reader of his own text, as it were. In the latter work the narrator speaks about himself directly to the

reader. There is no interaction between author and narrator and (because almost no time has elapsed between narrated event and its narration) no possibility for interaction between the narrator and his past incarnation.

7. Still, it is clear that *Childhood* has a didactic component and that Tolstoy the moralist was already present in his first published work. He says as much in a diary entry for November 30, 1852: "Since it is a novel about an intelligent, sensitive man who has lost his way, it will be instructive" (46: 151).

8. Tolstoy evidently retained a sentimental attachment to childhood and to his first work to the very end of his life. In 1910 he told V. Bulgakov: "When I was writing *Childhood*, it seemed to me that prior to me no one had ever felt or expressed all the poetry and wonder of childhood" (quoted in Ostrovsky, p. 158).

9. Lejeune, p. 14.

10. Gunn provides an excellent definition of the bond that grows up between reader and writer of an autobiographical text: "The reader experiences the autobiographical text as an occasion of discovery: of seeing in the text the heretofore unexpressed or unrecognized depth of the reader's self—not as a mirror image, nor even as a particular manifestation of some shared idea of selfhood, but as an instance of interpretive ability that *risks* display. . . . In a word, the reader discovers the *possibility* of selfhood through interpretation" (p. 19).

11. Morson, *Boundaries*, p. 48.

12. Ibid., p. 50.

13. The term "autobiographical novel" is Pascal's; it is used throughout his article, "The Autobiographical Novel." Lejeune uses the phrase "roman autobiographique" in *Le pacte autobiographique* (see p. 25). The term "poetic autobiography" is used in Spengemann, *The Forms of Autobiography*. The term "memoir novel" belongs to Romberg, as used in his *Studies in the Narrative Technique*.

14. Spengemann goes to the other extreme. In using the term "poetic autobiography," he tries (unsuccessfully, in my opinion) to subsume all autobiographically based writing (whether in third or first person, whether or not the narrator is identified with the author) into the category of autobiography. This produces a situation in which almost every work of the nineteenth and twentieth centuries can be considered an autobiography.

15. Pascal, "The Autobiographical Novel," p. 147.

16. In *When the Grass Was Taller*, Coe provides an excellent interpretation of why writers often prefer to write their childhood accounts in fictional forms: "To write the story of *another* child—and more especially, to write in the third person—does not commit the writer to the detailed and factual exactitude demanded if he should choose to write about himself directly. The 'autobiographical novel of childhood' . . . permits adjustments to that precarious balance between literal and symbolic truth that is so difficult to maintain in the autobiography pure and simple" (p. 86). In Russia, the form that was used to write about "another child" was not the third-person novel, but rather the first-person pseudo-autobiography.

17. For example, Tolstoy might well have read an unsigned article in *The Contemporary* that discussed the theory of autobiography and analyzed a number of Russian and European examples. *Sovremennik*, 1850, vol. 24: 56–61.

18. Quoted in Makashin, 1: 50.

19. In fact, however, at least in Russia the genre worked best when the author was sufficiently well known for readers to notice the autobiographical connections between author and narrator almost immediately.

20. Pascal, *Design and Truth*, p. 71.

21. Bakhtin uses the term "chronotope" in his essay "Formy vremeni i khronotopa v romane." As is usually the case with Bakhtin, he never gives a strict definition of the term. Instead, in the course of the article, he defines it through examples ranging from classical literature through Rabelais. See Bakhtin, pp. 121–290.

22. The presence and power of what I call the "author's voice" in the work of Tolstoy is discussed extensively in Morson, *Hidden in Plain View*, pp. 9–36. Morson calls this phenomenon Tolstoy's "absolute language."

23. In this respect the pseudo-autobiography can be profitably analyzed in terms that Genette has developed for discussing Marcel Proust. Describing the unity of Proust's magnum opus, Genette says: "There is something of the collage or, better, of the patchwork in *Remembrance*, and its unity as a narrative is more . . . a unity after the fact, all the more insistent because it is late in coming and laboriously constructed of materials taken from all places and epochs" (p. 174). This unity "after the fact," produced by the relationship of all three

voices in the text, is precisely the kind of unity that the reader of the pseudo-autobiography perceives.

24. In criticism of the trilogy it is customary to note only two voice positions in the text (those of the narrator and of the child) and to observe their interaction. See, for example, Christian, pp. 34–36; Bilinkis, pp. 11–15; and Dieckmann, pp. 31–45 (of these three, Dieckmann's analysis is the best). This type of analysis lumps what I call the author's voice together with the narrator's, despite differences in style and content. On the other hand, one can go to the opposite extreme and attempt to identify every different voice position in the text, without worrying about whether the differences are meaningful. This is what Zweers does in his book, *Grown-up Narrator and Childlike Hero*. In particular, see his discussion of "linguistic and structural devices," pp. 72–112.

25. Aksakov, *Detskie gody Bagrova vnuka*, in *Sobranie sochinenii v piati tomakh*, 1: 274. This is as complete an edition of Aksakov as there is. Whenever possible, further citations from his works will be made in the main text by reference to the volume and page number from this edition.

26. Mandel'shtam, vol. 2, p. 55.

27. Romberg, pp. 33–36. Romberg defines the epic situation as "the narrator's situation when he is telling his story." "To the extent that it is markedly present . . . it supplies the answer to important questions about epic time and why the novel is narrated, and it also provides effective support for that illusion of reality which it may be the purpose of the novel to evoke."

28. Bunin, *Sobranie sochinenii*, 6: 83. All further citations from the works of Bunin will be made in the text by reference to the volume and page number from this edition.

29. Belyi, *Kotik Letaev*, p. 9. Further citations from *Kotik Letaev* will be indicated in the text by reference to the page numbers from this edition.

30. In twentieth-century pseudo-autobiographies (especially in *Kotik Letaev* and *The Noise of Time*), the child's voice becomes more autonomous. It will frequently begin to speak without the benefit of a narrative frame. The reader must decide when the child's perspective begins and ends. This potential ambiguity is one of the things that makes texts like those by Mandel'shtam and Belyi so complicated.

31. Hamburger, pp. 64–81.

32. "We are equipped to explain first-person narration as a part of the general category 'narration' rather than of discourse, because it is never the I alone, but the *I-you* pair that marks discourse" (Banfield, p. 145).

33. Hamburger, p. 81.

34. There are many reasons why a child's perspective was preferred for the narrator's past incarnation. The first is that it allowed for a maximum difference between the time of narration and the time of narrated events. This created a situation in which memory, the ultimate hero of any autobiographically oriented work, could be given almost free play. The second is clearly the feeling that children are more perceptive than adults. The English poet Humbert Wolfe states this almost universally accepted idea succinctly at the beginning of his autobiography: "What is vivid in a child's mind? All its apprehensions of objects are obviously fresher and more intimate than those of the adult. Sight is clearer, sound sharper, touch more sensitive, taste and smell more immediate" (p. 1). The third reason for choosing a child's perspective had to do with the special status of the child in the Russian gentry family. I discuss this question in Chapter 3.

35. Note how quickly the narrative switches from second to first to third person and from past to present tense. Transitions of this kind are more common in Russian than in English, but this quantity of shifts in a couple of long sentences is unusual even in Russian.

36. Not all pseudo-autobiographies are nostalgic. If a pseudo-autobiography is not nostalgic, the recreation of past scenes in the voice of the past incarnation can have the force of a nightmare. Dostoevsky uses this device frequently in *Notes from the House of the Dead*: "Our prison stood at the very edge of the fortress, right by the fortress wall. It would happen that you would look through a crack in the fence out onto the wide world: perhaps you'd see something there?— and all you'd see was the edge of the sky and the high earth wall, overgrown with weeds, and, day and night, the guards would walk back and forth along that wall. And you'd think that the years will pass and you'll come back to look in the exact same way" (4: 9).

37. Sentences of this type can also be tied to recollections of nature or landscape, even in those pseudo-autobiographical novels that are not primarily nostalgic in tone. "It often happened—the sun would

set, fiery rivers would pour into the heavens and they would burn, and golden-red ash would fall to the velvet green of the garden, then everything around would get palpably darker, broaden, and swell, flooded with the warm twilight" (Gorky, 15: 179). Further citations from the works of Gorky will be indicated in the text by reference to volume and page numbers from this edition. This type of sentence was also used by writers of autobiography in much the same way. The following example is taken from the memoirs of A. V. Bolotov: "In the morning, it would happen, you'd run into grandmother's boudoir" (p. 14).

38. Of course, not all pseudo-autobiographies use the iterative with the same degree of frequency. In fact, a number of them use it quite sparingly. Still, it appears in all of them and is potentially present in any nostalgic narrative situation. Not surprisingly, Genette finds the iterative to be the dominant mode of narration in the work of Proust: "The first three large sections of *Remembrance . . .* can without exaggeration be considered essentially iterative" (p. 149). His general definition of the mode and its uses (pp. 145–53) is excellent. However, the importance of the iterative in the Russian pseudo-autobiography does call into question Genette's contention that Proust's use of the technique is qualitatively different from that of his predecessors.

39. Tolstoy, 46: 150–51. By this I think he meant that the message of *The Four Epochs of Development* was supposed to come through the inner logic of the story without the help of a "commentator." This was not to be the case with the proposed novel about a landowner, in which Tolstoy had definite and specific points he wanted to get across.

40. A diary entry for March 20, 1852, indicates just how close the voice I call the author's in the trilogy could be to Tolstoy's own: "Vanity is an incomprehensible passion . . . it is a kind of moral disease like leprosy—it does not just destroy one part, but maims the whole—little by little, unnoticed, it sneaks in and then it develops throughout the organism" (46: 94).

41. See p. 11 above.

42. Leont'ev, p. 228.

43. Bruss, p. 10.

44. Eikhenbaum is an example of a critic who sees outside influences to have been crucial: "In the period of *Childhood* Tolstoy is a

follower—and a rather timid follower" (*Lev Tolstoy*, p. 86). On the other hand, Chuprina goes so far as to practically dismiss them altogether. See Chuprina, especially chap. 7, pp. 116–48.

45. Tolstoy prepared this list in 1891 in response to a query from a publisher, M. M. Lederle. It can be found in Tolstoy, 66: 67.

46. For a fuller discussion of Tolstoy's debt to Rousseau, see Markovitch.

47. Constant, p. 35.

48. Letter of Sismondi to Madame d'Albany, October 14, 1816. Quoted in the introduction to Constant's *Adolphe*.

49. For a more detailed discussion of the connections between *Childhood* and *David Copperfield*, see Christian, pp. 27–30.

50. Nostalgia is a driving force in the Russian pseudo-autobiography. It is generally less important in European versions, which, as a rule, grow from the confessional model. That is, European pseudo-autobiographies and autobiographies look back at the past either having overcome it or ruing it. This fact was noted (at least in relation to the English tradition) by Greenwood: "Although it is not, strictly speaking, autobiographical, *Childhood* has that nostalgia without sentimentality which is peculiarly characteristic of Russian aristocratic memoirs such as those of Aksakov and Herzen. The oppression and rancour which mar so many English middle- and upper-class memoirs are conspicuously absent" (p. 25).

For Tolstoy and his followers in Russia, the remembrance of things past is a pleasant activity in and of itself. Tolstoy made this characteristic comment on the subject in a diary entry for March 26, 1852: "I just reread my old diary for July, 1851. . . . In the diary I found many pleasant memories—pleasant just because they are memories" (46: 92).

51. Eikhenbaum, *Molodoi Tolstoy*, pp. 71–72.

52. Eikhenbaum, *Lev Tolstoy*, p. 80, and *Molodoi Tolstoy*, pp. 65–66.

53. The same holds true for various other autobiographies and first-person narratives that appeared in the journals at about this time. These include the "Notes of Tal'ma: Written by Himself" and Vonliarliarsky's "Vospominaniia o Zakhare Ivanyche." The former is the autobiography of a well-known French actor that does not deal with childhood, and the latter is simply a first-person narrative describing the travels of an adult Russian through Europe.

54. Bolotov does describe the years when he was a child, but he cannot be said to discuss childhood. He never tries to recreate the child's perception of the world. As a result, he treats his own memories no differently from his father's disappointments and his mother's illnesses, often combining descriptions of all three in a single paragraph.

55. A comparison of "Iul'iana Terent'evna" and *Childhood* illustrates the gulf that separates a pastiche composed of bits and pieces of literary material that were "in the air" from an original work that uses its predecessors as a point of departure. Kulish's story has neither a ring of autobiographical truth to it nor anything to say about childhood as such. Good contemporary readers, like I. S. Turgenev, immediately noted the difference between the competent conventionality of Kulish and the first-class literary talent of Tolstoy. The problem with an early formalist reading like Eikhenbaum's is that it fails to differentiate between the presence of source material and the way it is used in a specific text.

56. As always, there are a number of possible exceptions to be cited. In "Forgotten Beginnings," Zirin demonstrates the existence of a group of "girlhoods" that were written prior to the appearance of the pseudo-autobiographies of Tolstoy and Aksakov. These include the first section of Nadezhda Durova's *Kavalerist-devitsa* (1836), Avdot'ia Panaeva's *Semeistvo Tal'nikovykh* (1848), and Nadezhda Sokhanskaia's *Avtobiografia* (1848). To this list could be added Evgeniia Tur's first-person novel, *Plemianitsa* (1851). Of these works only *Kavalerist-devitsa* and *Plemianitsa* were published before 1852. Durova's description of childhood is excellent, although not psychologically deep. While Tur's novel, which was heavily influenced by *David Copperfield*, does describe the narrator's childhood extensively, this childhood cannot in any way be construed as Russian. The narrator is the daughter of a German and is brought up by a French stepmother and an English stepfather. With qualifications, then, one can agree with Gusev when he says: "If one does not count the wonderful pages devoted to Oblomov's childhood in Goncharov's novel, then one can say that Tolstoy's novella was the first attempt in Russian literature to express the inner life of a child artistically" (1954, p. 398).

57. Tolstoy's concept of the golden age is rather different from the traditional one. In the idylls of earlier generations there were no moments of unhappiness: nothing interrupted the bliss of those who

dwelt in the ideal land. Tolstoy was too much a realist to write an idyll of this sort. He recognized that tragedy and unhappiness are potentially present at any time of life. However, he seems to have felt that moments of tragedy are essentially irrelevant to childhood's ultimate happiness, because the child's innate purity allows him to soar above the details of everyday life.

58. One could claim that the sentence, "How much those sounds say to my heart!" is in the narrator's voice. Although this interpretation is possible, it is not obligatory, since there is no information present in it that the child could not have known, no emotion that he could not have felt.

59. As usual, Eikhenbaum seems to have been the first to make this discovery: "The lack of a plot and his interest in details caused the movement of the novella to become organized not in terms of years or even of days, but of hours. . . . In fact, the composition of *Childhood* is organized around the juxtaposition of separate scenes that are linked by lyric commentary and 'generalizations'" (*Lev Tolstoy*, p. 87).

60. There is, of course, one important event in *Childhood* (the death of Nikolai's mother), but even this moment of action is treated in a peculiarly unnovelistic fashion. At one moment she is alive, bidding farewell to her husband and children, at the next they receive a letter informing them she is ill, and, finally, they arive home just before she dies. The death itself takes place offstage and is included not out of any narrative necessity (there is no need for a death to move the plot forward) but as a point around which a number of set scenes can be arranged, and as a convenient end point for the book.

61. One could also compare the structure of *Childhood* to that of a lyric poem rather than to that of a novel. As in a poem, the connections between sections are linked more to the mood of the text than to the inexorable forward motion of a plot line.

62. Recall also the passage I discuss earlier in which the child thinks of Sonechka in terms of "sweet dreams and memories."

63. The trilogy is not the only example in Tolstoy's oeuvre of a work that became more autobiographical as it was being written. The most famous case is, of course, *Anna Karenina*. The autobiographically based Levin does not even appear in the early drafts. In the course of writing he became more and more central until, in the final version, he is as important as Anna herself.

64. Ginzburg, p. 299.

65. Goldenveizer, p. 175.

66. Indeed, as Markovitch has noted, it runs through Tolstoy's entire oeuvre: "Like Rousseau, Tolstoy believes in the possibility of a 'return to nature,' and in the happy consequences for humankind that would result from it. In order to be good and happy, a person must quit society and its prejudices, must draw closer to the solitude of the fields, the natural life, must become a wild man in the manner of Rousseau" (p. 208).

67. According to Hubbs, this connection is not unique to Russian autobiography, but rather reflects an enduring mythological pattern in Russian culture: "The desire for a woman savior is expressed in a constant adulation of the ethical strengths of the good woman and the refusal to consider the virtues of male heroism" (pp. 230–31). Heldt notes some of these same tendencies in Russian fiction: "The Russian heroine is generally taken as a marvelous given of nature, a being in whom not only her own and her family's future, but the future hope of Russia resides" (p. 12). For my discussion of how such mother myths were translated into gentry autobiographies, see Chapter 3, pp. 96–99.

68. Bakhtin, p. 259.

69. To some extent, of course, Tolstoy was aware of his influence, both in the realm of fiction and in that of autobiography. A. P. Beliaev, for example, sent his (Tolstoy-influenced) memoirs to the master for comments, and notes that Tolstoy encouraged him to publish them. Tolstoy also read the memoirs of A. K. Chertkova. In his diary for 1909, he characterized the work (which, among other Tolstoyan moments, begins with an epigraph from *Childhood*) as "very good."

70. Dostoevsky, 25: 32.

Chapter 2

1. It is almost certain that he was familiar with the issue of *The Contemporary* in which it appeared. In a diary note for 1854, Aksakov's daughter, Vera, speaks of the family sitting together and rereading the "fat" journals. One work she specifically mentions is Kulish's "The Story of Iul'iana Terent'evna," which appeared in the issue of *The Contemporary* prior to that in which *Childhood* appeared. See Aksakova, p. 22.

2. In a letter to Turgenev dated December 20, 1857, Aksakov

says: "Tolstoy and I see each other frequently and friendlily. I have come to love him deeply" (quoted in *Russkoe obozrenie*, 1894, no. 12: 595).

3. Mashinsky, p. 391.

4. Tolstoy, 47: 112. In a letter to V. P. Botkin, also from January 1857, Tolstoy again expressed his admiration for Aksakov's work: "I heard two noteworthy literary works: Childhood Reminiscences of S. T. Aksakov, and Ostrovsky's A Profitable Situation. All of the former seemed to me to be better than the best parts of A Family Chronicle" (60: 156).

5. Panaev, p. 171.

6. Aksakov, *Sobranie sochinenii* (Moscow, 1895), 2: iv–v.

7. Such an unconscious projection would be in keeping with Bagrov's self-description in *Childhood Years*. At one point he describes how he read the stories of *Arabian Nights* and then retold them to his sister and nanny. But in his retellings he added, without consciously realizing what he was doing, many details that were not in the original. When he then read the actual stories he was shocked: "I myself was amazed not to find things in the book that, it seemed to me, I had read in it and that had become completely fixed in my head" (1: 433). His fascination with the fairy tale can also be seen in his inclusion of the story "The Scarlet Flower" in *Childhood Years*.

8. Some characteristics of Bagrov's narration (particularly the high melodrama of the section entitled "Maksim Maksimovich Kurolesov," and the rise, fall, and rise of Sof'ia Nikolaevna) could also be understood in reference to the conventions of the Gothic novel and sentimentalism. It should not be forgotten that Aksakov belonged to a generation that had grown up reading such novels, and it is not surprising that their influence should appear in his work. For more on the connection between the Kurolesov chapter of *A Family Chronicle* and the Gothic novel, see Durkin, pp. 121–32. Durkin also notes some fairy-tale elements in *A Family Chronicle* but does not analyze them fully (see Durkin, pp. 135–37).

9. At one point his strength is actually called "bogatyrskaia" (1: 121).

10. Anonymous, "Khudozhestvennye storony 'Semeinoi khroniki,'" *Russkaia beseda*, 1856. Reprinted in Pokrovsky, p. 170.

11. Of course, the search for the typical was characteristic of the realist novel in Europe as well. However, the tendency to use literary

types in order to comment on the social scene was particularly strong in Russian criticism. Some of the most well known examples of readings in which literary characters are seen as typical of Russian society are N. A. Dobroliubov's articles "What Is Oblomovitis?" and "The Country Life of a Landlord in the Old Days, as Reflected in *The Childhood Years of Bagrov's Grandson."* In *Chernyshevsky and the Age of Realism*, Paperno shows how the heroes of Chernyshevsky's *What Is to Be Done?* became models for the behavior of a whole generation of young Russians.

12. Tolycheva, p. 665.

13. Apropos of the differences between *A Family Chronicle* and *Memoirs*, it should be mentioned that Aksakov was quite annoyed that critics insisted on connecting the two. In a letter to Turgenev on February 18, 1856, Aksakov complained: "I would merely wish that some kind person would tell Mr. Critic that it is the height of indelicacy to aver in print that the personages who appear in the 'Chronicle' are the same as those in my 'Memoirs.' Does not my statement that the 'Chronicle' has nothing in common with the 'Memoirs' deserve the respect of those who write about my book? . . . I won't even mention the fact that silly encomiums place me in a kind of guilty position, and that they seem to find me sympathetic to the patriarchal lifestyle of the Bashkirs" ("Pis'ma S.T.," no. 12: 580). In this complaint Aksakov expresses a lack of desire to have his family personally connected to the exploits of previous generations, and, equally important, he asserts that the statements of his narrator do not necessarily agree with his own.

14. Aksakov, "Pis'ma S.T.," no. 12: 590.

15. Aksakov, "Pis'ma k M. A. Maksimovichu," p. 840.

16. For example, when Bagrov speaks of a story he read in the magazine *Detskoe chtenie*, the author kindly tells the reader the issue number should he care to look it up for himself (1: 323).

17. Thus, in a discussion of fishing, Aksakov supplies definitions for a couple of terms describing the parts of a net (1: 363).

18. Sometimes the narrator can show both past and future reactions to the natural world almost simultaneously. Describing summer at Sergeevka, the narrator explains: "At that time I appreciated nature more strongly than during the trip to Bagrovo, but not nearly as strongly as I was to appreciate it a few years later" (1: 353).

19. It should be noted that narrative interjections are not the only

means used to make the reader notice the novelty of a situation. The child's voice can do so as well. In the following quote, a common scene (a musical performance) is viewed through the eyes of the child in a masterful example of defamiliarization before Tolstoy: "Spoon in hand, mouth gaping, and eyes bulging, I turned into a statue and looked at that pack of people, that is at the orchestra,—they were all moving their hands nimbly back and forth and blowing with their mouths and thence flew wonderful, delightful, magical sounds, at one moment dying down and at the next turning into the roar of a storm or even into thunderclaps" (1: 510).

20. In a letter to Turgenev: "There's no faking under the guise of a child here and no moralizing" ("Pis'ma S.T.," no. 12: 590–91).

21. Mashinsky, p. 427.

22. In the course of the novel, there are a number of scenes in which Bagrov speaks admiringly of the ability and talent of serf laborers. Indeed, Bagrov romanticizes and idealizes field labor. He even tries his hand at it once and is embarrassed to discover that he is not able to do the work as well as the serfs. An attraction to peasant work was typical for many of the more conservative gentry (especially those with patriarchal or slavophile leanings), who always preferred the rural peasantry to the urban *raznochintsy*: one has only to recall the mowing scene in *Anna Karenina,* Tolstoy's own habit of working with his peasants, and Bunin's description of field work in *The Life of Arsen'ev* to see just how widespread the phenomenon was.

23. One has merely to remember the importance of the road in *Dead Souls*. There, however, the road is primarily an instrument by which Chichikov gets from one situation to another. Despite a number of hymns to the road, it is important for its symbolic, not its literal, value. On the other hand, the road did in fact have, in Gogol's opinion, healing abilities. In a letter to M. P. Pogodin of October 17, 1840, he said: "Having gotten to Trieste, I began to feel better. The road, my only medicine, had had its effect this time as well. I could already move about" (11: 315).

24. The child makes the same kind of uncomprehending judgments in relation to his mother's distaste for anything having to do with the work of the estate. Having seen the peasants in the fields, he tries to explain his amazement to his mother: "With my usual animation and excitement, I told my mother everything I had seen. I described the peasants' tasks with rapture, but, not for the first time, I

was distressed to see that my mother listened to me quite indifferently, and called my desire to learn peasant chores childish fantasies" (1: 428).

Coe, in "Mother Russia and the Russian Mother," uses these scenes of mutual misunderstanding in an attempt to prove that Aksakov depicts a mother "quite ruthlessly devouring her son" (p. 54). While Coe quite rightly points out that the mother/son relationship in *Childhood Years* is not without problems, he vastly overstates its negative elements. He is able to do so because he fails to see their relationship in its contemporary context. Instead, he claims: "The mother advances rapidly to a position which, to a modern psychologist, could be held to reveal a degree of emotional sadism" (p. 54). Unfortunately for Coe's argument, however, Aksakov was not versed in twentieth-century psychological jargon, and, being of sound eighteenth-century stock, he was not paralyzed by his mother's overprotectiveness. Instead, Aksakov seems to have outgrown his early neuroses (if he had them at all), and, by the time he wrote his pseudo-autobiography, he was able to see both the positive and the negative sides of his mother. Coe, by excerpting only the negative sides and by interpreting them in twentieth-century terms, gives a distorted picture of the mother/son relationship in *Childhood Years*. This is connected to his generally incorrect views on the subject of mother/son relationships in nineteenth-century Russian autobiography.

25. He could do so in *Memoirs* because he was surer of his more recent memories and had clearly come to terms with them. His earliest memories were far less clear and, perhaps in some ways, more painful.

26. Letter to M. A. Maksimovich on April 10, 1856 ("Pis'ma k M. A. Maksimovichu," p. 838).

27. In another letter to Maksimovich, on May 3, 1857, Aksakov wrote: "I think I wrote you about my work. It's supposed to be (I hope it will be) an artistic representation of my childhood years, beginning from the third and going to the ninth year of my life" ("Pis'ma k M. A. Maksimovichu," p. 840).

Chapter 3

1. Autobiographies written by members of the Russian gentry class did, of course, exist well before the 1850's. But such famous works as E. R. Dashkova's *Memoirs*, A. T. Bolotov's *Notes*, or I. I.

Dmitriev's *View of My Life* contained only brief sketches of early memories and show no indication of an appreciation for the specificity of childhood experience. After the appearance of Tolstoy's and Aksakov's pseudo-autobiographies, however, the childhood became a standard feature of such works; indeed, many gentry autobiographies were reduced simply to descriptions of childhood, leaving out completely the account of adult life that had formerly been their raison d'être.

2. I have drawn the gentry autobiographies used in this study from a range of sources. In order to get a preliminary list of gentry autobiographies, I consulted P. A. Zaionchkovsky's magisterial *Istoriia dorevoliutsionnoi Rossii v dnevnikakh i vospominaniiakh*. I was able to consult approximately 70 percent of the works he cites. However, I discovered that Zaionchkovsky's bibliography, massive as it is, is incomplete, and to supplement it I resorted to a search of the shelf lists of the New York Public Library Slavonic Division and Widener Library. In addition, Zaionchkovsky does not list works published outside of Russia / the Soviet Union. For materials published by émigrés, I found Liudmila Foster's bibliography a helpful, if incomplete, source. For a complete list of my sources, see the bibliography to this volume.

3. Aside from the anomalous works discussed in Chapter 1, note 56, I have been able to find only two gentry autobiographies written before 1860 that devote a significant amount of space to the author's childhood. Both Anna Evdokimovna Labzina's *Vospominaniia* (written in 1810, first published in 1903) and Ekaterina Aleksandrovna Khvostova's *Zapiski* (written in 1836–37, published in 1869) were completely unknown when *Childhood* was published. Although both Labzina and Khvostova describe their early years, their memoirs give no indication that they felt that the places, persons, and memories of childhood were in some way privileged. Instead, childhood leads directly into later life without being considered a qualitatively different stage.

4. The mechanisms by which this transformation occurred parallel those that Emerson has described in *Boris Godunov: Transpositions of a Russian Theme*: "Masterpieces in a given genre, powerful conceptualizations of a certain sort of time and space, inevitably contain more than a given epoch can absorb. When these works are built upon in later times, different aspects of form emerge as significant and thus encourage a different response, specific 'counterventions.' A theme is

freed from one context into another, and this liberation is the first step in transposing a theme" (p. 9).

5. Given access to the manuscript versions of these autobiographies, one could conceivably answer this question. At least one could see at what stage in the process of writing the gentry myths of childhood appeared. Unfortunately, it is extremely unlikely that any manuscript material relating to these works has been preserved. Given the reality of Russian life in the twentieth century, I doubt that there are many trunks stuffed with the papers of gentry families lying around in attics in the Soviet Union.

6. It should be noted that the literary conventions I am discussing here pertain to first-person accounts of childhood. They did not necessarily hold for the portrayal of childhood in lyric poetry or third-person fictional accounts. Thus, while it was possible to speak about childhood in Russian in terms other than those used by Tolstoy and Aksakov, it was not possible to write an autobiography about one's own childhood without taking them into account.

7. I did not specifically ignore autobiographies written by members of the upper and lower ranks of the gentry class. It just happens that such works are quite rare. One suspects that members of the lower rank of the gentry did not generally write autobiographies because the men lacked the leisure time and the women were often semiliterate. I do not know why the wealthiest aristocrats rarely wrote about childhood, but, in any case, they did not.

8. In 1834 there were 16,740 such families in European Russia. They comprised 13 percent of all serfowners. In 1858, on the eve of emancipation, there were 19,930 such families making up almost 20 percent of all serfowners. See Blum, pp. 368–69. Tolstoy's family was slightly wealthier than this.

9. The former serfs were willing to work as an agricultural proletariat because they had to pay the government a sum of money (over a period of time) for the land they had been "given" when they were freed. They were called "temporarily obligated" peasants during this period. Because a peasant family's own lands were generally not large or fertile enough to produce the surplus needed to pay off their debt to the government, some members hired themselves out as laborers on the lands of their former owners. For a good English-language discussion of the extremely complex details of the emancipation, see Robinson, pp. 64–93.

10. As a rule, the gentry ran their estates rather inefficiently. After emancipation, when the free labor they had counted on disappeared, their economic position slipped. Even so, most of them clung to their old ways of life, first borrowing, then gradually selling off assets to pay their most immediate debts. Thus, although the emancipation should have marked the end of the gentry way of life, in fact, estate life, especially those of its aspects that a child would have perceived, changed little until the very end of the nineteenth century. Nevertheless, with each passing generation, writers of gentry autobiography perceived that the traditional gentry way of life was being lost. It was their instinctive feeling of loss that helped trigger the production of nostalgic autobiographies about childhood.

11. Fet, p. 39.

12. Vereshchagin, p. 96.

13. Vigel', 1: 89.

14. Anonymous, no. 8: 258.

15. For the position of children in the culture and literary culture of other European countries, see Pfeiffer, Kuhn, and Chombart de Lauwe.

16. It is interesting to note that gender does not seem to make any difference in gentry accounts of childhood. Male and female autobiographers recount the same myths and describe the same sorts of situations. This is perhaps a function of the fact that up until approximately the age of ten, boys and girls seem to have been treated more or less equally. After this time their paths diverge radically, and gender differences begin to play a significant role.

17. V. N. Davydov, p. 77. Compare this passage to the ones cited in my analysis of chap. 15 of *Childhood* (1: 63–66).

18. Semenov-Tian-Shansky, p. 103.

19. Lelong, 1913, bk. 2, no. 7: p. 103.

20. B—n, no. 5/6: 159.

21. S. V. Mengden, no. 5: 327.

22. Kornilova, p. 8.

23. Dostoevsky, 3: 178. One can also hear echoes of the gentry myths of childhood in a speech by Madame Ranevskaia in "The Cherry Orchard": "Oh my childhood, my purity! I slept in this nursery, and I looked out at the orchard from here. Every morning happiness woke up along with me" (Chekhov, 9: 620).

24. Trubetskoy, p. 6.

25. Levitov, p. 162.

26. Pomialovsky, p. 61.

27. The literary and social influence of Chernyshevsky's *What Is to Be Done?* shows that nongentry behavioral models could successfully enter the Russian cultural consciousness if they were properly packaged. See Paperno.

28. That the decision to describe childhood in negative terms was part of a specific ideological stance can be seen in the case of at least one famous "nihilist," the mathematician S. V. Kovalevskaia. Kovalevskaia's biographer has this to say on her subject's supposedly unhappy childhood: "When Kovalevskaia set down her recollections of the period of Miss Smith's domination in *Memories of Childhood*, she tended to emphasize the unhappy aspects of her situation. . . . However, the adult Kovalevskaia sometimes indulged in a tendency toward self-dramatization, and her *Memories of Childhood* are highly colored by that trait. From the observations of other people, and even from many of Sofia's own comments, one gets the impression that her childhood at Palibino was not so gloomy as she often liked to portray it. . . . Those who knew Kovalevskaia during this period describe her as lively, gay, impulsively affectionate, with a happy, ringing laugh" (Koblitz, pp. 16–17). I, of course, would interpret Kovalevskaia's tendency to remember the negative aspects of her childhood not in terms of her tendency to "self-dramatization," but rather as an expression of her desire to repudiate her gentry past and the myths associated with it.

29. The one area in which these dissident accounts of childhood have had a strong influence is in twentieth-century historical scholarship. Because Soviet historians have generally desired to prove that life before the Revolution was unpleasant, they have republished and annotated the autobiographies of such radical members of the gentry class as A. I. Herzen, S. V. Kovalevskaia, V. I. Taneev, E. N. Vodovozova, T. P. Passek, and, of course, Prince Kropotkin. Nor is it a coincidence that gentry autobiographies that describe a happy pre-Revolution childhood have never been republished. Because negative or ambivalent accounts have been more readily available, historians have used them to create a picture of Russian gentry childhood. This, for example, is just what Manning does in *The Crisis of the Old Order in Russia* (see pp. 39–42). In order to prove that childhood in nineteenth-century Russia was perceived as an unhappy experience, she has

chosen, wittingly or not, to analyze only the works of this small group of disaffected aristocrats. Needless to say, their perceptions of childhood were no more typical of the Russian gentry as a whole than were the rest of their lives; no one would claim that Herzen or Kropotkin were typical members of the gentry class.

The evidence I have collected also seems to contradict Dunn, who asserts: "Childhood in Russia in the period from 1760 to 1860 was an ordeal, a precarious existence fraught with obstacles to both physical and psychological development" (p. 385). In fact, Dunn is dealing with evidence drawn from a wide variety of sources and covering childhoods on all levels of society. The fact that many members of the gentry class saw childhood as a golden age does not mean that childhood was happy for most Russians. The myth of the happy childhood is a literary/autobiographical one, whose characteristics are not necessarily directly related to actual conditions. On the other hand, when Dunn talks specifically about gentry childhoods and family life in his article, it is clear that he has made the same basic mistake as Manning. It would take too much space here to show what I find incorrect in Dunn's work, but anyone who knows his argument will understand my objections to it after they have read this chapter.

30. Passek, 1: 108.

31. The letter from Panteleev to Chernyshevsky is quoted in Saltykov-Shchedrin, 17: 540.

32. Ibid., p. 73.

33. Ibid., p. 80.

34. In "Mother Russia and the Russian Mother," Coe makes the startling assertion that the typical mother figure for Russian culture is "singularly unsatisfactory, perverse and treacherous" (p. 53). There are a number of reasons why Coe is wrong, but I will only mention four of them here: (1) he fails to distinguish between mother figures typical for fiction and for autobiography; (2) he fails to notice a historical progression in the portrayal of mothers; (3) he fails to appreciate the relation between the social class of a Russian writer and his/her portrayal of the mother figure; and (4) instead of reading what autobiographers actually say about their mothers, he interprets the child/mother relationship in terms of late-twentieth-century assumptions about proper "parenting" techniques.

Error (1) allows Coe to substitute literary traditions for autobiographical ones. With one exception, all the texts he cites are fictional. Because he does not read Russian autobiographies (especially those from the nineteenth century), he fails to realize that the autobiographical tradition is very different from the fictional one and that, therefore, his supposedly universal pattern is not universal at all. Error (2) causes him to ignore the fact that almost all failed mother portraits date from the twentieth century. He cites only two nineteenth-century texts: Tolstoy's *Childhood* (he dismisses the description of Irten'ev's mother as "blatantly inauthentic" [p. 45] but does not explain why inauthenticity automatically makes something an unsuitable model; in fact, it is precisely the inauthentic halo with which Tolstoy surrounded Irten'ev's mother that made her a popular model for gentry autobiography), and Aksakov's *Childhood Years*. Error (3) ensures that Coe will miss the class and ideological divisions that separate gentry portraits of childhood (with their generally perfect mothers) and those nongentry portraits (usually by twentieth-century autobiographers) by people like Gorky and Paustovsky. Finally, error (4) allows him to read his own perspective, one that was likely not to have been present in the minds of the authors, into literary texts. Thus, although Bagrov clearly loved his mother despite her obvious faults, Coe chooses to concentrate almost exclusively on the negative aspects of their relationship.

Coe's command of psychological jargon is impressive, but he fails to see that his over-interpretation of *Childhood Years* does not correspond to the way in which nineteenth-century Russians saw the work. While his interpretation may be perceptive from a psychological viewpoint, it is an interpretation that is historically flawed. It is precisely the "imperceptive critics" who "frequently quote the *Detskiye gody* as the supreme example of an idealized mother/child relationship" (p. 56) who express the view that was typical for Russian readers until well into the twentieth century.

35. In comparison with their West European counterparts, Russian gentry mothers seem, in general, to have been more actively concerned with raising their children. In part, the isolation of the Russian estate helps explain the relative abundance of contact between mothers and children. In the country, mothers had no place to go, and they tended, therefore, to spend time with their children.

36. Anonymous, pp. 246–47. An almost identical statement occurs in the memoirs of Shestov: "The most important place in my memories belongs to my mother." He goes on to call her "a vessel of love and selflessness" (p. 167).

37. Fet, p. 39.

38. Benois, p. 48.
39. Kornilova, p. 33.
40. Ibid., p. 94.
41. Grot, p. 24.
42. Nikolai Rostov is a perfect example of this kind of Russian nobleman in imaginative literature.
43. Karpinskaia, p. 857.
44. Glinsky, p. 63.
45. Osorgin, p. 17.
46. Kropotkin, p. 48. I use the Russian text of Kropotkin's *Notes* because it seems to be more complete than the original English version.
47. Fet, p. 39. For a good general discussion of card playing, gambling, and the gentry class, see Lotman, "Tema kart."
48. These phenomena form a major thematic background to Nekrasov's post-emancipation poem, "Who Lives Well in the Land of Rus'?"
49. Glinsky, p. 72.
50. Benois, p. 48.
51. Chombart de Lauwe devotes an entire subchapter to the theme of death. See *Un monde autre*, pp. 389–96.
52. Salov, bk. 7, p. 3.
53. B—n, no. 4, p. 175.
54. Kornilova, p. 128.
55. Grot, p. 31.
56. Ibid., p. 35.
57. Lelong, 1913, bk. 2, no. 7, p. 99.
58. While at least one exception can be found to all the other myths of childhood, there is not a single instance in gentry autobiography or pseudo-autobiography of anything less than ideal relations between gentry child and nanny.
59. Vereshchagin, p. 34.
60. Ibid., p. 48.
61. Lelong, 1913, bk. 2, no. 6, p. 786.
62. Chertkova, p. 175.
63. Tyrkova-Vil'iams, p. 38.
64. Ibid., p. 167.
65. Lelong, 1913, bk. 2, no. 6, p. 787.
66. L. E. Obolensky, p. 113.

67. Anonymous, p. 258.

68. Shatilov, no. 4, p. 220.

69. Pisemsky's play *A Bitter Fate* and Turgenev's novel *Fathers and Children* offer two of the most eloquent treatments of the subject in Russian literature.

70. L. E. Obolensky, p. 112.

71. I realize, of course, that the Russian Revolution, when it came, was every bit as violent and uprooting as the American Civil War. I believe that Russian émigré's were able to idealize pre-Revolution childhood because their nostalgia could be expressed through models that had been developed in less turbulent times, whereas Southern U.S. aristocrats of the 1860's and 1870's lacked such models.

72. The idealization of serfdom by gentry autobiographers in the second half of the nineteenth century was in marked opposition to the views of their parents. As one historian noted: "By the mid-1850's, defense of serfdom was neither fashionable nor respectable in educated society, and scarcely anyone, it was said, could be found who was willing to argue in behalf of its preservation" (Emmons, pp. 33–34).

73. Unlike the myth of the happy childhood and myths of the mother and father, the "happy peasant" seems to have been created independently of Tolstoy and Aksakov. It should be noted that they wrote their pseudo-autobiographies before emancipation, a period when the potential contradiction between serfdom and individual happiness was not felt quite as sharply. The happy peasant is clearly not a convention for Russian literature as a whole in this period. There are plenty of examples of unflattering presentations of serfdom throughout the nineteenth century. Some of the grimmest include Grigorovich's *Anton Goremyka*, some of the stories in Turgenev's *Notes of a Hunter*, and Leskov's story "The Toupee Artist."

74. Grot, p. 6.

75. Karpinskaia, p. 857.

76. Kornilova, p. 32.

77. Thus, Vodovozova, who devotes pages to an unmasking of the horrors of conditions on pre-emancipation gentry estates, excepts her own parents: "People like my father, with his broad intellectual interests, with his humanitarian relationship to his family and his serfs, were rare exceptions" (1: 32–33).

78. Vereshchagin, p. 58.

79. Glinsky, p. 63. The manifesto announcing the emancipation of the serfs was proclaimed on February 19, 1861.

80. Shatilov, no. 1, p. 192.

81. Anonymous, no. 8, p. 261.

82. Grot, p. 23. Another example of the same phenomenon can be seen in the memoirs of Von-Ritter: "I always find it funny when I hear tales of various 'atrocities' which, in the old days, landlords committed against their serfs. I find it especially funny when our young people, who could not have even known those times, start to go on about this. . . . But I am not usually as amused by our young people who get carried away . . . as I am angered whenever I happen to pick up old magazines (which are fortunately, by now, long forgotten) with their expositions of episodes from the days of serfdom" (p. 63). Von-Ritter specifically calls these attacks the malicious inventions of "liberal writers."

83. Bunin, "Iz zapisnoi knizhki'," in *Literaturnoe nasledstvo*, no. 84, vol. 1, pp. 388–89.

84. One autobiographer described an estate of this kind as follows: "It was located on the banks of a picturesque river, and it had an old-fashioned wooden house that had been built, as was frequently the case in the old days, not all at once, but gradually: additions had been added on as they were needed. Thanks to this, the house had no architectural style whatsoever" (Shatilov, no. 1, p. 168).

85. Fet, p. 193. For an extremely long and detailed description of a typical middle-rank gentry house and grounds, see Beketova, pp. 685–97.

86. Grot, p. 9.

87. Ibid.

88. Kropotkin, p. 74.

89. For a good description of the gardens of Russian estates and a discussion of their meaning, see Likhachov, chap. 5.

90. Anikst and Turchin, p. 132.

91. In fact, this theme dates back to classical antiquity. It was a favorite of Horace, for example. It was, however, its Enlightenment incarnation that exercised a direct influence on the Russian tradition.

92. Anikst and Turchin, after illustration no. 130.

93. Ibid., after illustration no. 108.

94. The first pages of Karamzin's story "Poor Lisa" make a fine illustration of the way sentimentalist authors described the natural world.

95. Goncharov, p. 103. Other quotes from this work will be noted by page numbers in the text. The diction of passages like this one owes a great deal to such "golden age" poetic pastorals as Batiushkov's "My Penates" and Pushkin's "The Little Town."

96. Herzen, 4: 74.

97. Glinsky, p. 73.

98. According to Coe, an ability to commune with nature is one that many autobiographers feel they had as children. See Coe, *When the Grass Was Taller*, p. 129.

99. Lelong, 1913, bk. 2, no. 7, p. 67.

100. Kamensky, p. 11.

101. Slavutinsky, pp. 238–40.

102. Sabaneeva, p. 2.

103. Vereshchagin, p. 53.

104. Glinsky, p. 73.

105. Chertkova, p. 81. The translation of the beginning of Pushkin's lyric "Winter Evening" is from Arndt, p. 195.

106. *Stolitsa i usad'ba*, 1915, no. 33: 3.

107. Ibid., 1914, no. 6: 6.

108. Vrangel', pp. 18–19.

109. Chertkova, p. 97. The sound "zh" in Russian is written with a single letter. The word "zhuk" means "beetle."

110. Karpinskaia, p. 863.

111. Lelong, 1913, bk. 2, no. 6, p. 790.

112. Ibid.

113. Kornilova, p. 102.

114. Kropotkin, p. 82.

115. The gymnasium did not become an educational option for girls until the very end of the nineteenth century. In the mid-nineteenth century, girls were generally kept at home longer than their brothers and then received some years of education/finishing school at private establishments called "pansions." As a rule, the pansions specialized in foreign languages, music, and etiquette, although there were some, especially in Moscow and Petersburg, that provided a broader curriculum.

116. Lotman, *Roman A. S. Pushkina*. See particularly the section entitled "The Education and Service of Noblemen" (pp. 42–54).

117. Salov, bk. 9, p. 63. Salov was born in 1834, so he is describing the situation in the mid-1840's.

118. In 1824 the total number of students enrolled in gymnasia in

Russia and the Ukraine was 3,416. The gymnasia were open to all social classes (except serfs), and, if the breakdown by class for 1887 is any indication, the children of the gentry made up about half of the students. Assuming that the figure of a half is more or less accurate throughout the century, then there were approximately 1,700 members of the gentry class in gymnasia in 1824. Continuing to use the assumption that half the students were from the gentry class, a census of gentry students enrolled in gymnasia can be obtained as follows: 1836, 5,500; 1847, 8,000; 1854, 7,000; 1863, 13,000; 1876, 18,500; 1887, 21,000; 1891, 22,000. These figures are based on tables in Brokgaus and Efron, 8: 703–4.

119. Kamensky, p. 13.

120. Salov, bk. 7, p. 11. This sentence, incidentally, sounds almost as if it came from chap. 3 of Tolstoy's *Childhood*: "Papa said that we'd had enough sitting around in the country, that we weren't little anymore, and that it was time for us to get a serious education" (1: 12).

121. In fact, there is a whole genre of Russian "schoolboy memoirs," in both third and first person. As a rule, the heroes of these memoirs are either the children of the poorer gentry or those of the *raznochintsy*. The genre has been a rather productive one in Russia; it includes Kushchevsky's *Nikolai Negorev*, Garin-Mikhailovsky's *Detstvo Temy*, Kassil's *Konduit*, Chukovsky's *Gimnasium*, and Dobychin's *Gorod En*. I do not treat them extensively here because they concentrate less on the child himself and more on the school environment. In fact, they can be said to contain myths of school, rather than myths of childhood.

122. Glinsky, p. 61.

123. Kropotkin, p. 82.

Chapter 4

1. The notes to the most recent critical edition of Gorky contain large numbers of references to contemporary comparisons of Tolstoy and Gorky. See, for example, 9: 546 and 15: 579–81. Contemporaries were also quick to note down and publish the transcripts of meetings between the two. A typical present-day formulation of the problem appears in Krasnov, pp. 49–63. He starts his article with the statement: "The theme of Tolstoy and Gorky is one of the most attractive in the history of literature."

2. See the notes to the most recent critical edition of Gorky's works, 9: 536.

3. Most important, as was noted in an early review by V. L'vov, Gorky's "Confession" is "an attempt to reach a different decision and to indicate a way out, not for himself, but for everyone" (quoted in Gorky, 9: 546). Of course, on the other hand, it could be argued that Tolstoy's "Confession" was equally meant to serve as the indication of a "way out" for all of humankind.

4. In fact there is still one more link in the chain. Gorky claims to have written the section of the essay from which this quote was taken immediately upon hearing of the death of Tolstoy in late 1910. That just happens to coincide with the beginning of his work on *Childhood*. Thus, he implies that the death of Tolstoy led him to recollect the conversation in which Tolstoy had requested a generalized autobiography and, therefore, that this recollected conversation provided the stimulus to begin work on his trilogy.

5. The definition of parody that I use here is derived from Tynianov's famous article, "Dostoevsky i Gogol" in *Arkhaisty i novatory*, p. 455, and from the same author's "O parodii" in *Poetika, istoriia literatury, kino*, pp. 284–310. For Tynianov, a parody is any work that orients itself against an earlier work, author, or genre. As he succinctly states: "All parody rests in dialectic play through the use of the device. If the parody of a tragedy is a comedy, then the parody of a comedy can be a tragedy" ("Dostoevsky i Gogol," p. 455).

6. It is interesting that Gorky himself was evidently of two minds about calling the work *Childhood*. When it was first published, in the newspaper *Russkoe slovo* (starting in late August 1913), it bore this title. However, when preparing a separate edition of the work at almost the exact same time, Gorky proposed a change in the title: "I'm sending you the 4th chapter of sketches; they should be entitled *Grandmother*, and not *Childhood*. Would you agree to change the title?" (from a letter of mid-September 1913 to his editor, Blagov; quoted in Gorky, 15: 575). A few days later, however, Gorky changed his mind again and wrote back to Blagov: "Having thought it over I find that I disturbed you for nothing and that I shouldn't change the title. We'll leave it as it is: *Childhood*" (15: 575).

7. Considering the clear orientation of Gorky's work toward Tolstoy, it is surprising how little serious work has been done comparing the two. It may be that the very obviousness of the connection has

prevented scholars from examining it closely. Typically, when speaking of the two works, critics limit themselves to vague generalizations. Thus, for example, Piksanov says only: "It goes without saying that Tolstoy's autobiographical trilogy was a major instructive model for Gorky when he wrote his glorious autobiographical trilogy" (p. 34). Mikhailovsky compares Gorky and Tolstoy from time to time but, despite some good observations, his work is marred by a teleological viewpoint that sees Tolstoy's *Childhood* as merely an imperfect attempt to do what Gorky perfected. See Mikhailovsky, pp. 33–86. English-language criticism has been, if anything, even more unhelpful. A partial exception is Cohen's dissertation, "The Genre of the Autobiographical Account of Childhood."

8. Borras makes an interesting comparison between Gorky and Tolstoy when he speaks of the death of Aleksei's father: "He never enters the narrative except as recalled by other people, and everything they remember about him is good. In this way Gorky creates in his novel a dream of fatherhood which he never knew in reality" (pp. 135–36). This implies that Gorky was trying to create a "father myth" that might counter the "mother myth" of the Tolstoyan gentry tradition. Of course, in his novel *The Mother*, Gorky created a "mother myth" of his own that was not autobiographically based.

9. In *Childhood* he is present at the death of his father, of "the Gypsy," of Aunt Natal'ia, of "Uncle Peter," and of his mother. In *Among the People* he sees at least five more deaths (15: 221, 248–49, 448, 475, 512).

10. This characteristic feature was noted by one of the early reviewers of Gorky's *Childhood*, V. Kranikhfel'd. Speaking of Tolstoy's Irten'ev, he says: "The poorer his impressions of the external world, the richer his inner moral life became." On the other hand, what is important for Gorky is "the external world and the richness of the impressions gleaned from it" (15: 580). Incidentally, when Gorky does "tell," it is in passages that are ideologically, not psychologically, motivated.

11. The following sentence is typical of this attitude: "Everyone enjoys recalling the places where he grew up" (Slavutinsky, p. 238).

12. It should be noted that here, as in other passages, Gorky shows an ambiguous attitude toward childhood as such. While he is obviously attacking the gentry myths of childhood as inapplicable to the real world in which he and most Russians grew up (and hence, as

false representations of childhood in reality), he retains a belief in the basic innocence of the child's soul.

13. The only exception to the generally negative attitude toward nature in the trilogy is the scene in *Among the People* when Aleksei goes to the forest with his grandmother. There he says: "The forest evoked a feeling of spiritual peace and comfort in me; all of my disappointments, everything unpleasant disappeared in that feeling" (15: 256). In part this exception is possible because the charm of the forest is not overlaid with any reminders of urban life. More important, the boy's appreciation of nature is tied to his grandmother's almost supernatural understanding of the forest. Still, even here, the idyll is tempered by the knowledge that winter will come and make such expeditions (which were undertaken to find nuts and mushrooms to be sold in the city) impossible.

14. From all accounts, Gorky's wish to write an "autobiography" (either real or fictionalized) dates back to the beginnings of his literary career. A background of the history of the creation of *Childhood* appears in Gorky, 15: 573.

15. The "democratic" writers of the nineteenth century were mostly the sons of priests and petty officials and had, as a rule, little childhood contact with "the people." Gentry writers often made fun of their socialist competitors, who claimed to speak for the people but did not really know them because they had never lived among them. Because of their childhood contact with the peasants, the gentry class always claimed to understand the Russian people better than the "democratic" opposition did. Of course, Gorky's knowledge could not be questioned since he was, to some extent, "the people." One of the reasons for the title of the second volume of the trilogy, *Among the People*, may well have been that it forcefully asserted Gorky's personal knowledge of the "real" Russians.

16. The narrator's dislike of reminiscing (the favorite activity of gentry pseudo-autobiographers and autobiographers) is telling in this regard. He experiences a vaguely unpleasant feeling listening to the stories of various workers on the banks of the Volga: "I hear—'it was,' ' it is,' 'it always was,' and it seems to me that this evening these people had come to the last hours of their life,—everything has passed, there won't be anything else. This separated me from Bashkin and Trusov" (16: 15).

17. His interest in creating a general model comes out even more

strongly in a letter he wrote just before beginning work on *Childhood*: "We should really occupy ourselves with a study of the roots of the psyche and worldview of our people" (quoted in Mashinsky, p. 476).

18. This letter is published in Medvedev, *M. Gorky o detskoi literature*, p. 143.

19. Avdeenko, p. 659. I am indebted to an unpublished paper by S. Wolohan of the University of California, Los Angeles, for this reference. Wolohan discusses a number of what she calls "*bezprizornik* tales," including Panteleev's *Len'ka Panteleev* and Voinov's *The Waif*, in addition to Avdeenko's work. Wolohan shows convincingly the extent to which the *bezprizornik* tale marks a continuation of Gorky's interpretation of childhood in Soviet literary and autobiographical culture: "But the most crucial identification of all . . . is the identification of the *bezprizornik* with Gorky himself. Gorky, as known to the *bezprizorniki* through his stories, and especially through the autobiographical *Detstvo* trilogy, became the ultimate prototype for the *bezprizorniki*" (p. 13).

20. These citations are taken from a 1934 *Pravda* article by S. Marshak entitled "Deti otvechaiut Gor'komu." The article is republished in Medvedev, *M. Gorky o detskoi literature*. Both letters are reproduced on p. 220 of that edition.

21. In the years immediately following the Revolution, Gorky's life also became the standard model for the autobiographies of Soviet writers. For example, Gorky's influence can clearly be seen in the autobiographical sketches that Russian writers prepared for a 1924 anthology edited by Lidin, entitled *Literaturnaia Rossiia*. Of the 28 writers in the book, not one describes childhood as having been happy. This is despite the fact that a number of these writers were from the gentry class. On the other hand, seven of them describe childhoods in obviously Gorkyan terms. The most impressive example is Aleksei Remizov, an émigré and a writer not usually associated with Gorky: "I passed my early childhood near the factory in a group of factory and simply vagabond 'street' kids. . . . It was on the streets that my first vernal thoughts, with dreams of the salvation of mankind and of a universal explosion, originally blazed into life" (pp. 31–32). Once again, I am not suggesting that these writers had to lie about their past in order to fit Gorky's model. However, the authority of that model unquestionably helped them to recall certain childhood memories and to suppress others.

22. Gladkov, p. 14.

23. Ibid., p. 215.

Chapter 5

1. I use the term modernist here to refer to all of the important artistic movements of the early twentieth century, including Symbolism, Futurism, Acmeism, and their offshoots. Although in other respects these movements may have had little in common, they shared a lack of interest in the questions concerning the nature of childhood that were important for realist writers.

2. A lack of interest in childhood was characteristic of the futurists, who, in keeping with their forward-looking ideology, tended not to delve deeply into the distant personal past. The early acmeists focused primarily on the lyric moment of immediate perception. For them, childhood was unimportant because the child was not fully conscious of the concrete world and, therefore, the child's voice was an inappropriate one for acmeist poetic expression. By the 1920's and 1930's, however, some of the former futurists and acmeists did become more interested in exploring their early years. Examples of this new-found concern include Pasternak's *Safe Conduct*, Mandel'shtam's *The Noise of Time*, and Tsvetaeva's autobiographical prose fragments.

3. Cited in the notes to Blok, p. 761.

4. Ivanov, p. 230.

5. The first four lines contain references to the "mineia" (the book of saints' lives used in church services). This book is read from beginning to end and then repeated. The concept of childhood as repetition, an idea so closely linked to the symbolists' cyclical theories of history, also plays a role in Blok's "Recompense": "Sons reflected in fathers: / A little fragment of a clan— / Two or three links,—And the secrets / Of the darkened past are clear" (p. 531).

6. In the present state of Belyi studies, it is almost heretical to assert that *Kotik Letaev* and *The Baptized Chinaman* have anything to do with the native Russian literary tradition. Instead, contemporary critics have paid almost exclusive attention to the connections between the novels and the thought of Belyi's sometime mentor, the anthroposophist Rudolph Steiner. In particular, I have in mind the work of Alexandrov, Elsworth, and Kozlik. Unfortunately, while declaring that the presence of anthroposophical motifs in these works leads to a multitude of possible readings, these critics have, by plac-

ing Belyi so firmly in the Steinerian camp, either implicitly or explicitly set his works all but off limits to those readers not immersed in anthroposophical doctrine. Elsworth, for example, states this opinion quite succinctly at the end of his chapter on *Kotik Letaev*: "Aesthetically *Kotik Letaev* is in no way inferior to *Petersburg*; indeed there are grounds for regarding it as Bely's most perfectly achieved work in prose. If it is nevertheless a less important work than *Petersburg* that is because of its dependence on a doctrine to which most readers neither have nor desire access" (p. 137).

Yet Steiner was clearly not a writer of imaginative literature and could not have been expected to provide Belyi with a model for the literary expression of anthroposophic thought. Belyi had to come to his mode of expression on his own, influenced by his intuition and by the literary tradition. Although I fully agree that images and ideas drawn from Steiner are crucial for *Kotik Letaev* (and, to a much lesser extent, for *The Baptized Chinaman*), I think that these works should also be examined in the light of the Russian tradition of pseudo-autobiographical novels. Many new facets emerge when they are read not merely as Belyi's personal transformation of Steiner's myths, but as a new answer to the questions that generations of Russian writers and autobiographers had been asking about the meaning and purpose of childhood.

7. Belyi, Na *rubezhe*, pp. 165–66.

8. Alexandrov's summation is typical: "As one might expect, Bely could not acknowledge his occult beliefs publicly in the Soviet Union in 1929. Thus in the memoir he attempts (unsuccessfully) to give a purely physiological motivation for the occult imagery that fills the work" (*Andrey Bely*, p. 153).

9. Obviously this observation is not new. Both Elsworth and Alexandrov have noted it without stating it explicitly. However, both of them feel that the child's gradually increasing ability to grasp the real world and his gradually diminishing ability to enter the realm of "memory of memory" represents a loss. This may be true for Steiner's system and it may even have been true for Belyi as an individual. However, within the novel, it seems to me that the child's loss of pre-natal worlds is more than balanced by his talent for making creative use of his memory. It is only the loss of past worlds (with a concomitant acquisition of the real world) that can stimulate the memory to recall them and the desire to record them in words.

10. The introduction to Kozlik's monumental study presents the most detailed survey of those elements of anthroposophic philosophy most important for Belyi. See Kozlik, 1: ix–c.

11. See Belyi, "Formy iskusstva." Belyi's position was evidently derived from his reading of Schopenhauer.

12. Belyi, "Budushchee iskusstvo," in *Simvolizm*, p. 453.

13. The connection between the two worlds is generally marked by the use of the word *vposledstvii* ("later on"). It is used for this purpose at least six times in the first chapter alone.

14. Belyi had, in fact, previously made use of the image of the point in the prologue to his novel *Petersburg* (1916).

15. It is interesting that, although Kotik has some idea of time even at this early age, he does not measure it in larger incremental units until he is older. In fact, he begins to do so only in *The Baptized Chinaman*, when he is six years old: "I remember the events of the year and the form of the regular months from just that time: yes, from October (I was born in October)" (p. 52).

16. There may also be distant echoes of Hindu creation myths underlying the child's first utterance. The Hindu god of fire is called "Agni," and, in some Indian legends, the actions of this god are linked to the creation of the world.

17. Steinberg, p. 161.

18. The child's untenable position between the warring factions becomes even more heartrending in *The Baptized Chinaman* because the older child understands it more completely: "—so why does papa yell at me when, out of fear that mama might wake up, I get my thoughts all mixed up;—you listen—you're guilty; you don't listen—you're guilty:—Guilty without end; guilty alone; guilty without end, guilty without cause" (p. 170).

19. Elsworth, paraphrasing C. Anschuetz, describes this process as follows: "One very astute critic of *Kotik Letaev* has argued that 'the action of the novel consists of the child's acquisition of language' to articulate the pre-natal experiences he recollects, but that as he learns speech, so he unlearns recollection" (p. 130). I would add, however, that the acquisition of the word gives Kotik the power not only to recreate the world of "memory of memory" but to create any world he chooses. That is, in some sense, the word is stronger than recollection because it can create that which memory is unable to recall.

20. The connection between early childhood experience and a spe-

cifically Biblical conception of earthly paradise (as opposed to the unspecified venues of nineteenth-century golden-age portraits) is typical for Ivanov's "Early Childhood" as well. In the last line of stanza 17, he mentions "My original childhood heaven!" This is connected with the first line of the next stanza, in which his window is said to have looked out "onto the territory of Eden." Later, in stanza 28, the poet says: "I've been three springs in heaven, and I haven't / Met the Serpent yet; but even so / Thick curtains are falling / On my primordial Eden."

21. This jealousy seems to be brought on, in part, by what can only be called a proto-sexual relationship between Kotik and his nanny: "And Raisa Ivanovna takes off her dress every evening; and—her slip: in front of me! She takes off her stockings: she stands in her shift; she even: takes me to sleep with her.—'Oy, oy, oy!'—'What's going to happen to her because of this?'" (p. 252). This sexual connection was pointed out to me by Professor John Kopper of Dartmouth College.

22. Both Elsworth (p. 130) and Alexandrov (p. 170) discuss this aspect of the novel's connections to anthroposophy.

23. Alexandrov, for example, finds this a matter of great concern and tries to solve the problem in an original if not altogether successful way (as he himself obviously realizes): "Apart from the rare occult passages in the work, what evidence is there that Bely is still operating within a world view that is a continuation of that in *Kotik Letaev?* The answer lies, I believe, in the significant role that alliteration and meter play in the prose of *The Baptized Chinaman* . . . the appearance of passages filled with sound repetitions and a recognizable meter in *The Baptized Chinaman*—many passages of which are written in regular amphibrachs—is an indirect expression of an occult worldview even when overt occult imagery is absent. The problem is that when the reader is presented with only such abstract and relatively mute phenomena as meter and alliteration, it becomes very difficult indeed to speak of the specific nature of man's links to the transcendent" (pp. 183–84). Kozlik does not even bother to try to connect the two works. In fact, he hardly mentions *The Baptized Chinaman* in his three volumes.

24. Even the "occult" passages in *The Baptized Chinaman* could be interpreted without recourse to Steiner's theories. The most important of them, which are drawn from the Bible, can be seen as the precocious child's self-projections rather than as dimly remembered moments from a previous life.

25. According to Kozlik, the "fire-breathing father" is an element of the Aztec world that is the base mythological text for *Kotik Letaev*. He mentions this connection specifically in 3: 789. For the lengthy discussion on the role of Aztec mythology in *Kotik Letaev*, see 2: 571–80.

26. In *The Noise of Time*, Mandel'shtam goes even farther than Belyi. He insists that a child's life is, for all intents and purposes, constructed not from direct experience but from cultural artifacts. Naturally, he uses Tolstoy and Aksakov as his point of departure: "I could never understand the Tolstoys, the Aksakovs, the Bagrov grandchildren enamored with their family archives and epic recollections of domestic life. I repeat—my memory is not loving but inimical, and it works not to reproduce the past but to distance it. A *raznochinets* doesn't need memory; all he has to do is tell us about the books he has read,—and his biography is ready" (Mandel'shtam, vol. 2, p. 99).

Chapter 6

1. A. V. Bolotov, p. 6.

2. Ibid., p. 11.

3. Nabokov, pp. 40–41.

4. There is, of course, one other work of Russian émigré literature that brilliantly continues the pseudo-autobiographical tradition: Nabokov's *The Gift*. In the first chapter of the novel, Fyodor Godunov-Cherdyntsev, the work's sometime first-person narrator and the displaced scion of a Russian gentry family, reads a review (actually, the review is a figment of his hopeful imagination) of his first book of poetry: a collection devoted to childhood. The putative reviewer describes the collection in terms that precisely define the peculiar mix of the general and the specific so characteristic of the pseudo-autobiography: "The author sought, on the one hand, to generalize reminiscences by selecting elements typical of any successful childhood—hence their seeming obviousness; and on the other hand he has allowed only his genuine quiddity to penetrate into his poems— hence their fastidiousness" (p. 21).

5. Bunin, *Ustami Buninykh*, 2: 184.

6. Bunin, "Kniga moei zhizni," in *Literaturnoe nasledstvo*, no. 84, vol. 1, pp. 383, 384.

7. This search for the time before memory begins is also reminiscent of Fyodor Godunov-Cherdyntsev's description of the pseudo-autobiographical project in *The Gift*, although Nabokov firmly re-

jects the mysticism of Belyi's and Bunin's conception: "These are all my very earliest memories, the ones closest to the original source. My probing thought often turns toward that original source, toward that reverse nothingness. Thus the nebulous state of the infant always seems to me to be a slow convalescence after a dreadful illness and the receding from primal nonexistence becomes an approach to it when I strain my memory to the very limit" (p. 23).

8. Quoted in Baboreko, p. 49.

9. There are a number of possible sources for the name Arsen'ev. It is well known, of course, that this was Lermontov's mother's family name. Her estate was in Tula province, not far from where Bunin grew up. I suspect, however, that the choice may have had more to do with a book published in Tula in 1903. Called *Rod Dvorian Arsen'evykh 1389–1901*, it goes back into the "mists of time" to search for the origins of the real Arsen'ev family. It begins with a note from the editor that sounds not unlike the statement of Bunin's narrator: "The Arsen'ev clan is glorious, both due to the antiquity of its extraction and because of its loyal service to the Tsars and the Fatherland" (p. 1).

10. The theme of physical exile as a stimulus to childhood memories is of crucial importance for the narrator of *The Gift*. In the first chapter, Godunov-Cherdyntsev wonders what it would be like to return some day to his family estate in the Russian countryside. Having considered this he concludes: "But there is one thing I shall definitively not find there awaiting me—*the thing which, indeed, made the whole business of exile worth cultivating*: my childhood and the fruits of my childhood. Its fruits—here they are, today, already ripe; while my childhood itself has disappeared into a distance even more remote than that of our Russian North" (pp. 37–38; italics mine; the phrase "the fruits of childhood" refers, of course, to the book of poetry that Godunov-Cherdyntsev has produced).

11. It is precisely this peculiarity of the Russian cultural mind that allowed later autobiographers to use the literary childhoods of Tolstoy and Aksakov as models.

12. Such passages are also common in gentry autobiography and in third-person narratives. Thus, for example, the scene in *War and Peace* (vol. 2, pt. 3, chap. 2) where Natasha looks out her window at the moon is quite similar to the passages cited above.

13. Gusdorf, p. 115.

14. Quoted in Baboreko, p. 48.

15. In fact, according to a scholar who has had access to the manuscripts of the novel, Bunin took great pains to make the final version less autobiographical than the drafts: "While working on the novel (even including the final correction of the manuscript), Bunin strove to avoid excess autobiographicalism. . . . Bunin made approximately a quarter of all the cuts in the manuscript at the expense of biographical detail" (Averin, p. 68).

16. Bunin, "Kniga moei zhizni," in *Literaturnoe nasledstvo*, no. 84, vol. 1, p. 382.

17. Bunin, "K vospominaniiam o Tolstom," in *Literaturnoe nasledstvo*, no. 84, vol. 1, pp. 396–97.

18. Bunin quotes from Pushkin's 1829 lyric "A Winter Morning."

19. Bunin, "Rech' na iubilee 'Russkikh Vedomostei,'" in *Literaturnoe nasledstvo*, no. 84, vol. 1, p. 318.

Conclusion

1. For example, the battle between the "innovators" and the "archaists" began as primarily a linguistic one, but it eventually took on much broader ideological overtones. Uspensky describes the process as follows: "One can say that these arguments [about the literary language] occupied a central place in the Russian cultural life of that time. They took on broad social meaning, absorbing ideological, political, and religious problems. One or another linguistic position became a kind of banner that allowed one to define, as it were, a person's party affiliation" (p. 5).

2. Barthes, pp. 142–43.

3. The tendency to confuse the realms of literature and life during certain periods (most notably Romanticism and Symbolism) is well documented, but this phenomenon is rarely noted in the second half of the nineteenth century. Indeed, Lotman specifically denies the existence of this tendency in the second half of the nineteenth century: "In losing to some extent the element of play, art stops leaping over the footlights, it no longer steps off the pages of the novel into the realm of the author's and readers' real lives. However, the disappearance of the poetics of behavior was not destined to be long. Having disappeared with the last of the Romantics in the 1840's, it was resurrected in the years between 1890 and 1900" ("The Poetics of Everyday Behavior in Russian Eighteenth Century Culture," in Lotman and

Uspensky, p. 252). At first blush this claim seems valid. The conventions of Realism are certainly less extravagant and harder to identify. It is, therefore, more difficult to document their extra-literary influence. Nevertheless, despite Lotman's assertions to the contrary, realistic literary conventions were imitated by the reading public. In fact, they may have been absorbed by an extremely large reading public precisely because they seem not to be conventions. Only a special kind of reader could see himself as a Romantic hero or herself as a Symbolist "beautiful woman," but it was quite easy for members of the Russian gentry class, both male and female, to identify with the childhoods described by Tolstoy and Aksakov.

4. The tendency of ideologies to crystallize precisely at moments when a dominant cultural group is under attack is eloquently expressed by Geertz: "In polities firmly embedded in Edmund Burke's golden assemblage of 'ancient opinions and rules of life,' the role of ideology, in any explicit sense, is marginal. . . . But when, as in revolutionary France . . . those hallowed opinions and rules of life come into question, the search for systematic ideological formulations, either to reinforce them or to replace them, flourishes" (p. 218).

5. A recognition that bipolar models recur constantly in Russian thought is the basis for an article by Lotman and Uspensky, "The Role of Dual Models in the Dynamics of Russian Culture," in *The Semiotics of Russian Culture*, pp. 3–36. However, for some reason Lotman and Uspensky end their discussion of dual models with the eighteenth century, leaving the impression that this system was somehow inoperative in the nineteenth century.

6. An example of the attempt to put some of the ideas ultimately derived from Chernyshevsky into action was the attempt by members of the non-noble intelligentsia "to go to the people" in the 1870's. The abject failure of this project was primarily due to their inability to differentiate the realistic from the utopian.

7. Osorgin, pp. 34–35.

Bibliography

Works preceded by an asterisk (*) are autobiographical sources and have been annotated by the author.

Aksakov, S. T. "Pis'ma k M. A. Maksimovichu." *Kievskaia starina*, 1893, no. 4: 829–40.

———. "Pis'ma S. T., K. S., i I. S. Aksakovykh k I. S. Turgenevu." *Russkoe obozrenie*, 1894, no. 8: 460–84; no. 9: 5–38; no. 10: 478–501; no. 11: 7–30; no. 12: 599–601.

———. *Sobranie sochinenii v piati tomakh.* 5 vols. Moscow, 1966.

*Aksakova, V. S. *Dnevnik, 1854–55.* St. Petersburg, 1913. Not about the author's childhood.

Alexandrov, Vladimir. *Andrey Bely: The Major Symbolist Fiction.* Cambridge, Mass., 1985.

———. "Kotik Letaev, The Baptized Chinaman, and Notes of an Eccentric." In John E. Malmsted, ed., *Andrey Bely: Spirit of Symbolism.* Ithaca, N.Y., 1987.

*Almedingen, E. M. *Fanny.* New York, 1970. Based on the first-person notes of the author's aunt, Francine Hermione de Poltoratzky. Original notes written 1913. Positive memories of childhood.

Anikst, M. A., and V. S. Turchin, eds. *...v okrestnostiakh Moskvy: Iz istorii russkoi usadebnoi kul'tury XVII–XIX vekov.* Moscow, 1979.

*Anonymous. "Iz nedavnogo proshlogo." *Russkaia starina*, 1910, vol. 143, no. 8: 246–66; no. 9: 441–59. Author born in mid-1850's. Positive memories of childhood.

Ariès, Philippe. *L'enfant et la vie familiale sous l'ancien régime.* Paris, 1973.

Arndt, Walter. *Pushkin Threefold.* New York, 1972.

Avdeenko, A. *Ia liubliu.* Moscow, 1967.

Averin, B. V. "Iz tvorcheskoi istorii romana I. A. Bunina 'Zhizn' Arsen'eva.'" *Buninskii sbornik*. Orel, 1974.

Axthelm, Peter M. *The Modern Confessional Novel*. New Haven, 1967.

*B—n, S. "Vospominaniia." *Russkaia shkola*, 1911, no. 4: 155–76; no. 5/6: 127–59; no. 7/8: 163–92; no. 9: 79–95. "My dear, irretrievable childhood" (5: 159).

Baboreko, A. *I. A. Bunin: Materialy dlia biografii*. Moscow, 1967.

Bakhtin, M. M. *Literaturno-kriticheskie stat'i*. Moscow, 1986.

Banfield, Ann. *Unspeakable Sentences: Narration and Representation in the Language of Fiction*. Boston, 1982.

Barthes, Roland. *Mythologies*. Tr. Annette Lavers. New York, 1972.

Becker, Seymour. *Nobility and Privilege in Late Imperial Russia*. Dekalb, Ill., 1985.

*Beketova, M. A. "Shakhmatova. Semeinaia khronika." In *Literaturnoe nasledstvo, Aleksandr Blok*, 1982, no. 92, 4 vols. Vol. 3. Not about the author's childhood. Discusses the material and personal surroundings that helped form Blok's character.

*Beliaev, A. P. "Perezhitoe i peredumannoe s 1803 goda." *Russkaia starina*, 1880, vol. 29, no. 9: 1–42. Author born in 1803. Grew up on country estate. "Carefree and happy childhood" (p. 10).

Belyi, A. "Formy iskusstva." *Mir iskusstva*, 1902, no. 12.

———. *Kotik Letaev*. Munich, 1964.

———. *Kreshchenyi kitaets*. Munich, 1969.

———. *Na rubezhe dvukh stoletii*. Letchworth, Hertfordshire, 1966.

———. *Simvolizm*. Moscow, 1910.

*Benois, Alexandre. *Memoirs*. Tr. Moura Budberg. London, 1960. Author born in 1870. A city childhood that is not discussed in depth.

Bilinkis, Ia. S. *O tvorchestve L. N. Tolstogo*. Leningrad, 1959.

Blok, A. A. "Vozmezdie." In *Stikhotvoreniia*. Leningrad, 1955.

Blum, Jerome. *Lord and Peasant in Russia from the Ninth to the Nineteenth Century*. New York, 1969.

Bocharov, S. "L. Tolstoy i novoe ponimanie cheloveka. 'Dialektika dushi.'" In *Literatura i novyi chelovek*. Moscow, 1963.

*Bolotov, A. T. *Zapiski*. St. Petersburg, 1871. Author born in 1738. Almost no description of childhood.

*Bolotov, A. V. *Sviatye i greshnye: Vospominaniia byvshego cheloveka*. Paris, 1924. Author born in 1866. Childhood takes place on family estates in Orel and Tula provinces. "All of this is dear, but distant legend; an irretrievable, good, old, carefree time, insouciant childhood" (p. 11).

Borras, F. M. *Maxim Gorky: The Writer*. Oxford, 1967.

Brochier, Hubert. "Psychoanalyse et désir d'autobiographie." In Claudette Delhez-Sariet and Maurizio Catani, eds., *Individualisme et autobiographie en Occident*. Brussels, 1983.

Brokgaus, F. A., and I. A. Efron, eds. *Entsiklopedicheskii slovar'*. 82 vols. St. Petersburg, 1890–1904.

Bruss, Elizabeth. *Autobiographical Acts: The Changing Situation of a Literary Genre*. Baltimore, 1976.

Bunin, I. A. *Literaturnoe nasledstvo*. Eds. A. N. Dubovnikov and S. A. Makashin. No. 84, 2 vols. Moscow, 1973.

————. *Sobranie sochinenii*. 9 vols. Moscow, 1965–67.

————. *Ustami Buninykh*. Ed. Militsia Green. 3 vols. Frankfurt am Main, 1977.

————. *Vospominaniia*. Paris, 1981.

Chateaubriand, Vicomte de. *René*. In *Oeuvres complètes*, vol. 3. 12 vols. Paris, 1861.

Chekhov, A. P. *Sobranie sochinenii v dvenadtsati tomakh*. 12 vols. Moscow, 1960–64.

Chernyshevsky, N. G. "Detstvo i otrochestvo. Sochinenie Grafa L. N. Tolstogo. Voennye rasskazy Grafa L. N. Tolstogo." In S. P. Bychkov, ed., *L. N. Tolstoy v russkoi kritike*. 2d ed. Moscow, 1952.

*Chertkova, A. K. *Iz moego detstva*. Moscow, 1911. Author born in early 1860's. Childhood takes place in the country on the upper Volga. Chertkova was the wife of one of Tolstoy's chief disciples, V. G. Chertkov. Her happy memories are clearly modeled on Tolstoy's *Childhood*.

Chombart de Lauwe, Marie Jose. *Un monde autre: l'enfance*. Paris, 1971.

Christian, R. F. *Tolstoy: A Critical Introduction*. Cambridge, Eng., 1969.

Chuprina, I. V. *Trilogiia L. Tolstogo 'Detstvo,' 'Otrochestvo,' 'Iunost'.'* Saratov, 1961.

Coe, Richard N. "Mother Russia and the Russian Mother." *Proceedings of the Leeds Philosophical and Literary Society, Literary and Historical Section*. Vol. 19, pt. 6. December 1984, pp. 44–67.

————. *When the Grass Was Taller: Autobiography and the Experience of Childhood*. New Haven, 1984.

Cohen, Elliot. "The Genre of the Autobiographical Account of Childhood—Three Test Cases: The Trilogies of Tolstoy, Aksakov, and Gorky." Ph.D. diss., Yale University, 1973.

Cohn, Dorrit. *Transparent Minds: Narrative Modes for Presenting Consciousness in Fiction*. Princeton, 1978.

Connolly, Julian W. *Ivan Bunin*. Boston, 1982.

Constant, Benjamin. *Adolphe*. Paris, 1867.

*Davydov, N. V. "Iz pomeshchich'ei zhizni proshlogo stoletiia." *Golos minuvshego*, 1916, no. 2: 164–200. This account is primarily about the author's parents. Few details about own childhood.

*Davydov, V. N. *Rasskaz o proshlom*. Moscow, 1931. Author born in 1849. Childhood passed in small town in Kherson province. "My childhood was happy, joyful" (p. 77).

Dieckmann, Eberhard. *Erzählformen im Frühwerk L. N. Tolstojs, 1851–1857*. Berlin, 1969.

*Dmitriev, I. I. *Vzgliad na moiu zhizn'*. Moscow, 1866. Author born in 1760. Memoir written in 1823. Almost nothing about childhood.

Dobychin, L. *Gorod En*. Moscow, 1935.

Dostoevsky, F. M. *Polnoe sobranie sochinenii v tridtsati tomakh*. 30 vols. Leningrad, 1972–.

Drobat, L. S. "O trilogii Tolstogo." In *Iasnopolianskii sbornik, 1980*. Tula, 1981.

Dunn, Patrick P. "'That Enemy Is the Baby': Childhood in Imperial Russia." In Lloyd deMause, ed., *The History of Childhood*. New York, 1974.

Durkin, Andrew. *Sergey Aksakov and Russian Pastoral*. New Brunswick, N.J., 1983.

*Durova, Nadezhda. *Kavalerist-devitsa*. Leningrad, 1985. First published 1836. Author born in 1783. Childhood unhappy. Durova's tomboyish tendencies were suppressed by her mother.

Eagleton, Terry. *Criticism and Ideology*. London, 1976.

Eikhenbaum, B. M. *Lev Tolstoy: Kniga pervaia, piatidesiatye gody*. Leningrad, 1928.

———. *Molodoi Tolstoy*. Berlin, 1922.

Elsworth, J. D. *Andrey Bely: A Critical Study of the Novels*. Cambridge, Eng., 1983.

Emerson, Caryl. *Boris Godunov: Transpositions of a Russian Theme*. Bloomington, Ind., 1986.

Emmons, Terence. *The Russian Landed Gentry and the Peasant Emancipation of 1861*. Cambridge, Mass., 1968.

Evseeva, T. I. "Psikhologiia rebenka v trilogii L. N. Tolstogo 'Detstvo. Otrochestvo. Iunost'.'" In *L. N. Tolstoy kak pedagog*, vol. 2. Tula, 1969.

*Fet, A. A. *Vospominaniia*. Moscow, 1983. Author born in 1820. Childhood passed in Orel province. Ambivalent memories of childhood.

Foster, Liudmila A. *Bibliography of Russian Emigré Literature, 1918–1968*. 2 vols. Boston, 1970.

Fowler, Alistair. *Kinds of Literature: An Introduction to the Theory of Genres and Modes*. Cambridge, Mass., 1982.

Gavrilov, A. I., et al., eds. *Buninskii sbornik*. Orel, 1974.

Gazdanov, Gaito. *Vecher u Klèr*. Ann Arbor, 1979.

Geertz, Clifford. *The Interpretation of Cultures*. New York, 1973.

Genette, Gérard. *Figures III*. Paris, 1972.

Ginzburg, L. Ia. *O psikhologicheskoi proze*. Leningrad, 1977.

Girard, Alain. *Le journal intime*. Paris, 1963.

Gladkov, F. V. *Povest' o detstve*. Moscow, 1980.

*Glinsky, B. B. "Iz letopisi usad'by Sergeevki." *Istoricheskii vestnik*, 1894, vol. 58, no. 10: 57–85. Author born in late 1850's or early 1860's. Happy childhood takes place on country estate in "T" province (probably Tula).

Gogol, N. V. *Polnoe sobranie sochinenii*. 14 vols. Moscow, 1940–52.

Goldenveizer, A. V. *Vblizi Tolstogo*. Moscow, 1959.

Goncharov, I. A. *Oblomov*. Leningrad, 1978.

Gorky, M. *Polnoe sobranie sochinenii v tridtsati piati tomakh*. Ed. M. L. Leonov et al. 35 vols. Moscow, 1968–82.

Greenwood, E. B. *Tolstoy: The Comprehensive Vision*. London, 1975.

*Grot, N. P. *Iz semeinoi khroniki*. St. Petersburg, 1900. Author born in 1825. Childhood takes place on estate in Riazan' province. "We were the happiest of children" (p. 17).

Guillen, Claudio. *Literature as a System: Essays Toward the Theory of Literary History*. Princeton, 1971.

Gunn, Janet. *Autobiography: Toward a Poetics of Experience*. Philadelphia, 1982.

Gusdorf, Georges. "Conditions et limites de l'autobiographie." In *Formen der Selbstdarstellung*. Berlin, 1956.

Gusev, N. N. *Lev Nikolaevich Tolstoy: Materialy k biografii s 1828 po 1855 god*. Moscow, 1954.

Gusev, N. N., et al., eds. *L. N. Tolstoy v vospominaniiakh sovremennikov*. 2 vols. Moscow, 1960.

Gustafson, Richard. *Leo Tolstoy, Resident and Stranger: A Study in Fiction and Theology*. Princeton, 1986.

Hamburger, Käte. *The Logic of Literature*. Tr. Marilynn J. Rose. Bloomington, Ind., 1973.

Heldt, Barbara. *Terrible Perfection: Women and Russian Literature*. Bloomington, Ind., 1987.

*Herzen, A. I. *Byloe i dumy*. In *Sochineniia v deviati tomakh*, vols. 4–5. Moscow, 1956. Most of this famous autobiography is devoted to Herzen's adult years. In English exile he fondly recalled memories of summers on his father's country estates, although, overall, his memories of childhood were ambivalent.

Hobsbawm, Eric. "Introduction. Inventing Traditions." In Eric Hobsbawm and Terence Ranger, eds., *The Invention of Tradition*. New York, 1983.

Hubbs, Joanna. *Mother Russia: The Feminine Myth in Russian Culture*. Bloomington, Ind., 1988.

Iablokov, M. T., ed. *Rod dvorian Arsen'evykh 1389–1901*. Tula, 1903.

Iokar, L. N. "Gorky za chteniem knig o L. Tolstom." *Russkaia literatura*, 1973, no. 3: 151–61.

Iser, Wolfgang. *The Implied Reader: Patterns of Communication in Prose Fiction from Bunyan to Beckett*. Baltimore, 1974.

Ivanov, V. I. "Mladenchestvo." In *Sobranie sochinenii*, vol. 1. Brussels, 1971.

Jauss, Hans Robert. *Toward an Aesthetic of Reception*. Tr. Timothy Bahti. Minneapolis, 1982.

*Kamensky, S. *Vek minuvshii*. Paris, 1958. Author born in 1883. Generally happy childhood in the town of Tambov.

*Karpinskaia, Iu. N. "Iz semeinoi khroniki." *Istoricheskii vestnik*, 1897, vol. 70, no. 12: 853–70. This account is about estate life in general and does not really deal with the author's childhood.

Kassil', Lev. *Konduit i Shvambraniia*. Moscow, 1959.

Kataev, V. P. "Trava zabven'ia." In *Almaznyi moi venets: Povesti*. Moscow, 1981.

*Khvostova, E. A. *Zapiski*. Moscow, 1869. Written in 1836–37. Does not deal with childhood.

Koblitz, Ann Hibner. *A Convergence of Lives*. Boston, 1983.

*Kornilova, O. I. *Byl' iz vremen krepostnichestva*. St. Petersburg, 1890. Author born in 1840's. Childhood on country estate south of

Moscow. "I have retained the most joyous memories of my child-hood" (p. 8).

Korolenko, V. G. *Istoriia moego sovremennika*. In *Sobranie sochinenii v desiati tomakh*, vols. 5–7. Moscow, 1954–56.

*Kovalevskaia, S. V. *Vospominaniia detstva*. Moscow, 1960. Author born in 1850. Childhood on various country estates. Negative memories.

Kozlik, Frédéric C. *L'influence de l'anthroposophie sur l'oeuvre d'Andréi Biélyi*. 3 vols. Frankfurt, 1981.

Krasnov, G. B. "M. Gorky i literaturnaia traditsiia L. Tolstogo." In *M. Gorky i russkaia literatura*. Gorky, 1970.

*Kropotkin, P. A. *Zapiski revoliutsionera*. Moscow, 1966. Author born in 1842. Childhood spent in Moscow with summers in the country. Ambivalent memories of childhood.

Kuhn, Reinhard. *Corruption in Paradise: The Child in Western Litera-ture*. Hanover, N.H., 1982.

*Kuzminskaia, T. A. *Moia zhizn' doma i v Iasnoi Poliane*. Tula, 1959. Not primarily about the author's childhood.

Kuz'mychev, Ivan. "'Detstvo' i ego literaturnaia predystoriia." *Volga*, 1978, no. 8: 171–87.

*Labzina, A. E. *Vospominaniia*. 2d ed. St. Petersburg, 1914. Memoir written in 1810. Describes period of 1760's and 1770's. No child-hood description.

Larrain, Jorge. *The Concept of Ideology*. Athens, Ga., 1979.

Lejeune, Philippe. *Le pacte autobiographique*. Paris, 1975.

*Lelong, A. K. "Vospominaniia." *Russkii arkhiv*, 1913, bk. 2, no. 6: 778–808; no. 7: 52–103; 1914, bk. 2, no. 6/7: 370–407; no. 8: 535–56. Author born in 1841. Childhood on country estate in Riazan' province. "My dear, quiet childhood" (1913, bk. 2, no. 7: 103). This is one of the most extensive and best accounts of child-hood available.

Leont'ev, Konstantin. *Egipetsky golub'*. New York, 1954.

Levin, Dan. *Stormy Petrel: The Life and Work of Maxim Gorky*. New York, 1965.

Levitov, A. I. "Moia familiia." In *Sochineniia v odnom tome*. Moscow, 1956.

Lidin, Vl., ed. *Literaturnaia Rossiia: Sbornik sovremennoi prozy*. Mos-cow, 1924.

Likhachov, D. S. *Poeziia sadov*. Leningrad, 1982.

Lotman, Iu. M. *Roman A. S. Pushkina "Evgenii Onegin": Kommentarii.* Leningrad, 1980.

―――. "Tema kart i kartochnoi igry v russkoi literature nachala XIX v." In *Trudy po znakovym systemam*, vol. 7. Tartu, 1975.

Lotman, Iu. M., and B. A. Uspensky. *The Semiotics of Russian Culture.* Ed. Ann Shukman. Ann Arbor, 1984.

*L'vova, E. V. "Davno minuvshee." *Russkii vestnik*, 1901, vol. 275, no. 10: 399–416; vol. 276, no. 11: 76–89. Author born in early 1850's. A rare unhappy childhood as a result of the death of her father and subsequent family impoverishment.

Makashin, S. *Saltykov-Shchedrin.* 2 vols. Moscow, 1951.

Mandel'shtam, O. E. "Shum vremeni." In *Sobranie sochinenii v trekh tomakh.* Ed. G. P. Struve and B. A. Fillipov. 3 vols. Washington, D.C., 1967.

Manning, Roberta Thompson. *The Crisis of the Old Order in Russia: Gentry and Government.* Princeton, 1982.

Markovitch, Milan I. *Jean-Jacques Rousseau et Tolstoï.* Geneva, 1975.

Mashinsky, S. *S. T. Aksakov: Zhizn' i tvorchestvo.* Moscow, 1973.

Medvedev, N., ed. *M. Gorky o detskoi literature.* Moscow, 1952.

*Mengden, E. "Iz dnevnika vnuchki." *Russkaia starina*, 1913, vol. 153, no. 1: 103–31. Author born in 1825. Childhood on country estate. "The sunny days of my childhood" (p. 109).

*Mengden, S. V. "Otryvki iz semeinoi khroniki." *Russkaia starina*, 1908, vol. 134, no. 4: 97–116; no. 5: 325–48. Author born in mid-1860's. Childhood on estate in Tula province. "My happy childhood" (5: 327).

Mikhailovsky, B. V. "Avtobiograficheskaia trilogiia M. Gor'kogo." In *Literatura i novyi chelovek.* Moscow, 1963.

Morson, Gary Saul. *The Boundaries of Genre.* Austin, 1981.

―――. *Hidden in Plain View: Narrative and Creative Potentials in 'War and Peace.'* Stanford, 1987.

Muramtseva-Bunina, V. N. *Zhizn' Bunina, 1870–1906.* Paris, 1958.

Muratova, K. D. *M. Gorky: Seminarii.* Moscow, 1981.

Musset, Alfred de. *La confession d'un enfant du siècle.* Paris, 1859.

Nabokov, Vladimir. *The Gift.* New York, 1963.

―――. *Look at the Harlequins!* New York, 1974.

*―――. *Speak, Memory.* New York, 1947. Author born in 1899. Idyllic childhood in Petersburg and on family estate near that city.

*Obolensky, L. E. "Kartiny proshlogo." *Istoricheskii vestnik*, 1906, vol.

105, no. 9: 771–89; vol. 106, no. 10: 104–32. Author born in early 1850's. Childhood takes place in the country. "Dear, distant childhood" (9: 773).

*Obolensky, V. A. *Ocherki minuvshego*. Belgrade, 1931. Author born in early 1870's. Childhood takes place in Petersburg and on family estate near Smolensk. Positive memories.

Okenfuss, Max J. *The Discovery of Childhood in Russia: The Evidence of the Slavic Primer*. Newtonville, Mass., 1980.

*Osorgin, M. *Vremena*. Paris, 1955. Author born in late 1880's. Childhood spent north of Moscow on the Volga. A strong and lyrical nostalgia for childhood permeates this account.

Ostrovsky, A., ed. *Molodoi Tolstoy v zapisiax sovremennikov*. Leningrad, 1929.

Panaev, I. I. *Literaturnye vospominaniia*. Moscow, 1950.

Panaeva, Avdot'ia. *Semeistvo Tal'nikovykh*. Leningrad, 1928.

Paperno, Irina. *Chernyshevsky and the Age of Realism: A Study in the Semiotics of Behavior*. Stanford, 1988.

Pascal, Roy. "The Autobiographical Novel and the Autobiography." *Essays in Criticism*, 1959, vol. 9, no. 2: 134–50.

———. *Design and Truth in Autobiography*. London, 1960.

*Passek, T. P. *Iz dal'nikh let*. 2 vols. Moscow, 1963. Author born in 1810. Childhood in countryside. She has mixed memories of childhood. Says that writing down childhood memories helped "bring her back to life" during a tragic period of her life (1: 76).

Pasternak, B. L. "Okhrannaia gramota." In *Vozdushnye puti*. Moscow, 1982.

Paterson, Janet M. "L'autoreprésentation: Formes et discours." *Texte*, 1982, no. 1: 177–94.

Pavel, Thomas G. *Fictional Worlds*. Cambridge, Mass., 1986.

Pfeiffer, John Richard. "The Child in Nineteenth-Century British Fiction and Thought: A Typology." Ph.D. diss., University of Kentucky, 1969.

Piksanov, N. K. "Tolstoy i Gorky: Lichnye, ideinye, i tvorcheskie vstrechi." In *Tolstoy i russkaia literatura*. Gorky, 1961.

Pokrovskaia, A. K., and N. V. Chekhov, eds. *Materialy po istorii russkoi detskoi literatury (1750–1855)*. Series 1, vol. 1. Moscow, 1927.

Pokrovsky, V. I., ed. *Sergei Timofeevich Aksakov, ego zhizn'i sochineniia: Sbornik istoriko-literaturnykh statei*. 2d ed. Moscow, 1912.

Pomialovsky, N. G. "Meshchanskoe schast'e." In *Sochineniia*. Moscow, 1951.

Raeff, Marc. *Origins of the Russian Intelligentsia: The Eighteenth-Century Nobility*. New York, 1966.

Reshetnikov, F. M. *Mezhdu liud'mi*. In *Sochineniia F. M. Reshetnikova v dvukh tomakh*, vol. 1. St. Petersburg, 1890.

Robinson, Geroid Tanquary. *Rural Russia Under the Old Regime*. Berkeley, 1972.

Romberg, Bertil. *Studies in the Narrative Technique of the First-Person Novel*. Stockholm, 1962.

Rousseau, Jean-Jacques. *Les Confessions*. Paris, 1841.

Rynikov, N. A. *Avtobiografii rabochikh i ikh izuchenie*. Moscow, 1930.

*Sabaneeva, E. A. *Vospominaniia o bylom*. St. Petersburg, 1914. Author born in the 1830's. Childhood takes place on estate in Kaluga province. She sees childhood and its natural surroundings as the foundation of her entire "moral being" (p. 2).

Salaman, Esther. *The Great Confession*. London, 1973.

*Salov, A. I. "Umchavshiesia gody." *Russkaia mysl'*, 1897, bk. 7: 1–27; bk. 8: 1–25; bk. 9: 56–81. Author born in 1834. Childhood on father's estate in Penza province. Childhood is "a happy time" (8: 16).

Saltykov-Shchedrin, M. E. *Poshekhonskaia starina*. In *Sobraniia sochinenii v dvadtsati tomakh*, vol. 17. Moscow, 1975.

*Semenov-Tian-Shansky, P. P. *Detstvo i iunost'*. 7th ed. Petrograd, 1917. Author born in 1827. Childhood takes place on estate in Riazan' province. "Happy childhood" (p. 103).

*Shatilov, N. I. "Iz nedavnogo proshlogo." *Golos minuvshego*, 1916, no. 1: 165–201; no. 4: 205–25; no. 7/8: 171–87; no. 9: 21–39; no. 10: 45–71; no. 12: 119–39. Author born in 1850's. Childhood takes place on estates in the Crimea and in Tula province. Generally positive memories of childhood.

*Shestov, I. A. "Vospominaniia: Polveka obyknovennoi zhizni." *Russkii arkhiv*, 1873, no. 2: 166–200. Author born in 1820. Childhood takes place on estate in Smolensk province. Positive memories.

*Skariätina, Irina. *A World Can End*. New York, 1931. Author born in 1890's. Childhood in Petersburg and on estate in Orel province. Very positive memories of childhood.

*Slavutinsky, S. T. "Rodnye mesta." *Russkii vestnik*, 1880, no. 5:

198–240. Positive memories of childhood permeate author's being (p. 240).

*Sokhanskaia, Nadezhda. "Avtobiografiia." *Russkoe obozrenie,* 1896, nos. 6–12. Author born in 1823. Memoir written in 1848. Childhood on isolated country estate in the Ukraine. Childhood generally happy. "We had so much love, so many kisses and caresses!" (6: 483).

Spacks, Patricia Meyer. *Imagining a Self: Autobiography and Novel in Eighteenth-Century England.* Cambridge, Mass., 1976.

Spengemann, William C. *The Forms of Autobiography: Episodes in the History of a Literary Genre.* New Haven, 1980.

Steinberg, Ada. *Word and Music in the Novels of Andrey Bely.* Cambridge, Eng., 1982.

Stolitsa i usad'ba. St. Petersburg, 1913–17.

Stone, Lawrence. *The Family, Sex, and Marriage in England, 1500–1800.* New York, 1977.

Tal'ma, F. J. "Zapiski." *Panteon,* 1851, nos. 1–4.

*Taneev, V. I. *Detstvo i shkola.* Moscow, 1959. Author born in 1840's. Grew up to be important social democrat. Childhood takes place in Vladimir. Ambivalent memories.

Todorov, Tzvetan. *Les genres du discours.* Paris, 1976.

Tolstoy, L. N. *Polnoe sobranie sochinenii.* Ed. V. G. Chertkov et al. 90 vols. Moscow, 1928–58.

*Tolycheva, T. "Semeinye zapiski." *Russkii vestnik,* 1862, vol. 41: 665–705. Not primarily about the author's childhood.

Töpffer, Rodolphe. *La bibliotèque de mon oncle.* New York, 1898.

Tovrov, Jessica. "Mother-Child Relationships Among the Russian Nobility." In David L. Ransel, ed., *The Family in Imperial Russia.* Urbana, Ill., 1978.

*Trotsky, Leon. *My Life.* New York, 1930. Author born in 1879. Childhood takes place in poverty in Kherson province. Unhappy childhood.

*Trubetskoy, E. *Iz proshlogo.* Vienna, no date given, but based on internal evidence the book was published sometime between 1920 and 1923. Author born in 1863. Childhood takes place on country estate near Moscow. Extremely positive memories.

Tur, Evgeniia. *Plemianitsa.* Moscow, 1851.

Tynianov, Iu. N. *Arkhaisty i novatory.* Ann Arbor, 1985.

———. *Poètika, istoriia literatury, kino.* Moscow, 1977.

*Tyrkova-Vil'iams, Ariadna. *To, chego bol'she ne budet.* Paris, 1954. Author born in late 1870's. Childhood spent in Petersburg and on estate in Novgorod province. Happy childhood.

Uspensky, B. A. *Iz istorii russkogo literaturnogo iazyka XVIII–nachala XIX veka.* Moscow, 1985.

*Vereshchagin, A. V. *Doma i na voine.* St. Petersburg, 1885. Author born in mid-1850's. Childhood takes place in Novgorod province. Positive memories.

*Vigel', F. F. *Zapiski.* 2 vols. Moscow, 1928. Author born in 1787. Does not describe childhood.

*Vodovozova, E. N. *Na zare zhizni i drugie vospominaniia.* 2 vols. Moscow, 1934. Author born in 1844. Childhood spent in the Ukraine. Vodovozova was a member of the Petersburg populist intelligentsia. She found all aspects of gentry life, including her own childhood, to be disgusting.

Vonliarliarsky. "Vospominaniia o Zakhare Ivanyche." *Sovremennik,* 1851, vol. 27.

*Vonliarovsky, V. *Moi vospominaniia.* Berlin, 1939. Author born in 1852. Childhood spent on estate in Smolensk province. Positive memories of childhood.

*Von-Ritter, A. A. *Otzvuki minuvshego.* Moscow, 1892. Author born in late 1830's. "Happy childhood" takes place in countryside (p. 107).

Voronov, M. A. "Detstvo i iunost'." In *Povesti i rasskazy.* Moscow, 1961.

Vrangel', N. "Pomeshchich'ia Rossiia." *Starye gody,* July–September 1910, pp. 5–79.

Wasiolek, Edward. *Tolstoy's Major Fiction.* Chicago, 1978.

Wolfe, Humbert. *Now a Stranger.* London, 1933.

Wolohan, Sheila, "The *Bezprizorniki* in Soviet Culture." Unpublished paper, 1988.

Woodward, James A. *Ivan Bunin: A Study of his Fiction.* Chapel Hill, N.C., 1980.

Zaionchkovsky, P. A., ed. *Istoriia dorevoliutsionnoi Rossii v dnevnikakh i vospominaniiakh.* 4 vols. Moscow, 1976–86.

Zirin, Mary. "Forgotten Beginnings. Early Depictions of Russian Girlhood: Nadezhda Durova, Avdot'ia Panaeva, and Nadezhda Sokhanskaia." Unpublished, 1989.

Zweers, Alexander F. *Grown-up Narrator and Childlike Hero: An Analysis of the Literary Devices Employed in Tolstoy's Trilogy Childhood, Boyhood, and Youth.* The Hague, 1971.

Index

In this index an "f" after a number indicates a separate reference on the next page, and an "ff" indicates separate references on the next two pages. A continuous discussion over two or more pages is indicated by a span of page numbers, e.g., "57–59." *Passim* is used for a cluster of references in close but not consecutive sequence.

Library of Congress Cataloging-in-Publication Data

Wachtel, Andrew.
    The battle for childhood : creation of a Russian myth /
Andrew Baruch Wachtel.
        p.   cm.
    Includes bibliographical references.
    ISBN 0-8047-1795-8 (alk. paper) :
        1. Russian literature—19th century—History and
criticism.   2. Russian literature—20th century—History
and criticism.   3. Childhood in literature.   4. Literature
and society—Soviet Union.   I. Title.
PG3015.5.C55W34   1990
891.7'09354—dc20   89-29961
                                                         CIP

    ⊗ This book is printed on acid-free paper